Future Imperfect

FUTURE

A Blade of Grass 2014–15

Elizabeth M. Grady, editor

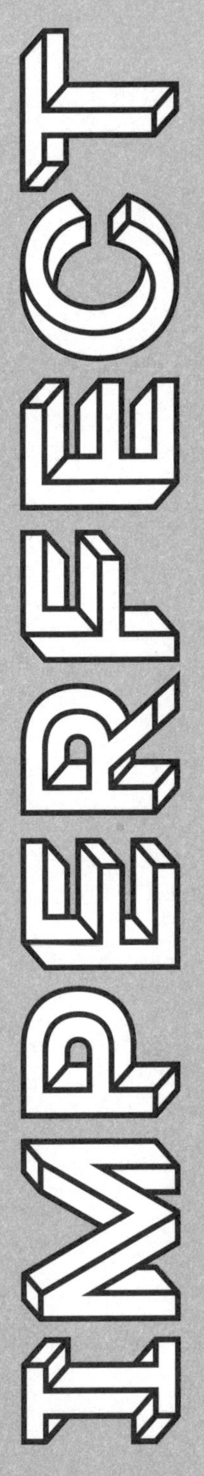

Part 1

IMPACT

Part 2

ETHICS

Part 3

EFFECTIVENESS

Artist texts by Elizabeth M. Grady
Artist biographies by Joelle Te Paske

Shelley Frost Rubin

Foreword: A More Perfect Future

In 2011 I founded A Blade of Grass in the belief that art can change lives in straightforward, practical ways. Art and creativity are cornerstones of cohesive, resilient communities, and can foster greater participation in civic life. Art should be everywhere, and for everyone, because artists reframe problems, help us see things differently, and introduce us to beautiful, novel, and complex experiences that expand our minds, so that we can imagine a world beyond what we already know.

A Blade of Grass supports socially engaged artists who make a difference. The fellowships we offer enable socially engaged art to become more visible, understandable, and appreciated by more people, both inside and outside the art world. From a mobile beauty salon serving homeless women, and grassroots efforts to clean contaminated topsoil using mushrooms in New York, to healing and wellness workshops in Oakland, this is art that belongs to the communities that make it.

Future Imperfect captures these projects often in the participants' own voices, and placed alongside some of the most notable thought leaders in socially engaged art, including Charles Esche, Tom Finkelpearl, Grant Kester, Rick Lowe, Gregory Sholette, Nato Thompson, and Christian Viveros-Fauné. These narratives encourage me to think more broadly about the roles of artists in civic life. I hope that they inspire you to re-imagine what art is, who it's for, and what it can do to change lives. By gathering and sharing stories of artists who are making social change, we create more opportunities for artists to participate actively in civic life as leaders and visionaries.

Deborah Fisher

Evolving the Institution

A Blade of Grass nurtures socially engaged art, and our primary vehicle for this support is our Fellowship program, which pairs $20,000 in direct support of a socially engaged art project with specific tools that are designed to describe the project, build audience and deepen understanding: regular co-assessment meetings with a cohort of like-minded Fellows; an ethnographic assessment that utilizes action research methodology; a short documentary film; and this publication, which presents these important Fellowship projects and seeks to ground them in a larger discourse about socially engaged art.

ABOG focuses exclusively on artists working directly in communities, in collaborative leadership roles, who enact a specific social change at an ambitious scale. This is important work that more and more artists are doing, and we began implementing the Fellowship knowing that thoughtful support of this type of work would require a radical rethinking of what an arts institution is, and the work it does. I want to focus on this rethinking process—the ways we have innovated the work we do because we only support social practice. There are exciting institutional challenges in this mandate. Socially engaged artists are nourishing the contexts in which their work is situated instead of relying on arts institutions to provide a social and physical context, so this work isn't well supported by exhibition spaces. We must support and build audience for it in other ways. The artists we support are enacting social change, and we have to be thoughtful about our relationship to that change. Are we defining a social justice agenda and choosing art that moves that agenda forward? Are we organizing our work around political content? Are we asking about the political implications of a genre or a form? The artists we support are evolving their own practice to engage power. We take inspiration from this, and relate more actively and creatively to our own power as an institution.

Context

A Blade of Grass is a presenter of socially engaged art, but it does not produce art projects or maintain a space for exhibitions. Rather, it supports artists where they work, in a way that creates a substantive, useful, and sensitive set of stories about the projects, and the contexts in which they reside. This is a unique orientation for an arts organization. Our top priority is to ensure that these projects, which are so dependent on their context for their meaning and value, can circulate within a broader discourse. But the projects themselves are delicate ecosystems of relationships, which we could easily distort. So we position ourselves just outside a project, in partnership with the artist, with a set of low-impact listening, viewing, and storytelling tools. Using these tools, we create and present a secondary body of work—an assessment, journalism and programs, a documentary, and this publication—*about* the projects.

The artist and the participants are the experts of this context and the project, and our job is to work with them to tell effective stories about it. We start by asking the artist detailed questions about the project—its goals, definitions of success, issues, relationships, and political sensitivities. We ask if there's anything we should do to avoid harming the project. We ask whether and how we can best visit it. We ask whom we can bring to it, and sometimes we ask how to best manage that interaction. For some projects, like Brett Cook's culminating Life Is Living festival, this is a non-issue because they are designed to be public. But in the case of SexEd's *Wearing Consent,* we really had to think through how to film and assess teenagers talking about sex, or for Jody Wood's *Beauty in Transition,* how to bring visitors to a very small salon in the back of an old ice cream truck that was specifically designed to give people who feel vulnerable an intimate experience. We even had to postpone documenting an artist's work because the "art part" was delayed by real-world imperatives of the project. Laurie Jo Reynolds' *Honeybun Comedy Hour* took a back seat to working on a political campaign to re-elect the Governor of Illinois, with whom she had partnered to close Tamms Supermax Prison. Instead of focusing on a video project, she campaigned. She had to respond to her political context and her goals—the meaning of her work depends on the act of closing the prison, and keeping it closed.

For each Fellowship project, the artist guided all access, assessment, and documentation efforts. Jan Cohen-Cruz or a field

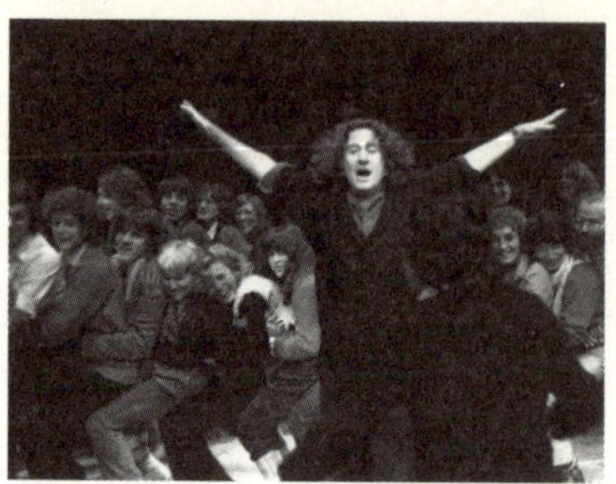

Augusto Boal conducts Theatre of the Oppressed exercises in Paris, 1975.

researcher under her supervision made three site visits to each project, and wrote a report that reflected their subjective experience of it, as well as that of the participants. RAVA Films similarly worked directly with artists to gain access, interview participants, and conduct interviews that were grounded in their subjective experience and the artists' goals and definitions of success. Interviews with participants for our Reports from the Field forum, public programs, and field trips gave us more understanding and experience with each project. This collection of multiple subjective insights gained through RAVA, Jan, and through our own visits and storytelling, constitutes a secondary narrative about the project that we shape and distribute. This secondary narrative is not objective—it is a synthesis of many subjective points of view, including our own. It originates from the access points provided by each artist, follows the artists' guidance, and amplifies the artists' and the projects' goals, relying heavily on the voices of the participants.

This publication is part of that secondary body of work, and its purpose is to contextualize these projects as part of a larger art movement. It is organized around an important online debate we hosted with Ben Davis, Tom Finkelpearl, Rick Lowe, and Nato Thompson, and includes essays by Charles Esche, Grant Kester, Laura Raicovich, Greg Sholette, and Christian Viveros-Fauné alongside in-depth descriptions of the Fellowship projects that rely on participants' voices to do most of the storytelling.

Other parts of this body of work that ABOG creates about the Fellowship projects serve to increase our knowledge, elevate the profile of the artists and social practice more generally, and increase audience. The ethnographic assessments Jan writes are critical feedback to artists about how their work is being perceived in their community, and they also serve an important role as fundraising, fact-checking, and case-making tools, for Fellows and for a wider field of practice and arts journalism. And the FIELDWORKS series of films is designed to give new audiences a taste that ignites their passion, so that more people can enjoy and take inspiration from the fantastic work our Fellows are doing.

In creating each of these stories about the projects, it is critical for all of us at ABOG HQ to remember that we are never presenting the work itself, nor do we have any control over it. Guided by the artists, we are carefully creating a secondary body of work that is built out of many points of view and operates in service of the artists' goals.

Liberatory Form

Artists are increasingly working with social justice issues, and many arts nonprofits and foundations are developing an interest in the intersection of art and social justice. We are part of this larger movement. We believe that all change is cultural change, and that art has significant political and civic impact. And we have a particular focus. We want to know how cultural change works.

How does art impact the political and civic landscape? What are the mechanics of cultural change? What is political practice? What's the difference between representing a political idea and enacting political change? Is there such a thing as a liberatory *form* of art, or are the politics of art always a function of its intention or content?

This notion of enacting change, and understanding how and whether art can serve a liberatory function by developing critical consciousness, is fundamental to our work. We believe that if we can more clearly articulate what artists are doing when they enact change, three important outcomes emerge. We increase the potential for political engagement and critical consciousness raising by supporting and telling stories about artists who are doing this type of work. We develop tools for understanding what constitutes excellent social practice. And we make a case for supporting more artists in more roles and contexts, particularly in leadership positions.

To articulate a specific social justice agenda would certainly clarify what kind of political engagement we are supporting and telling stories about in the short term, but we felt in crafting the Fellowship that this short-term clarity would cause us to sacrifice our mid- and long-range goals. In addition to gathering information about how social practice works, what artists are doing with it, and what its political and social effectiveness is, we would also have to reconcile the content of the work to our social justice agenda. We would be trying to talk and listen at the same time. We wondered whether our capacity to learn what social practice is, and about its capacity to raise consciousness and enact change, would be circumscribed or limited by the need to telegraph a social justice agenda. So we articulated an institutional bias toward the form of social practice rather than toward artistic content that articulates a specific social justice platform of ABOG. Our goal in doing this was to isolate formal aspects of social practice like dialogical approaches and co-creation, so that we could study these forms in terms of their social and political relevance.

This proved to be an effective stance, particularly for a young organization and a new program. It helped us understand how to effectively and completely support a cohort of artists, each of whom has their own theory of change and social justice agenda. It helped us understand our role, which is to support the artist as an agent of change. And we gathered experiential evidence that supports the writing of Augusto Boal and Paolo Freire, who are so often cited by the artists we support. Our data sample is small—only seven projects. But in those seven projects we can see, for example, how these seven artists negotiate oppression. We can see that many of the artists focus on creating a high-trust environment that's about a topic important to the participants, in which a risk is taken, but the risk has relatively low stakes. This creates the conditions Boal describes as "rehearsing for the revolution," or generating a strong emancipatory sensation in the participants that is aesthetic—it feels beautiful. But it could have the potential to be generalizable, or to inform future behavior. At the conclusion of year one, we can confidently assert that dialogical and co-created practices really do have a specific role to play in developing critical consciousness about the nature of oppression, and are therefore more likely to enact progressive, or liberatory, social change.

We want to be able to say more about this assertion. We want, as the years unfold, to be able to analyze the political potential of a project based on its form and craft. Is the project co-created or simply participatory? Is there a dialogical element? How were important details like community outreach or bridging cultural divides managed? What was its exit strategy? Were participants challenged creatively?

Taking the time to cultivate this sort of formal understanding is worth the short-term evasion of not articulating a social justice agenda that Rick Lowe rightly calls us out on in the very pages of this book! Rick's position is well taken. Because social practice is politically effective, he feels that a social justice agenda must be articulated. Otherwise, you are acting in support of all types of action—progressive and non-progressive. The danger is clear, but the possibility of clarifying and developing comparative qualitative information about the political aspects of many projects is important because we want more, and more interesting, and more effective, liberatory action.

Power

The artists we support almost always actively engage with institutional authority in some way. Jody Wood works in deep relationship with the shelter system in New York City. Laurie Jo Reynolds is pressuring the Illinois state legislature to close a prison and keep it closed, and Mel Chin's *Operation Paydirt* is, among other things, an effective lead advocacy and lawmaker education initiative. It helps ABOG to see this work as an evolution of institutional critique in contemporary art practice. Instead of

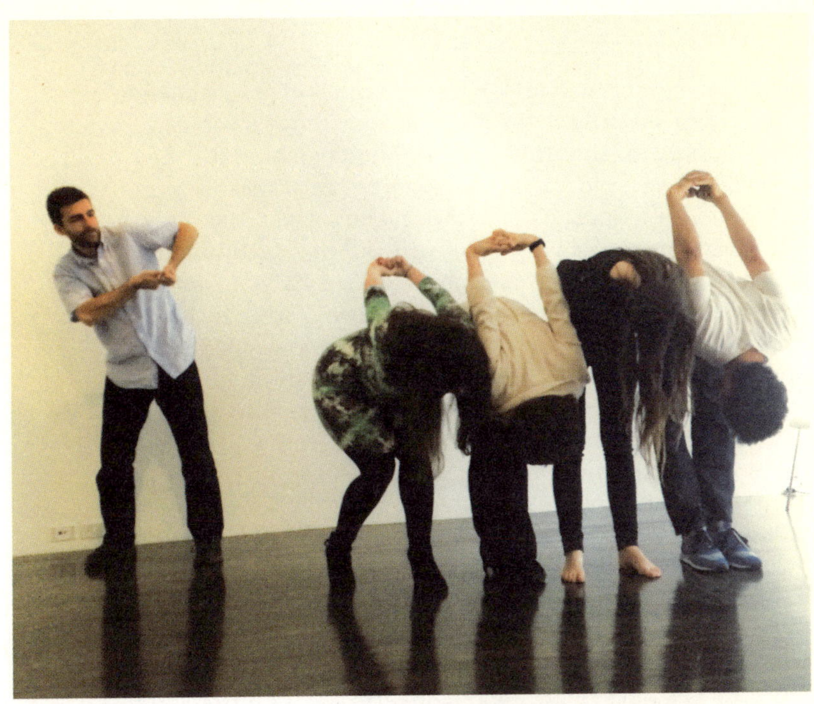

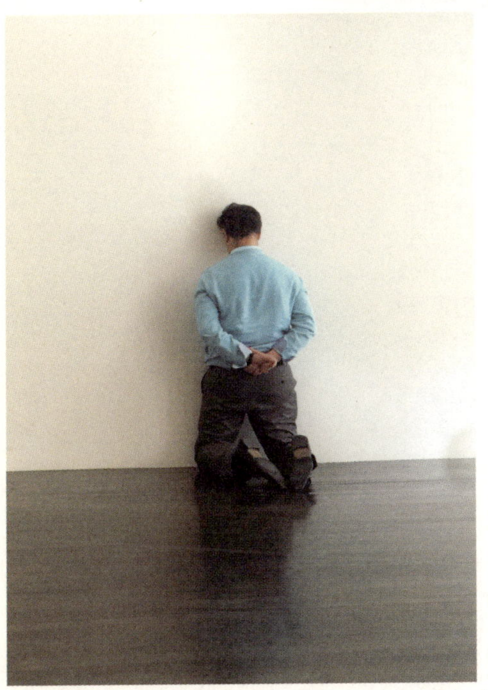

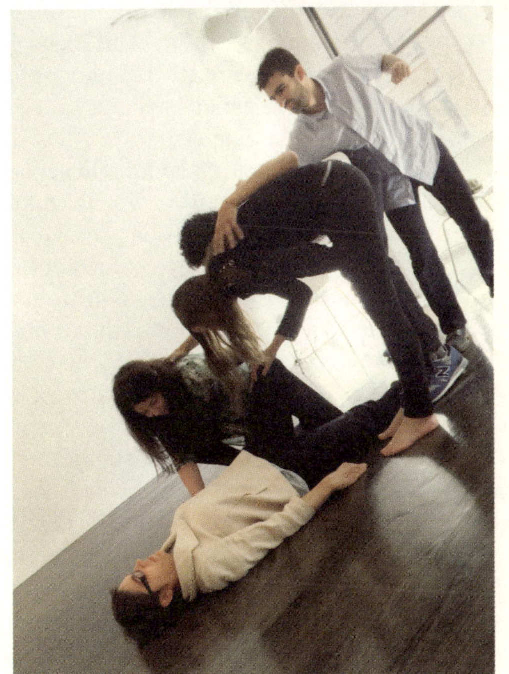

All: A Blade of Grass staff and Fellows perform Theatre of the Oppressed exercises.

critiquing the workings and power dynamics of the art institution from within, the artists we support are wielding power out in the world. This shift from artists critiquing power to artists using power is key to understanding why social practice is important, both from an art historical and social justice perspective. It also demands that we deal with our own institutional power differently. We can't simply create a context for artists we support to critique our institutional authority for us. Instead, we have to account for and develop a creative awareness about how we use our power. This accounting for institutional authority manifests in our relationships with the projects we support, and it informs all that boring back-of-the-house work that we feel less license to be creative about, like our leadership culture and fundraising strategy.

Because the artists we support are developing and using their own power instead of critiquing ours we have to reconsider the power dynamics that tend to flow between artists and arts institutions. Arts institutions typically work to amplify or engender specific types of power in partnership with artists. An institution is typically a platform that amplifies an artist's visibility and social capital, and does so in a way that enables critique and protects freedom of expression. Freedom, visibility, and social capital are great powers. But we find that the artists we support don't find these types of power as useful as artistic agency—the capacity to get things done in the world as an artist.

This difference between artistic freedom and artistic agency shapes much of our work as an institution. For an institution to protect or promote artistic freedom, it needs to create a physically or conceptually bounded institutional space that operates according to a familiar social contract in which art is separated from the world around it and elevated in some way, so that it may be considered "free." This paradigm won't work for us because socially engaged art rejects the idea that art happens within a bounded zone—rather, it inserts itself into existing social contracts out in everyday life. It is not protected, and the artists that we work with generally do not consider themselves completely free. They are more likely to consider themselves both ethically and politically bounded by the relationships and dynamics that they carefully tend within their projects, because their goal is not to express or represent an idea. It is to get something done. This means that we can't do some of the basic things other arts organizations do to help artists, like protect the art, because that would isolate it from its context. We are mindful of things like social capital and visibility, because positioning the artist as a singular genius instead of as a creative catalyst within a community could harm the delicate relationships that constitute their work. And we have to design a way of working that prioritizes artistic agency over artistic freedom. To take one example: our assessment is artist-driven—we don't look for anything the artist isn't asking us to look at. But it does serve as a record of the artists' accountability to a community of service. As such, it is a critical tool for artists as they make the case that they can play an important role in a non-art context, and that their work has an important role in daily life.

When we prioritize artistic agency, we hold up a mirror to our own agency, and are inspired to account for our own actions as an organization at all levels, from the way we select Fellows to the way we interact with our Board. Cultivating an institutional awareness of and creativity toward one's own power is risky, indirect, and completely satisfying work. To see one's power is to use it better. For example, the number of applications we receive is an important metric for ABOG HQ—it helps us declare that there is a need for more Fellowships. But when we realize that we have a responsibility to each of the 500+ artists who spends time on an application, we realize that we can't simply try to increase the number of applications. That would result in the waste of thousands of hours among hundreds of artists that could be spent creatively in the world! Instead, we invest in a two-stage process, particularly transparent criteria, samples, workshops and feedback, so that artists' time is respected and the quality and fit of the applications increase. And we measure this. We track both the total number of applications and the number of relevant applications—the ones that make the very first cut for "eligibility and basic relevance." We are proud of the way the fit and quality of applications have improved between 2014 and 2015, and feel that over time this method will yield satisfying quantitative and qualitative data—that we will see the relevance and quality of applications increase.

We also want to bring this sense of accountability inside, and grow support and leadership that deeply understands how important process and agency are to socially engaged art, and is committed to engaging these values. ABOG is lucky to have a particularly inquisitive Board culture that is accustomed to taking the social change goals of projects seriously, and helping artists amplify their work by providing legal or other types of professional expertise. This culture of thoughtful inquiry and participation makes board meetings much more fun, and the culture also acts as a constant rehearsal for the incendiary topics that inevitably arise when you support artists that are trying to change the world. Each Board member has taken a risk by signing on to act as a steward of an organization that helps artists try to enact social change. Sometimes artists take on problems that we're not quite ready to take on. Sometimes supporting artists means examining political topics that are particularly difficult. By developing this inquisitive culture, we gain the courage and insight that we need to truly embrace the work we support.

It is also critical that we allow our fundraising to be inspired by the art we support. Our fundraising strategy is grounded in two core ideas: movement building, and making a case for the value of socially engaged art to its many contexts and communities of service. Our first goal when we fundraise is to participate in the building of an ecosystem that includes us, but is larger than us. Ideally, this ecosystem will sustainably support artists as change agents in communities, imagine roles for artists, and enable and amplify the integration of art into everyday lives. The mantra of this ecosystem is *More Art for More People in More Places!* It values the specific social, civic and political value of art. This broadening of context and clear articulation of value is expansive. It broadens the potential audiences for this art, and positions more people who work on its support as participants. This position also enables a deeper existential shift from a scarcity mindset to an abundance mindset around fundraising, which is the most stressful and frustrating work that any arts nonprofit encounters. And we enact this shift whenever we take supporters on field trips to like-minded organizations' projects. We also enact it by positioning the Fellowship as a valuable tool for integrating artists into non-art contexts.

Looking Ahead

It's funny. ABOG's trajectory as an organization over the past four and a half years has been nothing less than meteoric, and the future is similarly bright. At this writing we are rolling out screenings of our FIELDWORKS film series; engaging in research about how ABOG Fellowships might serve specific contexts; and evolving our favorite feature, Reports from the Field, to include more live talks that feature the participants of projects. And yet, the first draft of this essay got scrapped because everyone said it sounded negative. From this, I learned how much I love problems! ABOG's success is entirely a function of the way we have embraced and grappled with the problems inherent to social practice, and seen them as opportunities. ABOG supports artists whose practice is to change the world. This is a bold and galvanizing proposition until you start thinking about it. In practice, it operates more like a riddle, or a Zen koan. Can artists change the world? What does that mean? Should they? How, and how much? In what ways? If an artist can change the world, can I change the world? Can we measure this type of change? Does it happen accidentally or on purpose? Is changing the world good art? How do we see it as art? What is its form? How does it circulate, and generate a discourse around itself? Is it possible to support it using the art world's existing relationship to wealth?

I could go on ... but I think I've illustrated my point.

It is true that by starting with these questions, my first draft made nurturing socially engaged art sound like a wearying burden. But by ending with them, I hope to communicate the degree to which these questions, and the problematic nature of this work, serve us—move us into the future. These questions are wonderful challenges to a status quo that is begging for change. There is a hunger for substance and relevance within the contemporary art discourse, which can sound an awful lot like a never-ending complaint about the power of the market. And there's a hunger for creativity and inspiration in the philanthropic landscape that is currently being met by things like TED talks. This introduces some inadvertent oversimplification—TED talks work because they reduce a complex idea into one compelling personal story. Does social practice replace the art market? I hope not. I like art objects, and 75% of my job is fundraising—I want financial resources to go to this art. I'm hopeful about the way the examples in this book can satisfy these hungers, and at the same time retain a sense of resistance in their very structures and forms. It is important that we can learn about these projects, but they cannot belong to us. They are elsewhere. They consist of relationships that are not ours. They are only meaningful if a transformation occurs inside another person, and it is very likely that none of us know that person. There is a beautiful, basic generosity to enabling this work because it truly is for others. And there is tremendous possibility in embracing that generosity and complexity, and continuing to refine our organizational position as deep listeners and translators of art that is not ours.

PART ONE

IMPACT

Distraction or Solution: How Does Socially Engaged Art Impact Communities?

On August 9, 2013, Deborah Fisher, Executive Director of A Blade of Grass, posted a link on her Facebook page to Ben Davis' article, "A Critique of Social Practice Art: What does it mean to be a political artist?," which appeared in issue #90 of the *International Socialist Review*. In it, referring to what he called "social practice", Davis asked, "Is this strand of art a starting point for addressing social problems, or a distraction that keeps us from seeing their true extent?" It generated a flurry of responses and counter-responses. The conversation began to gel together into a full-fledged debate that eventually included Davis on the value and practice of socially engaged art, which revolved in various ways around the general question of effectiveness.

This debate kicked off ABOG's now-regular Growing Dialogue online forum, in which artists, curators, critics and project participants are invited to publicly respond to important articles published on socially engaged art. Participants included Deborah Fisher, Nato Thompson, Gregory Sholette, Rick Lowe, and Ben Davis. ABOG's Executive Director kicks off this segment by picking up on one of Ben Davis' main inquiries.

Deborah Fisher
Davis is right to ask what separates SEA [Socially Engaged Art –Ed.] from other types of social action and social work. Why is its status as art important? What does calling it art accomplish?

Nato Thompson
The issue of whether or not something is art is not ultimately what is at stake. For many artists and non-artists, the concerns are much broader. If anything, socially engaged art points out the obvious fact that there is a crisis of cultural production. What we can do is realize that the social terrain is shifting and people are using culture in new ways to do stuff in the world. As opposed to wondering whether or not something is art, we must try to tease out how to navigate the crisis that is the incorporation of cultural production into the very machinations of power.

Deborah Fisher
There's a difference between asking if SEA is art or not, and asking what calling something art accomplishes and whether the designation of art is useful. SEA projects are often categorized and funded as art. This categorization creates a specific relationship to power; a pool of resources; a set of expectations about both meaning and efficacy. We are both complicit in this—Creative Time and ABOG are both arts organizations.

I don't think ABOG can take the political nature of this work seriously, fund it thoughtfully, and meaningfully assess these projects unless we are fully accountable to the power we have as funders, and the way art functions not only within a marketplace but as a symbol that distances the powerful from their own ideology. And I believe there are real opportunities to expand this dialogue past SEA as social work if we can be clear about the way art shapes our expectations of impact.

Nato Thompson
Many of these projects use cultural production, a word I like more than art, at some point in their process. Artists are not alone in using culture to do things. Using the symbolic, the formal, the poetic alongside the didactic, the infrastructural, and activist are simply contemporary ways of doing things. The field of SEA is often artists and activists catching up to the fact that a hybrid form of aesthetic and political production is how the world works.

Deborah Fisher
Davis draws a relationship between art and power and the social agenda of SEA projects. What does it mean to support projects that do not solve social problems?

Gregory Sholette
Ben Davis writes: “You cannot prevent innovations in art from eventually being given a capitalist articulation.”

And we are confronted with a conundrum. Does culture ever act to directly shape socioeconomic reality, or is it in turn always molded by these forces? And if capitalism is the totality of our existence, then how can any artistic practice be substantially “anti-capitalist” or “radical” or “subversive” and therefore let us call it “pro-human” or “pro-society”?

There can be no satisfactory answer to the conundrum of whether radical innovation—however defined—is or is not complicit with capital’s long march. As Mr. Davis certainly knows, interpretation and judgment are always subject to the same socioeconomic and historical forces that shape culture at any given moment. However they might, circumstances permitting, undermine or resist these forces, offering at the very least a momentary breach within the decadence of what Mr. Davis labels commercial art, an indignation if not exact wording I share. In the best of moments such practices cast a light, however weak, on an often less visible counter-historical tendency entwined with capitalist development itself. This "art history from below" is a realm of fragmented publics and working class fantasy generated in response to the alienating conditions of capitalism. Occupy and the Movement of the Squares undoubtedly brought this other cultural force, this missing mass or creative dark matter, into the fore.

Rick Lowe

One of the biggest concerns I have for the field of social and community engaged practice is that we don't have serious critical dialogue about the work being practiced and produced. And I'm not talking about dialogue that questions whether socially engaged work is art. I'm talking about dialogue about how our work relates to the issues of power, privilege, appropriations, exploitations, etc. I self-reflect on these issues daily in relation to my work, but it is valuable to confront them from different perspectives with different agendas. I'm excited to hear Ben Davis's perspectives, and eager to learn more of his perspectives on art that rises above "capitalist articulation", and the "completely different direction" that social practice might take as a result of critical debating.

Ben Davis

In her classic book on the topic, *Reform or Revolution*, Rosa Luxemburg started from the premise that reform and revolution are not opposed; there will have to be many, many small victories and tiny, inspiring acts that lead up to any movement that makes even modest systematic changes in society.[1]

A problem only arises when the fight for reforms becomes ossified into "reformism," that is, when the overall terms of social struggle are set by what is immediately possible and not what could be possible, thereby becoming an ideological brake. Sometimes it may be difficult to know where we find ourselves on that continuum, but to state at the outset that "reformism" is a challenge that socially engaged practitioners have to tangle with is to take them seriously as political actors. Some forms of activism are clearly more palatable than others to the powers that be, and will get more support precisely as a way of containing discontent. Given the recent anniversary of the March on Washington, I've been thinking a lot of the early Civil Rights movement: In the early 1960s, then-attorney general Robert Kennedy offered organizers from the Student Nonviolent Coordinating Committee a deal: "If you cut out this Freedom Rider and sitting-in stuff and concentrate on voter registration, I'll get you a tax exemption." What if they had taken the offer?[2]

As people living at the tail end of generations of rightward drift, we do not have much immediate experience of movements of mass protest. They have, however, been a key to every important social movement that has made any sort of advance. Given that "social practice" is clearly attracting some of the most sincere and motivated artists in the present, the question for me is how various forms of socially engaged art practice do or don't relate to such politics. I think that "social practice," in its various incarnations, can be an inspiring jumping off point and raise political horizons.

And yet ... let me give an example that haunts me, from the expanded field of cultural activism. In the wake of Hurricane Sandy, the remnants of the Occupy movement heroically organized to form Occupy Sandy. While government officials sat on their hands, scores of volunteers joined together across the boroughs to try to get some relief to devastated communities. Teaming up with my neighbors to bring hot food to a mosque in Coney Island or deliver bottled water and baby formula to blacked-out public housing blocks in the Rockaways was one of the most meaningful experiences of my political life. However, when I returned in the evening to my untouched Williamsburg apartment, I was distressed to log onto Facebook and see the graphic that was circulating, a stylized image of volunteers at work with the caption "Occupy Sandy: #WeGotThis." Here is my anguished Facebook post from that night (complete with unedited sentence fragments):

> What Occupy Sandy has done is inspiring... But the slogan "#WeGotThis" bugs me... I think we need to be honest that we definitely don't "have this." Volunteers are stepping in, heroically, where the system has failed people... But we don't have the generators, the earth movers, the massive stores of food, housing, blankets, and on and on needed to handle a crisis of this scale. People have lost their homes and lives. This just feels like focusing on how important it feels—and it is very important—and not the real state of the case, which is that the government NEEDS to be doing a lot more. That's why you still pay taxes, because you believe some public services are necessary, that they do things that we, even acting together, can't; not to start terrible wars and bail out crooks. The idea of crowd-sourced disaster relief, if that is what the future holds, is scary, not awesome.

Just as the natural disaster accelerates and dramatizes the crisis and neglect faced by marginalized communities in general, so do such moments accentuate and dramatize the dilemma of activism. We are facing terrifying ecological challenges, ever more deeply entrenched economic inequality, huge and ingrained structures of systematic racism ... Individuals or even small groups engaging in creative projects simply do not have the metaphorical generators or earth movers to turn these things around, and until the tide is turned activists and artists alike are going to be fighting an ever increasing number of battles in ever more embattled circumstances. That's the big picture against which this debate takes place for me. Of course, just as I would never say that we should not have taken food and blankets to people starving in the cold in the wake of Sandy, I would never say that we shouldn't engage in modest experimental initiatives to agitate to make things better—what else are we going to do? However, we can't be too self-satisfied about them; such initiatives should be critically hashtagged #WeDON'THaveThis. I think that conceptual shift makes a lot of difference.

One of the useful things about this approach is that it helps reframe the vexed debate over efficacy, which is for me perhaps better thought of in negative rather than positive terms. Thompson is correct that it is hard to judge the immediate impact of gestures that are symbolic. Building a culture of creative activism has value, as a base where ideas about social change can be fostered and, as Rick Lowe says of the *Project Row Houses*, as an example that can inspire bigger things, even if it doesn't actually solve everything itself. An art project needn't have any measurable immediate positive effect, as far as I am concerned. It does, however, need to avoid having one negative effect: There is clearly the danger, because of the very worthy nature of the projects involved, combined with the prestige and intellectual sheen that the art connection gives these things, that "social practice" substitutes rather than complements non-artistic activism in our minds. Addressing that danger is an obligation that goes with the territory. But as long as we start from that premise, then I think we are pulling in the same direction.

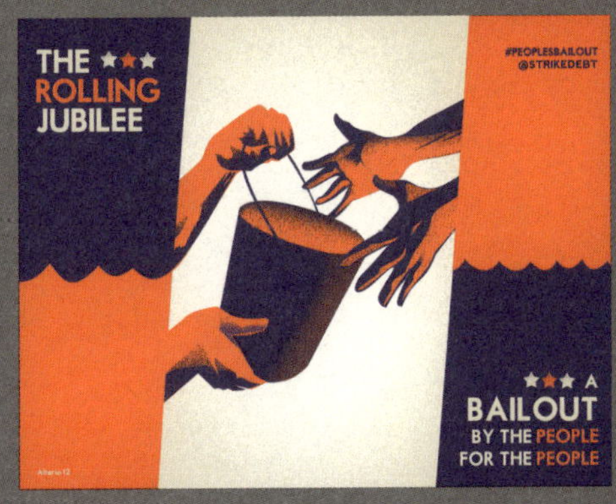

Joe Alterio, Rolling Jubilee poster.

Nato Thompson

Davis basically states that he is interested in questions of effectiveness not only with SEA but activism writ large. Well, who can argue with that?

I would like to give credence to the concern that some works of SEA are ultimately symbolic, in that the image of social commitment is merely a front for something else.

Activists, artists and critics alike might roll their eyes when a large institution gets involved in Sally Struthers-like social work. They sense an opportunistic desire to have the image of doing good, while the underlying commitment remains dubious at best.

Deborah Fisher

If SEA has a specific role to play in social change because it can reshape power, the last thing we want to do is collapse SEA into small-bore social work. A great artwork embraces paradox, and contains multiple, sometimes contradictory, truths. I think this quality gives a great SEA project the ability to reframe, reshape, or for a moment redistribute power. Strike Debt's *Rolling Jubilee,* for example, can infiltrate and destabilize power structures that feel monolithic precisely because it is not designed to solve the problem as much as it's designed to exist as a gesture and as a result at the same time. The *Rolling Jubilee* doesn't have to abolish all medical debt in order to do something important. It does most of its work on an aesthetic level. It is elegant to take the tactics of oppression and use them to deliver people from that oppression, and that elegance is inspiring. Straightforward social work cannot do this because social workers have totally different goals in terms of scale.

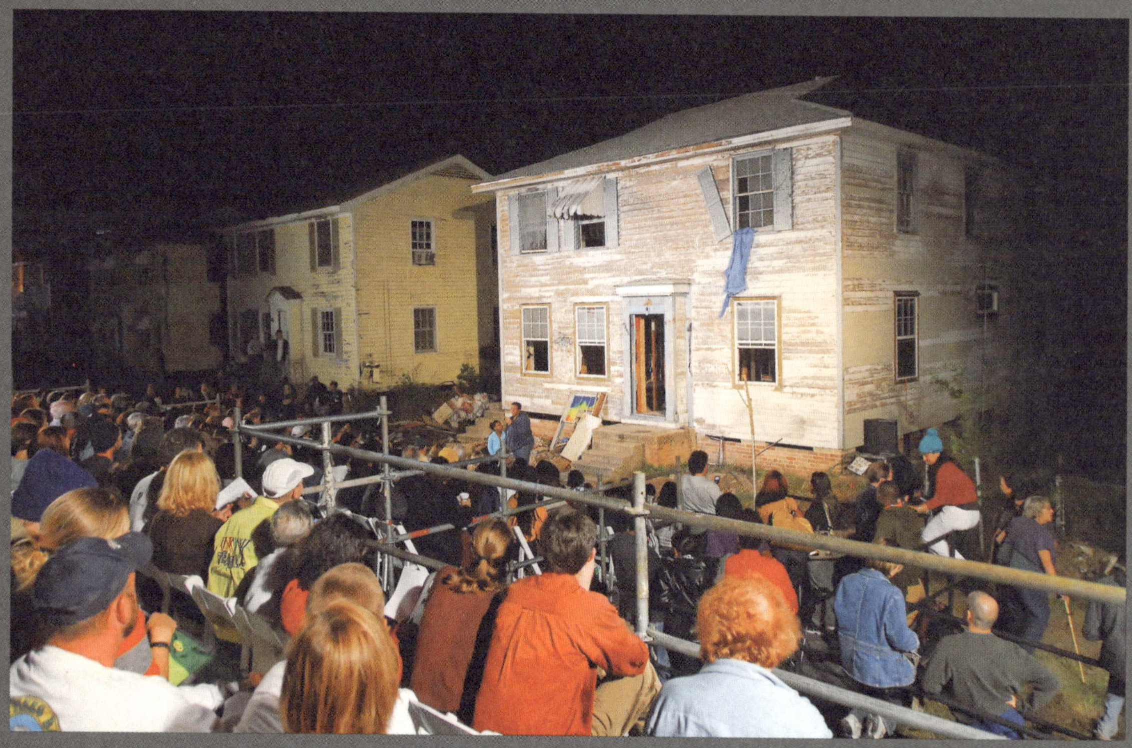

Paul Chan, *Waiting for Godot in New Orleans*, 2007.

Ben Davis

As it is being canonized, I see the concept of SEA contributing to confusion rather than clarifying stakes, by creating a hybrid category of art-politics. Lowe points out the need to define an "ethical agenda" for SEA, lest it become divorced from any tangible social mission; Fisher replies that A Blade of Grass doesn't "currently declare that we have a specifically progressive agenda" because the organization wants "to be open to projects that have a lot of very obtuse angles, or are taking an indirect course, or that perhaps don't quite know what they are doing, or are operating very responsively." If the demands of being open to artistic language are such that they diffuse even our ability to define ourselves in relation to something as general as a "progressive agenda," then I think we may have a looming problem.[3]

Fallen Fruit (David Allen Burns, Matias Viegener, and Austin Young), Urban Fruit Action, 2005. Inkjet print, 40 × 60 in.

Fallen Fruit was originally conceived by David Burns, Matias Viegner and Austin Young. Since 2013, David and Austin have continued the collaborative work.

Thompson's "Living As Form" show was a landmark, and helped crystalize my own thoughts on "social practice." That show deliberately expanded beyond the world of professional art, presenting Allora & Calzadilla's participatory public art project *Tisa* alongside the sit-ins in Tahrir Square, the Fallen Fruit collective's public, participatory jam-making project alongside WikiLeaks, Paul Chan's *Waiting for Godot in New Orleans* alongside the celebrations of Barack Obama's 2008 election in Harlem. This dizzying assortment of things is linked by the potency with which they mobilize symbolic discourse in public space. And yet I don't know what they have to do with one another as political phenomena. That's worrying, considering that the whole terms of the discussion imply that we are trying to escape the insularity and formalism of traditional art practice to enter into meaningful dialogue about how to change the world. It seems to me we are being recaptured by the art world's vagueness—its sneaky habit of transforming politics into a motif or talking point—in the very act of trying to escape it.

At the very same time, discussion of SEA seems defined by (largely unstated) *political* exclusions, seemingly to preserve the illusion of consensus about the progressive political value of the term. Once we include more challenging examples, it becomes clear that, without defining more specifically what we mean by "socially engaged," the category of "Socially Engaged Art" becomes a meaningless abstraction, easily

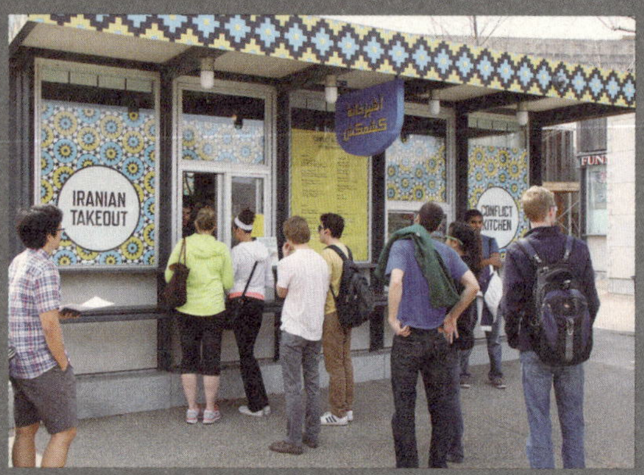

John Rubin and Dawn Weleski, *Conflict Kitchen*, Iran iteration, Oakland neighborhood of Pittsburgh, 2010–ongoing.

abused. The conservative activist James O'Keefe's infamous stunt, dressing as an outlandish pimp and tricking ACORN workers into embarrassing the agency on (heavily edited) film, is basically textbook Yes Men-style "tactical media" intervention. In fact, O'Keefe's prank would place very highly in the annals of SEA "effectiveness"—ACORN is no more, while the Bhopal gas victims that the Yes Men famously champion still await some modest justice from Dow Chemical.

I definitely agree with Thompson that one shouldn't take a one-size-fits-all approach to social change, and that there's plenty of room to challenge power on a lot of levels. But anything with real political stakes should inspire real political debate, and the false consensus implied by a vague term doesn't help.

Nato Thompson

For the present, it seems to me that SEA continues to mean art and politics work that in some way touches upon the social realm. I realize that this definition is extremely loose but, well, it is a pretty big tent. First we must define the field of this aesthetic engagement and then we can move toward the cultural realm outside the arts to actually tackle the uses of culture writ large. We are in the beginning phases of this. The avant-garde has historically always tried to move art outside the realm of art from Dada to Futurism to the Situationists, but what is particularly different in this historic period is that the tools of art are in use by all mechanisms of power. The sheer scale of cultural production over the last fifty years has made a large swath of the planet aware of the formal language of artistic action such as representation, reflexivity, site-specificity, participation and performativity.

1 See Rosa Luxembourg, *The Essential Rosa Luxemburg: Reform or Revolution and the Mass Strike*, edited by Helen Scott. Chicago: Haymarket Books, 2007.

2 Robert Kennedy, quoted in Ronald Steel, *In Love With the Night: The American Romance With Robert Kennedy*. New York: Simon and Schuster, 2000, p. 159.

3 The issue of ethics is taken up in the dialogue on effectiveness later in this book.

Christian Viveros-Fauné

Business Art, Reconsidered

> Making money is art, and working is art and good business is the best art.
> —Andy Warhol, *The Philosophy of Andy Warhol (From A to B and Back Again)*

About a hundred years ago, Marcel Duchamp took a urinal, put it on a pedestal in a museum, and called it art. Two years ago, inside a cramped Ecuadorean café in Queens, the Cuban artist Tania Bruguera repeated in conversation a remarkably invigorating idea that should prove just as memorable: It's time to return Duchamp's urinal to the bathroom.

Delivered in the context of a coffee colloquy, Bruguera's phrase struck me with the force of the newly obvious. The clincher for a statement she called her "Introduction on Useful Art," delivered in April, 2011, at the headquarters of *Immigrant Movement International*, Bruguera's evolving political-movement-cum-artwork, her words should serve as a rallying cry for thousands of a socially engaged artists and like-minded allies around the world.

Instead, her ideal of "Useful Art" and that of other artists with similarly social aims remains mired in an astoundingly academic set of disquisitions that bring to mind less Jacques Rancière and Jean Baudrillard than the Scholasticism of Don Scotus and Thomas Aquinas. How many socially engaged artists can dance on the head of pin? Can the Western-centric "aesthetic regime of art," as inaugurated by Friedrich Schiller and the Romantics, make room for a socially engaged art with real-world goals? Are such efforts truly art, or do they instead constitute—in the snooty terms used by Claire Bishop—merely "well-intentioned homilies that today pass for critical discourse on social collaboration"?

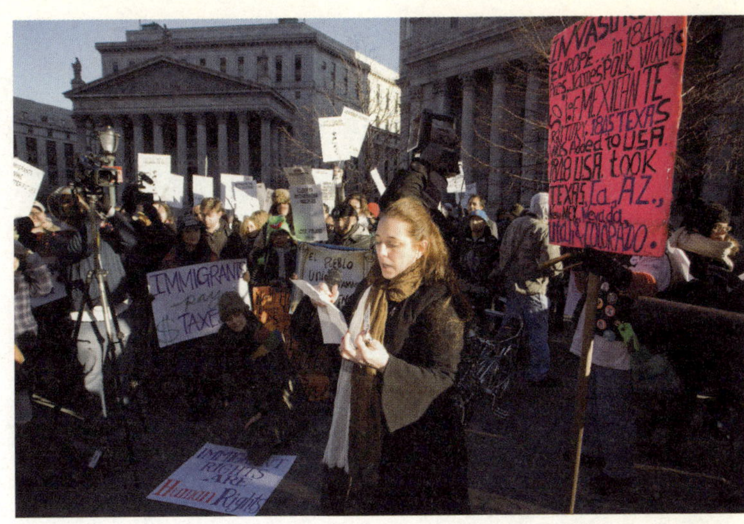

Tania Bruguera, *Immigrant Movement International*, Queens, NY, 2011.

And finally, to quote Ben Davis, is the idea of art as social practice "a starting point for addressing social problems, or a distraction that keeps us from seeing their true extent"?[1]

A great deal could be said here about the "paranoid consensus" that Eve Kosofsky Sedgwick rightly identified as dominating contemporary critical theory, especially the kind that relies on structuralism, psychoanalysis, and neo-Marxism for its worldview. To paraphrase Harold Rosenberg, a great deal of postmodern criticism, like postmodern art, calcified into reactionary convention long ago—constituted as it is by professions whose central aspect is the pretense of overthrowing themselves.

But the idea of this essay isn't just to point out the self-serving suspicions that characterize the increasingly totalizing nature of approaches like Marxist critique and criticality—one typically cries out for activist engagement of a vintage nature, while the other absurdly still demands the detachment of deconstruction—but mainly to call attention to what's missing from current discussions about socially engaged art. Five years after the start of the global economic crisis, much of the recent theoretical throat-clearing—enacted in the shadow of the most brazenly speculative art market in history—critically avoids one of the most fundamental advances in the art of this century: namely, the return of the idea of "business art" to avant-garde practice. This is not, mind you, the familiar art-as-an-asset-class version of "business art," but another beast entirely. This time it's for service.

A phrase first made popular by Andy Warhol's 1975 book *The Philosophy of Andy Warhol* and later abridged to just two words, "business art" has arguably come to be the dominant form of art in our time. Today, this juggernaut of commodity-based art drives not only the way art is made, but also the way it's promoted, marketed, sold and, ultimately, understood both by experts and the vast public. (Michael Findlay, in his 2012 book *The Value of Art*, refers to the phenomenon as "commercialism," the last art movement after Pop and postmodernism.)

One telling example of this form's most public face is the Tate Modern's 2009 show "Pop Life: Art in a Material World."

1 Claire Bishop. "The Social Turn: Collaboration and Its Discontents," *Artforum* 44 February 2006, 178–183.

Ben Davis. "A Critique of Social Practice Art: What Does It Mean to Be a Political Artist?" *International Socialist Review* 90 isr.org.

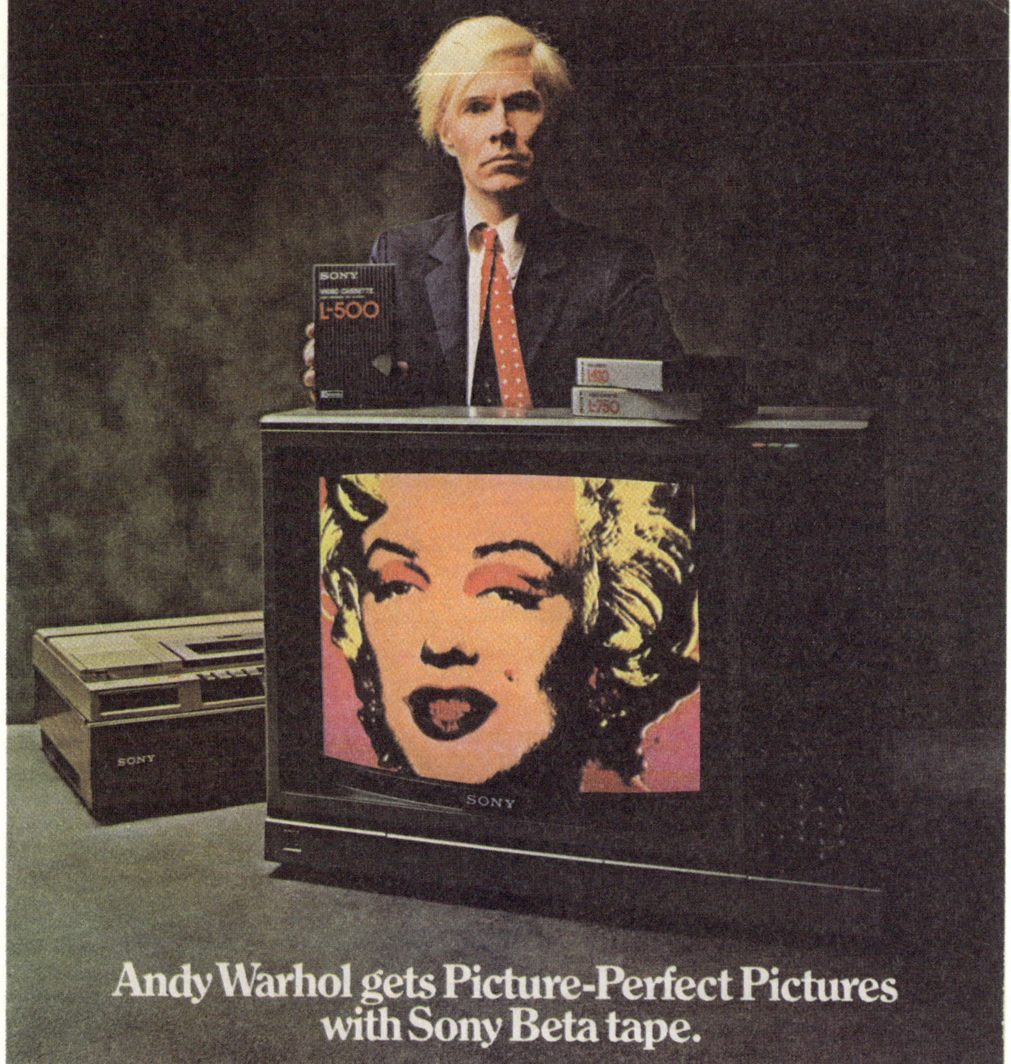

Andy Warhol, pop artist par excellence, looked slightly askance when we told him we'd like to transfer one of his original "Marilyn" prints onto Sony Beta tape and it would come out a Picture-Perfect Picture.

After all, every one of his prints shows incredible attention to color and subtle tonal relationships. And it's hard to imagine any video tape reproducing his vibrant colors perfectly.

But that's exactly what Sony Beta tapes do. They produce Picture-Perfect Pictures. As you can see from this *unretouched* closed circuit transmission.

There's a good reason for this. We're the ones who invented the Beta machine and the cassettes that go with it. We're the leader in the field. We set the standard. It's no wonder that Sony Beta tape is the largest-selling Beta tape in the world.

To create tape that captures brilliant color and delicate shading, we use a unique process. We polish each and every tape to a perfect mirror-finish. We have a special formula for perfect binding of the magnetic particles to the tape, for longer tape and head life.

And like all Sony products, each and every tape is inspected. Not just at the end. But all along the way.

Andy Warhol is quite impressed with Sony's Picture-Perfect Picture. And who could be harder to impress than the perfect picture artist? **SONY**

Shown: Sony Trinitron, KV-1945RS and Sony Betamax recorder, SL-5800. © 1981 Sony Corp. of America. Sony, Trinitron, Betamax are trademarks of Sony Corp.

Newsweek 9/14/81

Advertisement (Andy Warhol for Sony Beta cassette tapes), 1981.

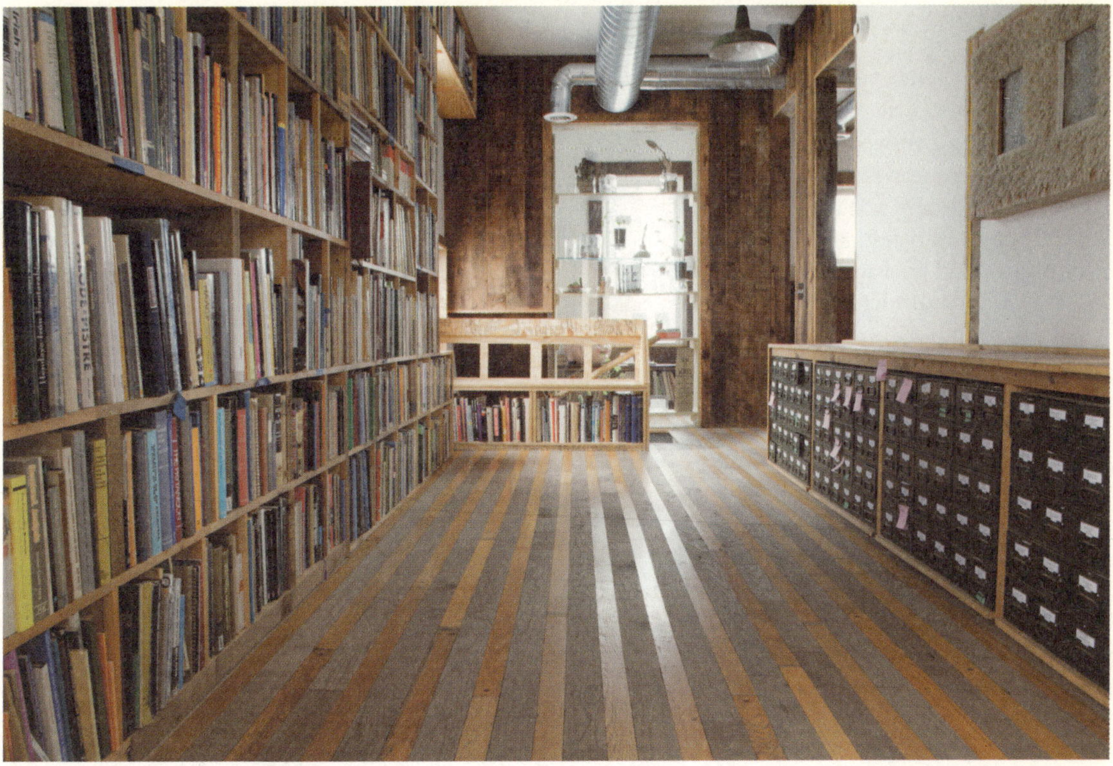

According to the exhibition's wall text, Warhol's business art philosophy "is reflected in the work of artists of subsequent generations who have infiltrated the publicity machine and the marketplace as a deliberate strategy." That show, along with a number of others (such as the Met's "Regarding Warhol") recounted the story of how figures like Richard Prince, Jeff Koons, Damien Hirst, Takashi Murakami, and other business artists achieved blue chip status (a condition far more important than fame or critical standing) by co-opting Warhol's tactics and vastly improving upon them. These tactics include the referencing of consumer products, practicing corporate-style branding and self-promotion, engaging in factory-like production, creating economic consortiums with like-minded investors, and, finally, treating art like an especially fungible instrument of high finance—or, more to the point, like modern-day hedge funds and alternate currencies.

Theaster Gates, *Archive House, Prairie Avenue Books*, 2014.

In a word, the 21st century has seen the rise of business art as a species of meta-art—a new form of contemporary art whose primary purpose is to shape the marketplace for its own commercial purposes. (Consider in this light Hirst's diamond-studded skull *For the Love of God*, as well as the November 2013 auction sale of Koons' *Balloon Dog*, set not-so-accidentally by Christie's

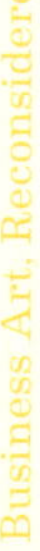

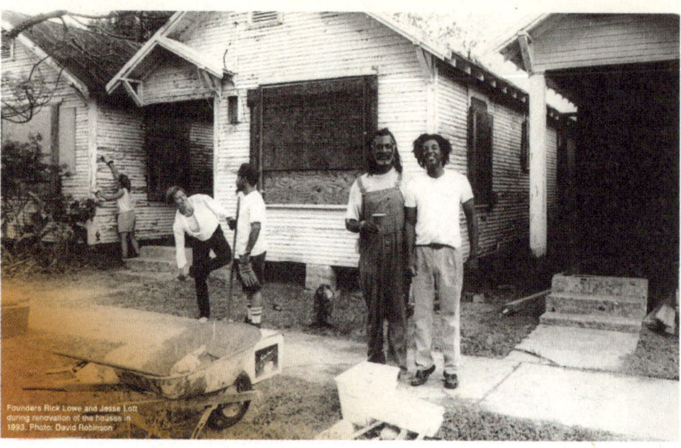

Rick Lowe and Jesse Loft, 1993.

and one of the artist's biggest collectors to hype his recent Whitney Museum retrospective.) The net effect of this phenomenon is nothing less than a revolution in artistic values: an assault that finally jettisons traditional humanistic and postmodern aesthetics to nakedly embrace the idea of art as an asset (now without the aid of passé irony); that univocally accepts the market as the ultimate arbiter of worth (both economic and symbolic); and that, finally, banks on the auction houses as a stock exchange to be readily manipulated by powerfully opaque interests (with virtually no oversight).

Today big money shapes and dominates the art world like at no time previously in history. In fact, the paradigm of 20th-century Warholian business art is so dominant as to have enunciated its own bald-faced 2006 corollary. Enter Sotheby's auctioneer Tobias Meyer's platinum rule: "The best art is the most expensive because the art market is so smart." The sentiment is so institutionally classist, so smarmily unfair and self-fulfilling, it's a wonder progressive artists and their supporters have not marched up to Sotheby's York Avenue offices brandishing torches and pitchforks.

Protest art and social practice, as Davis has properly pointed out, "grows out of a dispirited reaction to the commercial art industry's complicity with capital, and a corresponding, and altogether wholesome, hunger for an art that actually makes a difference." Not only are the questions it raises "very real," I would argue that the dilemmas pointed up by current social practice remain the most urgent issues affecting the "art industry" today. Not only are speculative actors much more open about their real economic interests than in the past—one writer referred to the current state of the art as "a vapid hellhole of investment-crazed pretentiousness"—but those who champion the connection between ethics and aesthetics in contemporary art appear to have found a stronger voice. Like the historical periods that engendered Marx's Eighteenth Brumaire and Joseph Beuys' idea of "social sculpture," the time is ripe for the kind of artistic and critical innovation that at once crystallizes and breaks with the current order of things. Despite the fact that some critics of socially engaged art have taken little notice, that is exactly what has taken place recently in the field of contemporary art.[2]

2 Simon Doonan. "Why the Art World Is so Loathsome," *Slate Magazine* 8, 2012.

Consider Bruguera's idea of "Useful Art" in light of the discussion of business art. An evolving experiment in which she and other artist volunteers founded a brick and mortar center for art and civil rights, *Immigrant Movement International* has not merely protested the status quo, it has also managed to conceive of the idea of collaborative art as a long-term project with an expansive social vision. Among other practical activities, it has served to help immigrants regularize their legal status, bring the issues of new arrivals to the US into the public sphere, meet regularly with local politicians, aid newcomers in constructing a sense of cross-national community—and, just as important, provide artists with an enhanced sense of ethical purpose. By harnessing art world institutional power (the center was funded by Creative Time for a period and continues to be supported by the Queens Museum) Bruguera and company have managed both to imbue critical aesthetics with an ethical mission, and to articulate an inspired response to art's ongoing commodification. Rather than using art as a convenient tool to service business, *Immigrant Movement International* has instead turned the business of art toward service.

One of several emblematic examples of artists moving toward direct "insertions" into what Brazilian artist Cildo Meireles would have termed "ideological circuits," this and other newfangled real world art interventions also put a premium on mobilizing actual political and financial power. To use Bruguera's parlance, such experiments no longer define art as "a space for signaling problems, but the place from which to create the proposal and implementation of possible solutions."

That is certainly one way to consider Theaster Gates' *Dorchester Projects,* an artist-led block improvement effort started in Chicago's South Side in 2007 that has rapidly evolved into a $20 million redevelopment scheme. A growing art project that includes turning an abandoned bank into a cultural center, creating an artist housing collaborative, and establishing a brand new 20,000 square foot "Arts Incubator," Gates' efforts amount to a wholesale revitalization scheme for the city of Chicago. Developed in partnership with the University of Chicago on the site of a boarded-up Walgreens, Gates' latest effort makes a powerful argument for taking advantage of market conditions, as well as private, municipal, and federal housing grants—not to mention the art world's guilt toward racially charged encounters—to trump the conventional capitalist calculus of risk and return.

"I have personal ambitions, as do a lot of people, to see this neighborhood alive," Gates told the *Chicago Tribune* at the March inauguration of the "Arts Incubator" joint venture. (It constitutes only part of a growing partnership between Gates and the university called the "Arts and Public Life Initiative.") "But what does the neighborhood want this block to look like? What does it want it to feel like? The thing I want to do is focus on getting this space as legible to the world as possible, to having this building act as a creative catalyst, both as a home to things happening inside and things radiating outward from it."

The success of Gates' projects, even missing impact statements—these would truly demonstrate effectiveness, identify target audiences, quantify numbers of people served, provide accurate demographics, justify programs in relation to wealth creation, etc.—make certain conclusions abundantly clear. Namely, that the efforts of this artist and those allied with him represent a paradigm shift for an art world used to seeing money deployed chiefly as a marker of financial and (now) symbolic value. His example may be emulated—to a lesser or greater degree, or perhaps even not at all—by other artists throughout the country, but it remains a groundbreaking innovation. Like a Keynesian capitalist with a redistributive mission, Gates has learned how to use—with a nod to the cultural critic Shannon Jackson—money as material.

So it is with what is undoubtedly the oldest and most developed service-oriented business art scheme in the country, Rick Lowe's *Project Row Houses*. Founded in 1993 by Lowe and six other artists in an effort to do something that was not just symbolic but that had a practical application, it has long had a marked real world impact upon its immediate community in Houston's Third Ward, while providing a stark example of art's transformative potential for forward-thinking artists around the world. As of its founding two decades ago, *Project Row Houses* comprised 22 houses spanning a block and a half. Today it occupies six blocks that are home to 40 properties, including exhibition and residency spaces for artists, administrative offices, a community gallery, a park, low-income residential and commercial spaces, and houses that provide homes and support for single mothers trying to get their lives back on track.

Developed largely in contrast to the commercial art world, *Project Row Houses* nonetheless participates not just in the for-profit world, but also in other much larger and more powerful business environments (among them, architecture, urban planning, real estate development and banking)—a fact that also distinguishes this and other similar ventures from previous examples of social practice. An official community development corporation with a $1 million annual budget, *Project Row Houses* has not only pioneered urban revitalization through the arts in this country, it has also helped incubate new businesses in a neighborhood that desperately needs the stability and social fabric these provide.

The commercial art world may be booming so much that, in the words Reuters blogger Felix Salmon, "it has stopped being a source of fascination and crazy numbers, and has started to become a source of sheer disgust," but a handful of artists have upended Andy Warhol's famous dictum about business art in the process. At a precisely the time when the art business perfectly reflects the values of the 1%, artists like Lowe, Gates and Bruguera have learned to use business art to uphold a set of opposing values: critical thinking, social and cultural usefulness, an expansion of art's possibilities in relation to real life, and a profoundly adaptive humanism.

If that's not returning Duchamp's urinal to the men's room—as well as providing art's best example of a genuinely dialectical turn during this money-besotted era—I don't know what is.

Gregory Sholette

Knots

1.

A tangle of questions from A Blade of Grass sends us deep into the weeds.

In the description for a recent public panel discussion they asked, among other things, "Is socially engaged art inherently progressive?" and "Is socially engaged art necessarily tied to progressive politics?"

If we answer yes to the first question, "Is socially engaged art inherently progressive?", we assert that progressive politics (however defined) is inseparably connected to socially engaged art. It's almost as if the two share the same DNA. Severing one from the other fundamentally deforms both.

If we respond positively to the second question, "Is socially engaged art necessarily tied to progressive politics?", another cultural topography comes into view. Art and progressive politics are connected, and yet each remains somehow autonomous from the other.

The search for certitude begins to resemble a Gordian knot, or more exactly a clever *trompe l'oeil* painting of a knot rendered by someone like René Magritte. Each set of questions and answers comes with its own implications. Each has its own historical references. Following one takes us towards a broad conception of art as an ameliorative form of free human labor. Following the other opens the door to asymmetrical power relations and the possibility that culture can be reduced to a political instrument. But what precedents might exist for this puzzle? I stare at the painted knot. Its braided coils are simultaneously a convoluted abyss and nothing more than a flat, pigmented surface. Into my head comes Kim Novak's coif in *Vertigo*. Down we go.

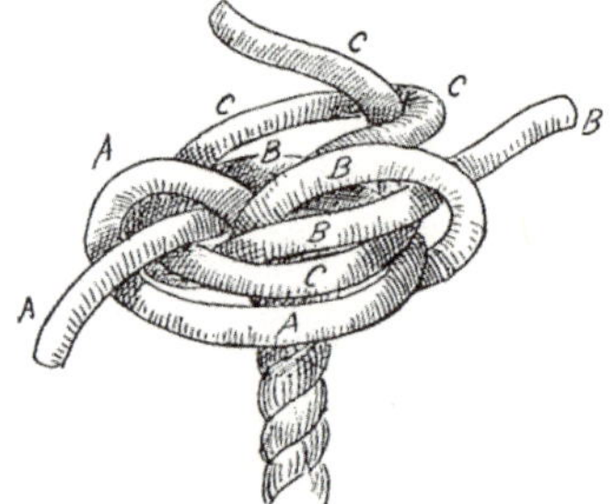

Hand copy of a well-known graphic of an endless knot.

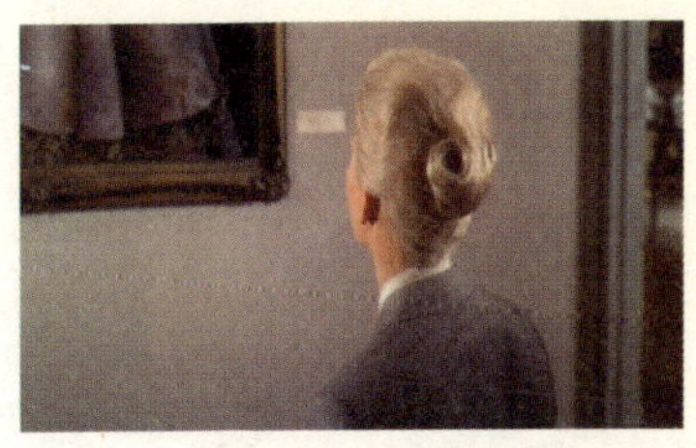

Kim Novak in *Vertigo*. Directed by Alfred Hitchcock, Paramount Pictures, 1958.

2. Deep Storage

Standing in the dimly lit basement of André Malraux's museum without walls, we rifle through an imaginary archive of mental images and documents related to art and politics. The going is slow. It's deep storage. What do we find? First, a hand colored photograph showing a group of men standing in front of a pile of rubble.

April 12, 1871. Gustave Courbet is arguing with his fellow Communards. He points to the Vendôme Column, insisting it's nothing but a "mass of melted cannon that perpetuates the tradition of conquest, of looting, and of murder."[1] Cables are tied to the Napoleonic spire. "Citizen Courbet expresses the wish that the National Defense government will authorize him to disassemble this column." The column falls to pieces. The moment is recorded on a photographic glass plate. The Communards are visible standing victorious beside massive cylinders that were once a monument to Napoleonic conquests. Within weeks the revolutionaries are rounded up and tried, and shot or expelled by a decidedly non-progressive military force. The short-lived socialist experiment is over. Charged with destruction of state property, Courbet is billed some 323,000 francs to rebuild the demolished memorial.[2] He flees the country never to return. The murderers go unpunished. The image rests in the archive.

Sometime in the year 1984, Eva Cockcroft reads from *Artforum*'s glossy pages, looking into the lens of a video camera. Produced by Paper Tiger Television, "Eva Cockcroft Reads Art Forum: Art and Language and Money" is focused on what was then, and what remains today, the world's leading trade magazine for commercial fine art. But artist, muralist and independent scholar Cockcroft focuses on a brief period of time in 1975 when two of *Artforum*'s most intrepid editors—John Coplans and Max Kozloff—turned art world renegades. They published what were then daring essays by people who boldly suggested art was not about transcendental truths. What is art? It is the cultural expression of specific economic, social and political regimes. Carol Duncan, Allan Sekula, Lawrence Alloway, Alan Wallach, Patricia Hills and Eva Cockcroft herself fleetingly became *Artforum* writers. It was Cockcroft and Kozloff who famously maintained that the CIA had been a secret proponent of 1950s action painting, using it as a "weapon" in the cold war. But when once-influential *New York Times* art writer Hilton Kramer suggested art dealers should boycott the magazine, the Coplans/Kozloff editorial moment was over. Kramer later co-founded the neoconservative journal *The New Criterion*. Meanwhile, Cockcroft's reading of *Artforum* was recorded on

1 James Panero. "A Monumental Problem." *The Wall Street Journal*, Sept. 24, 2012. Web. http://www.wsj.com/articles. April 18, 2014.

2 Bertrand Tillier. "La Colonne Vendôme déboulonnée." *L'Histoire par l'image*. Web. http://www.histoire-image.org/site/etude_comp_detail.php?analyse_id=60. April 18, 2014.

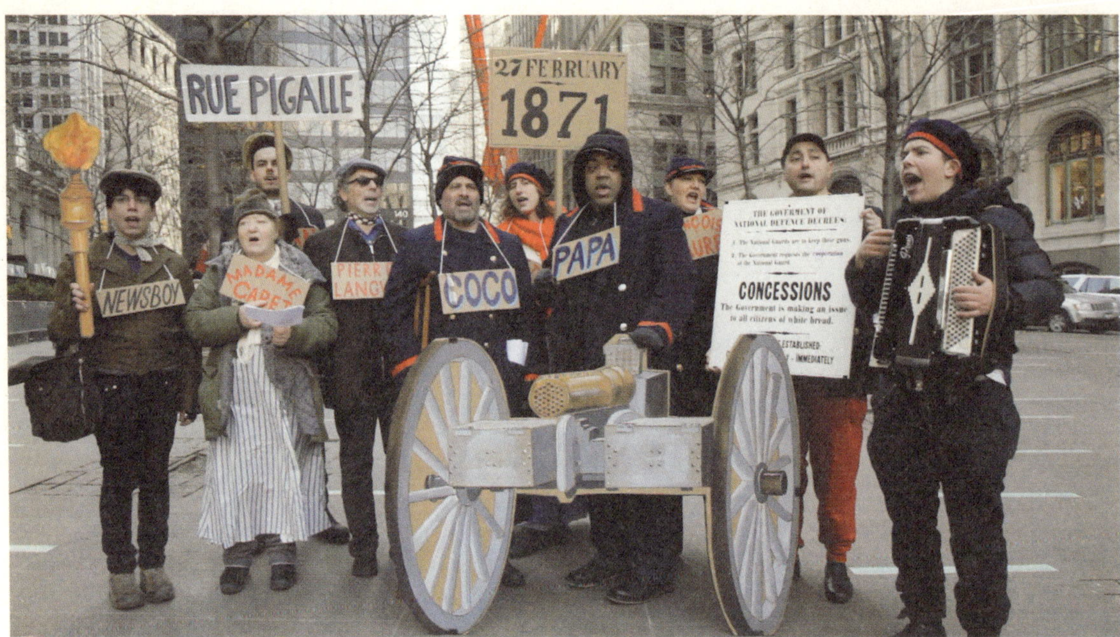

Zoe Beloff, *The Days of the Commune*, 2012.

U-matic three-quarter-inch magnetic tape, an outdated format today that is sometimes still used to view archived 1980s videos. Sometimes the equipment appears as cinematic props in the background of 1980s period films.

On January 7, 1935, three yellowed, handwritten letters from Walter Benjamin to Theodor W. Adorno turn up. Benjamin was on a short trip to Italy and Adorno was living in England but making regular visits to their native Germany. "I presume you are back and I will proceed to answer your long letter of December 17. Not without trepidation."[3] Benjamin starts off cautiously and later sheepishly asks if Adorno has read Bertolt Brecht's *Threepenny Novel* (1934) in which the poet and playwright revisits certain characters from his famed opera with Kurt Weill. Adorno's dislike of Brecht grew increasingly sharper over the years, pivoting on both a rivalry for Benjamin's friendship and the question of whether artistic form should ever be linked to progressive politics. "It is not the office of art to spotlight alternatives, but to resist by its form alone the course of the world, which permanently puts a pistol to men's heads." These are Adorno's words some 27 years after this correspondence, long after Benjamin had taken his own life while fleeing the Nazis. Again from the 1935 letter: "I am not looking beyond Easter. Brecht again asked me to come to Denmark and, indeed, right away. Now I will probably not leave San Remo before May in any case." A few months later Adolf Hitler begins to rearm Germany in violation of the 1919 Treaty of Versailles. As it turns out,

3 Walter Benjamin, Gershom Scholem, and Theodor W. Adorno. *The Correspondence of Walter Benjamin, 1910–1940*. Chicago: University of Chicago Press, 1994.

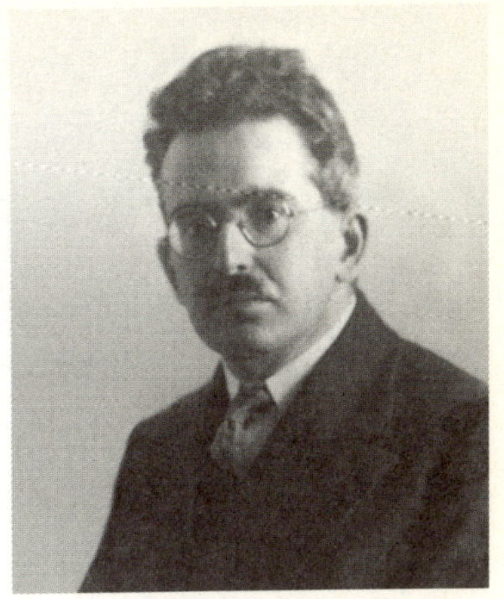

Identity photo of Walter Benjamin, 1928.

Georges Bataille saved these brittle sheafs of paper from destruction and they were not rediscovered until 1981. By then Adorno was also gone.

February/March 1982. The cover of a cheaply printed, 12-page, black-and-white magazine entitled *Upfront* raises its own questions about art and politics. "But Is It Art?" the headline reads. Then "A Not-So-Imaginary Dialogue" ensues. Two unnamed artists exchange views. The first insists, "Well, we're not just doing our thing while Reagan fiddles. The art we make isn't neutral; it isn't escapist; and it ain't necessarily pretty." This is obviously a socially engaged artist speaking to an imaginary gallery-based interlocutor. The latter responds, "That makes good political sense. But is it good art?" "Damn right it is," comes the unqualified reply. "If you include the art of pictorial resistance: words, sounds and images that touch and move people by challenging oppression with passion and imagination." But if you "define art's domain as timeless, universal, beyond history, isolated, out-of-touch, then it isn't our thing!" Written by the editorial staff of *Upfront*, this Platonic dialogue was printed in the newsletter of Political Art Documentation/Distribution (PAD/D), a "left-to-socialist artists' resource and networking organization" co-founded by Lucy R. Lippard, Jerry Kearns and others including myself.[4] PAD/D emerged out of the remnants of the post-1968 New Left. It echoed, though far less dictatorially, Mao Zedong's sentiments from 1943 linking art to class struggle: "There is in fact no such thing as art for art's sake, art that stands above classes, art that is detached from or independent of politics."[5] Our mission in the 1980s seemed equally clear. At a time of well-funded and well-organized right-wing backlash against the progressive gains of the 1960s, PAD/D sought to provide political leadership to cultural workers whose progressive outlook might otherwise remain disorganized and haphazard. *Après PAD/D vient le contre-révolution!* Scanned copies of the offset journal are online.

January 23, 1884. "The cause of Art is the cause of the people," declares a scraggly-bearded man in front of an affluent, though progressive, British audience gathered at the Leicester Secular Society in 1848.[6]

> Now once more I will say that we well-to-do people, those of us who love Art, not as a toy, but as a thing necessary to the life of man, as a token of his freedom and happiness, have for our best work the raising of the standard of life among the people ...

4 "Lippard Charitable Visits by the AWC to the MoMA and Met." Originally published by the Ad Hoc Women Artists' Committee and reprinted in *Get The Message*, 22. http://darkmatterarchives.net

5 "Mao Zedong Yan'an Forum Talks on Literature and Art, May 1943." *Open Hearing, Art Workers' Coalition Primary Documents*, 1969, 51.

6 William Morris. "Art and Socialism." Marxists Internet Archive. Web. April 18, 2014.

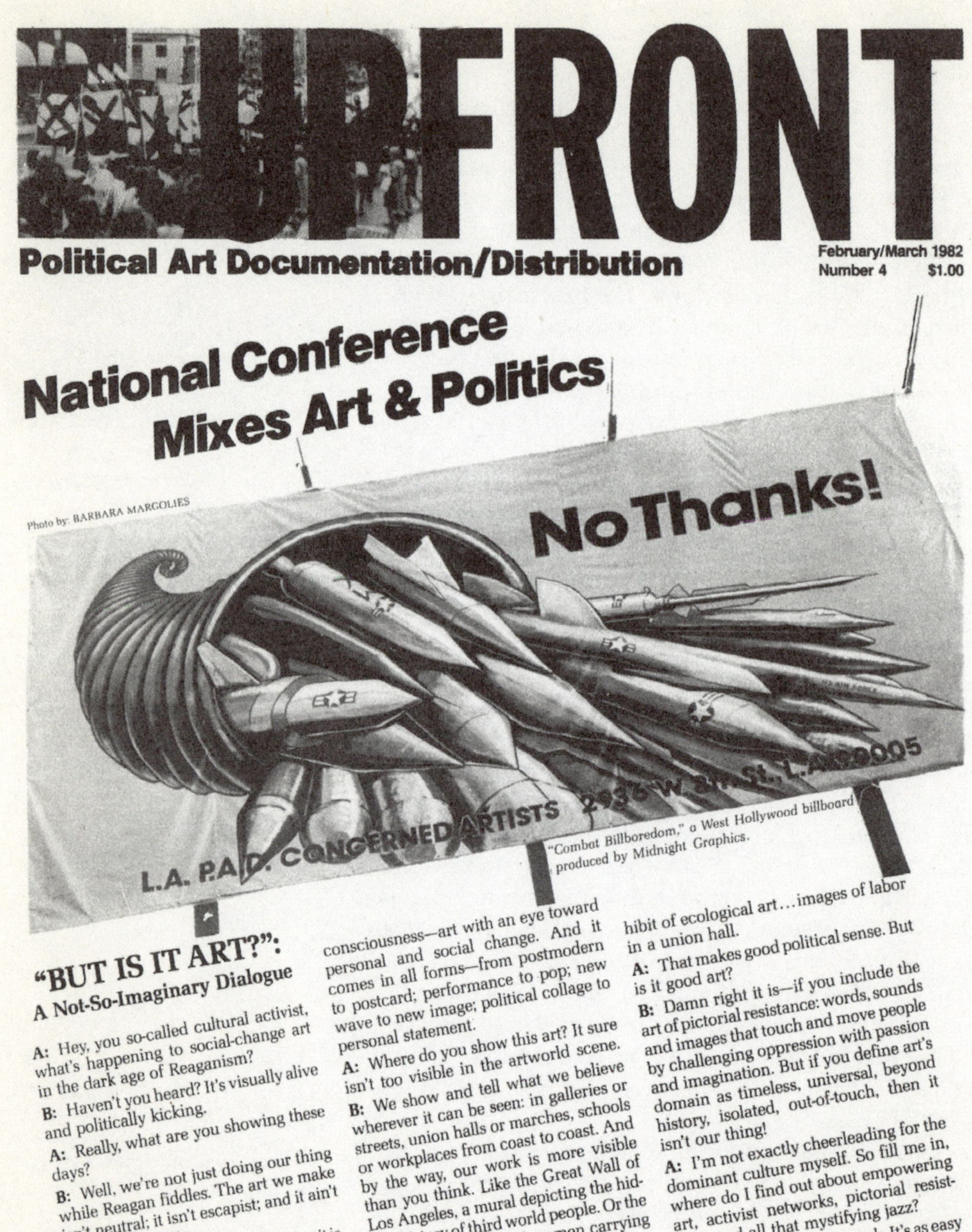

UPFRONT

Political Art Documentation/Distribution

February/March 1982
Number 4 $1.00

National Conference Mixes Art & Politics

Photo by: BARBARA MARGOLIES

"Combat Billboredom," a West Hollywood billboard produced by Midnight Graphics.

"BUT IS IT ART?": A Not-So-Imaginary Dialogue

A: Hey, you so-called cultural activist, what's happening to social-change art in the dark age of Reaganism?

B: Haven't you heard? It's visually alive and politically kicking.

A: Really, what are you showing these days?

B: Well, we're not just doing our thing while Reagan fiddles. The art we make isn't neutral; it isn't escapist; and it ain't necessarily pretty.

A: I know what it ain't. Tell me what it is.

B: It's all about concern, involvement, consciousness—art with an eye toward personal and social change. And it comes in all forms—from postmodern to postcard; performance to pop; new wave to new image; political collage to personal statement.

A: Where do you show this art? It sure isn't too visible in the artworld scene.

B: We show and tell what we believe wherever it can be seen: in galleries or streets, union halls or marches, schools or workplaces from coast to coast. And by the way, our work is more visible than you think. Like the Great Wall of Los Angeles, a mural depicting the hidden history of third world people. Or the parade of black-robed women carrying a coffin of illegal abortion devices. Or a video of FBI harassment... a gallery exhibit of ecological art... images of labor in a union hall.

A: That makes good political sense. But is it good art?

B: Damn right it is—if you include the art of pictorial resistance: words, sounds and images that touch and move people by challenging oppression with passion and imagination. But if you define art's domain as timeless, universal, beyond history, isolated, out-of-touch, then it isn't our thing!

A: I'm not exactly cheerleading for the dominant culture myself. So fill me in, where do I find out about empowering art, activist networks, pictorial resistance and all that mystifying jazz?

B: I thought you'd never ask. It's as easy as turning this page and getting into the "February 26th Movement."

—*Editorial Staff*

Cover of *Upfront: Political Art Documentation/Distribution*. February/March 1982.

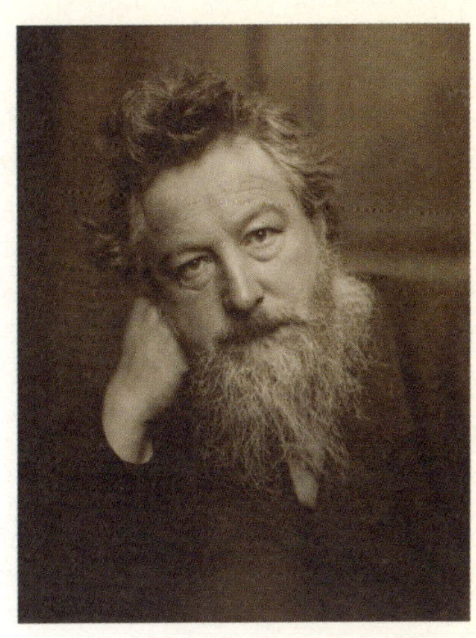

Frederick Hollyer, Portrait of William Morris, c. 1887. From J. W. Mackail, *The Life of William Morris*. London, New York and Bombay: Longmans, Green and Co., 1899.

Acknowledging his own class status, artist, socialist and entrepreneur William Morris called upon his comfortable peers to renounce their class privilege and help "return" Art, or perhaps more accurately artisanal production, to its place within the life and labor of the masses. "One day we shall win back Art, that is to say the pleasure of life; win back Art again to our daily labour." The roughness of the proletariat is not their natural condition, Morris avowed; it is the result of a degrading process of alienation brought about by the capitalist obsession with profits. If only the working person would be reintroduced to the ennobling balm of artistic production, it would rekindle his or her latent desire to live a cultural, full life. Meanwhile the wealthy have captured Art, squandered its transformative power, and reduced it to a mere plaything. For Morris, the task of freeing workers from capitalist wage slavery ran parallel to the act of freeing art from its upper-class prison. His 1884 lecture, "Art and Socialism," appeared that same year as a thin, inexpensive pamphlet sized so that a worker could slip a copy into a pocket and discreetly read it during his or her lunch break.

Here we pause, because this document is an especially intriguing precedent for our twisted problem. Why? Because for one thing Morris's idea of cultural and political revolution pivoted as much on art's emancipatory possibilities as it did on the moral resolve of the well-to-do toward their laboring brothers and sisters. "I offer a means of renouncing their class by supporting a Socialist propaganda in joining the Democratic Federation." According to Morris, by "re-aestheticizing" work and de-privileging art with a capital "A," the unimaginative drudgery of the factory would be abolished and an essential first step taken towards spreading socialist freedom amongst the masses. In this sense, he distanced himself from contemporaries such as Karl Marx and Frederick Engels who had little to say about art or moral imperatives, and who focused their emancipatory aspirations on the inherent contradictions of capitalism. But where would we locate Morris in our debate? Is socially engaged art inherently progressive, or is it only linked with progressive politics? In modified form Morris seems to answer yes to both questions. He was indeed seeking to forge ties between art and progressive politics, but he did so in the belief that his actions were reuniting art with its atrophied humanist values. Artistic labor, he assured, "is the true pleasure of life."

3. The Knot and the Cheese

I stare at the knot.

Clearly to some degree contemporary, socially engaged art practice conforms to Morris's idea about art and its positive effects on the daily life of the masses. We simply need to substitute underprivileged communities for laborers. Then again, much has changed since his lecture "Art and Socialism." Most art today is not artisanal or craft-oriented, at least not in the way Morris imagined. In fact, art is now quite unlike its antecedent in the 19th century, period. But debates covering basically the same ground have come and gone, and erupted anew, and disappeared again ever since.

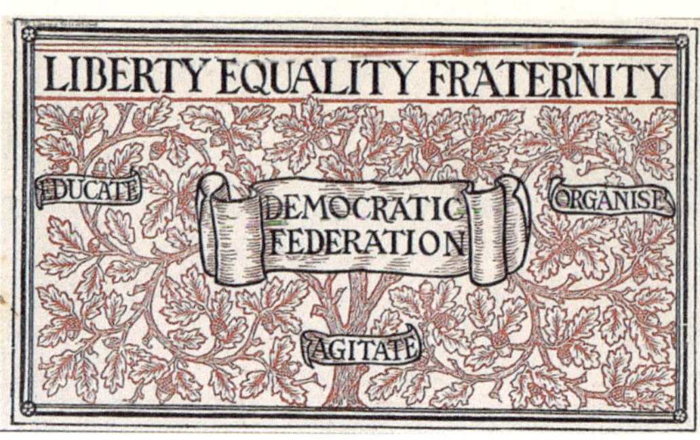

Democratic Federation membership card, c. 1880–1914.

The Democratic Federation was formed in 1881 by H.M. Hyndman, a leading British Marxist. In 1884, William Morris and others left to form the Socialist League.

And although all those cited in my imaginary archive would agree that there is an ever-present link between artistic engagement in society and notions of social progress (regardless if one is for or against the latter point of view), it would seem impossible to truly reconcile the Courbet/Brecht/ Cockcroft/Mao/ PAD/D position—that art is a tool of class interests and must therefore be placed at the service of progressive change or considered reactionary—with Morris's belief that artistic labor is inherently liberating because it allows for human expression. What made him tick? Morris would have been a teenager in 1848 during the so-called "Springtime of the Peoples," in which ad hoc revolutions spread across France, Germany, Denmark and the Austro-Hungarian Empire among other parts of the continent. Could there really be that much of a gap between the rising expectations of working class unionization in mid 19th-century Europe when compared with the numerous revolutionary defeats and instances of state repression that would follow? Besides, most of the progressive changes enacted would vanish in a few years. And so I stare at the knot again and wonder if perhaps the issue is not this thicket of snarled questions, but rather something more like recognition failure? After all, you cannot untangle a painting of a knot, you can only observe it, or compare it with other objects, or hang it in a museum. Oh, and yes of course, you can cut it up into smaller pieces.

Today it is all but impossible to only make a painting or a sculpture. No work of art can refuse social meaning now, any more than traces of our actions can escape being endlessly archived in cyberspace. Connectivity to networks of socialized production and communication are inescapable. It is a relatively new phenomenon. Recall Richard Serra's *Tilted Arc*, which was installed in front of the Jacob K. Javitz Federal Building in downtown Manhattan without any input from the men and women whose offices were adjacent to the sculptor's curving wall of rusting steel. Serra's art apparently gave no William Morris-like pleasure to their workday. Perhaps its austere presence even reminded them of the barren cubicles they spent so much of their lives housed within. In any case, they objected, suing the General Services Administration, which had commissioned the work, to have *Tilted Arc* carted off. It was removed in 1989. The following year an entirely new language appeared in the grant guidelines of the National Endowment for the Arts (NEA). From then on, artists proposing a public project would have to take into account the "community" their work would impact and seek to address "underserved communities." Like Kurt Vonnegut's ice-nine, which rapidly crystallizes water at any temperature, the new language of inclusivity and sensitivity and service to community spread to other agencies, foundations, and institutions. Since then the transformation has gained momentum and breadth.

For aspiring artists these days it is virtually *de rigueur* to attach some external narrative—national, biographical, communal, and on occasion, political—to even the most autonomous looking abstract image or object. It was not always so. Indeed, the entire artistic paradigm has shifted so quickly and so dramatically that it is no longer impertinent to speak seriously about art as a political or social or collective activity, as it was in the early 1980s. For example, in the 1980s PAD/D published a monthly calendar of upcoming radical art events called Red Letter Days. It was as much a way to announce these programs as it was a means of reinforcing the coming-into-being of socially engaged art in New York. But most Red Letter Days (and evenings) took place in non-mainstream venues such as union halls, school auditoriums or less visible alternative art spaces like Franklin Furnace. By contrast, over the course of the past two months as I have been working on this essay: a significant conference focusing on artistic collaboration took place at a mainstream academic institution; an exhibition opened at a major museum featuring an artist who invited high school students to cover its normally white walls in graffiti; another prime New York City art institution described its own biannual exhibition as composed of artists working in "interdisciplinary ways, artists working collectively, and artists from a variety of generations," and a third Manhattan museum was invaded by protesters who sought to call attention to human rights violations in the Middle East where this institution is building a new facility under terrible local labor conditions. The demonstrators dropped handmade dollar bills into its famed atrium, much as Abbie Hoffman and the Yippies did on the New York Stock Exchange in 1967.

And here are some more examples of this phenomenon to consider. Once denounced by *New Criterion* neoconservatives such as Hilton Kramer, PAD/D's archive of socially engaged art is now in the collection of the Museum of Modern Art. The radical approach to social art history that once led to the expulsion of Kozloff and Coplans from *Artforum* is today central to most academic programs. Brecht is part of the standard theater repertoire everywhere, and an entire industry has sprung up around Walter Benjamin's writings. Courbet's work has an entire room at the Metropolitan Museum of Art. And most of all, despite our polymorphous, deskilled, post-artisanal contemporary art world, Morris' belief in culture's ameliorative properties has been become a central tenet not only of the fast-growing arena of social practice art, but also the art world as a whole.

In other words, what if we "progressives" have already conquered the ideology of the art establishment, from its academic programs to its "serious" cultural institutions, biennials, art fairs, and so forth, but most of all, the way the art world imagines itself within its own international discourse? Of course there is still plenty of non-committed art, anti-social art, and even a bit of reactionary art. But here in this, our tiny, specialized corner of the culture industry, isn't the *lingua franca* of global art-speak inherently progressive? (Even if the actual political economy of art is anything but forward looking?) Which means what? That the knot is actually an optical illusion? A distraction? Something akin to Holbein's infamous anamorphic skull floating impertinently in front of us? Remember this *memento mori* only appears undecipherable when we stare at it straight on. Once we step to the side of the painting and look at it askew, the distorted image crystalizes. Can we look at this knot of questions on art and politics askew?

As Kerstin Stakemeier puts it, the capitalization of art that started around the 1960s also meant "its factual socialization."[7] In other words, once "Art" became an arena of ever-intensifying economic trade and investment, any remnant of autonomous production was forced to enter the thoroughly socialized disciplines of modern finance capital. Whatever independence once existed for art apart from the broader economic matrix ended. What remained, I would argue, is a knot of desire for art's dream of autonomous labor that is kept alive largely within its discourse. That is the good news. Projects like Caroline Woolard's BFAMFAPHD.com, W.A.G.E., Art and Labor, and the intensifying critiques of the Guggenheim Museum's franchise in the United Arab Emirates by groups such as Gulf Labor Coalition and Occupy Museums evince both the vitality of this progressive debate, as well as a renewed recognition regarding 21st-century capitalism. That is not to say that artists were never before asserting progressive politics—we need only look at the words and

7 "It is the real subsumption of artists under capital which transforms them into producers of contemporary art. And it is this process that in turn gave rise to the independent artist organizations of the 1960s and 1970s, while implicating artists in the dramatic social struggles of their time, including most notably the anti-Vietnam War movement. They participated in these political confrontations as one kind of 'producer amongst many.'" —Kerstin Stakemeier in Greg Sholette and Oliver Ressler, eds. *It's The Political Economy, Stupid: The Global Financial Crisis in Art and Theory*. New York: Pluto Press, 2013.

work of Morris or Daumier or even David to counter that notion. But even with the emergence of "deskilling" and "dematerialized" art in the 1960s—to cite Ian Burns and Lucy R. Lippard respectively—the artist/cultural worker as a "specialized producer" still always had one foot wedged tightly in the world according to William Morris, because even as conceptual artists outed painting as merely another commodity, they refused to embrace the idea that "art" was doomed to be nothing more than a luxury good. "There is our hope: the cause of Art is the cause of the people," Morris proclaimed. Eighty-five years later, Art Workers' Coalition demanded: "Art isn't entertainment. It should be free to anyone who is or might be interested." It would take another few decades to all but completely disenchant artists from their 19th-century ideals. And while I admit to now and then indulging my own Morris-like willful naïveté in this regard, there's no denying that the emergence of art-based hedge funds and Damien Hirst's platinum skulls is a symptom of art's ultimate transition into the cold realm of capital.

"Who will eat the cheese?" Marcel Broodthaers once asked about the machinations of the art world, his rhetoric flavored with more than a pinch of sarcasm. Who indeed? Without losing sight of the knot—for where would we be without it—perhaps we need to learn how to look simultaneously at it and beyond into the darkness of the art world's undereconomy where the most challenging questions loom into view? William Morris would no doubt agree.

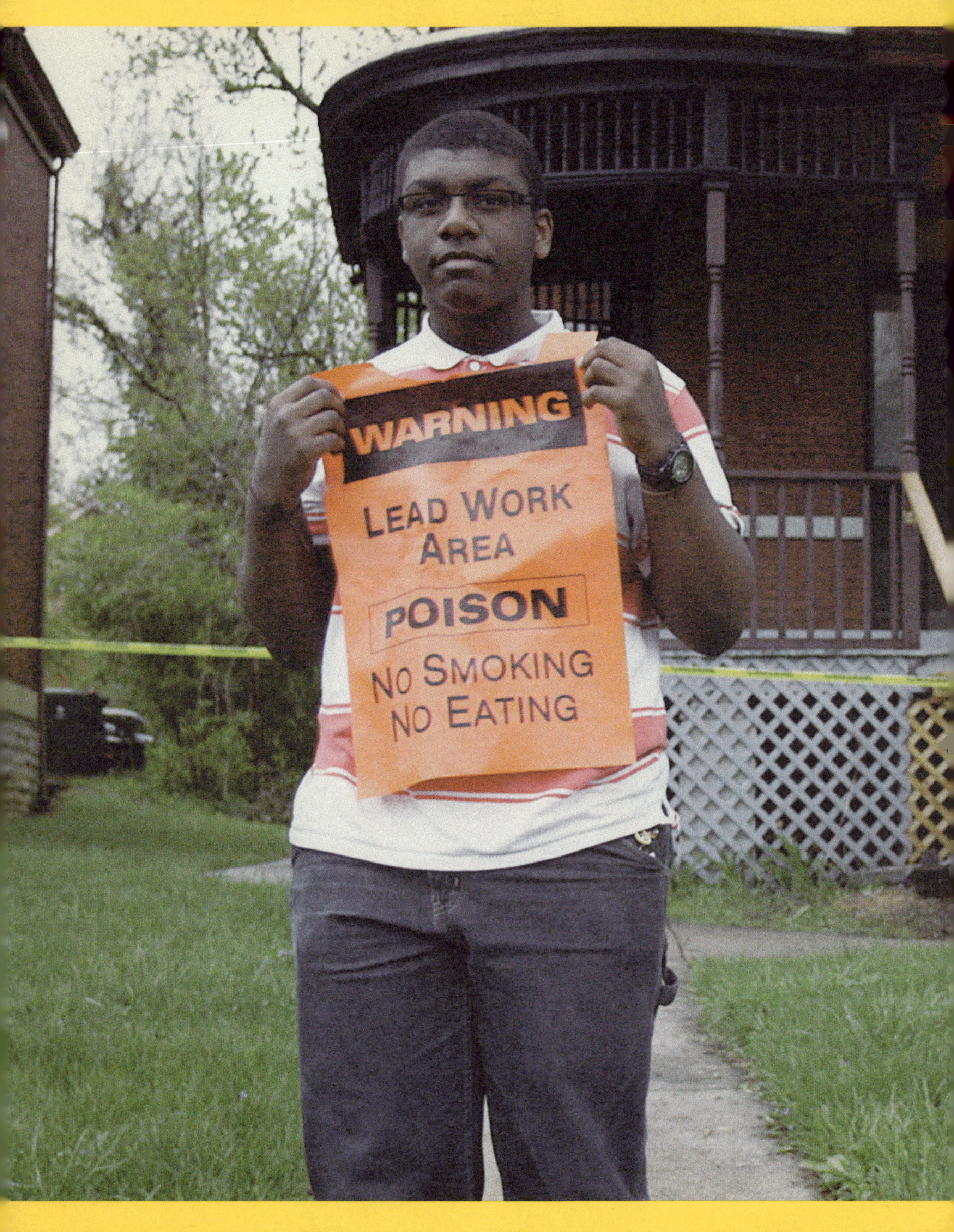
WARNING
LEAD WORK AREA
POISON
NO SMOKING
NO EATING

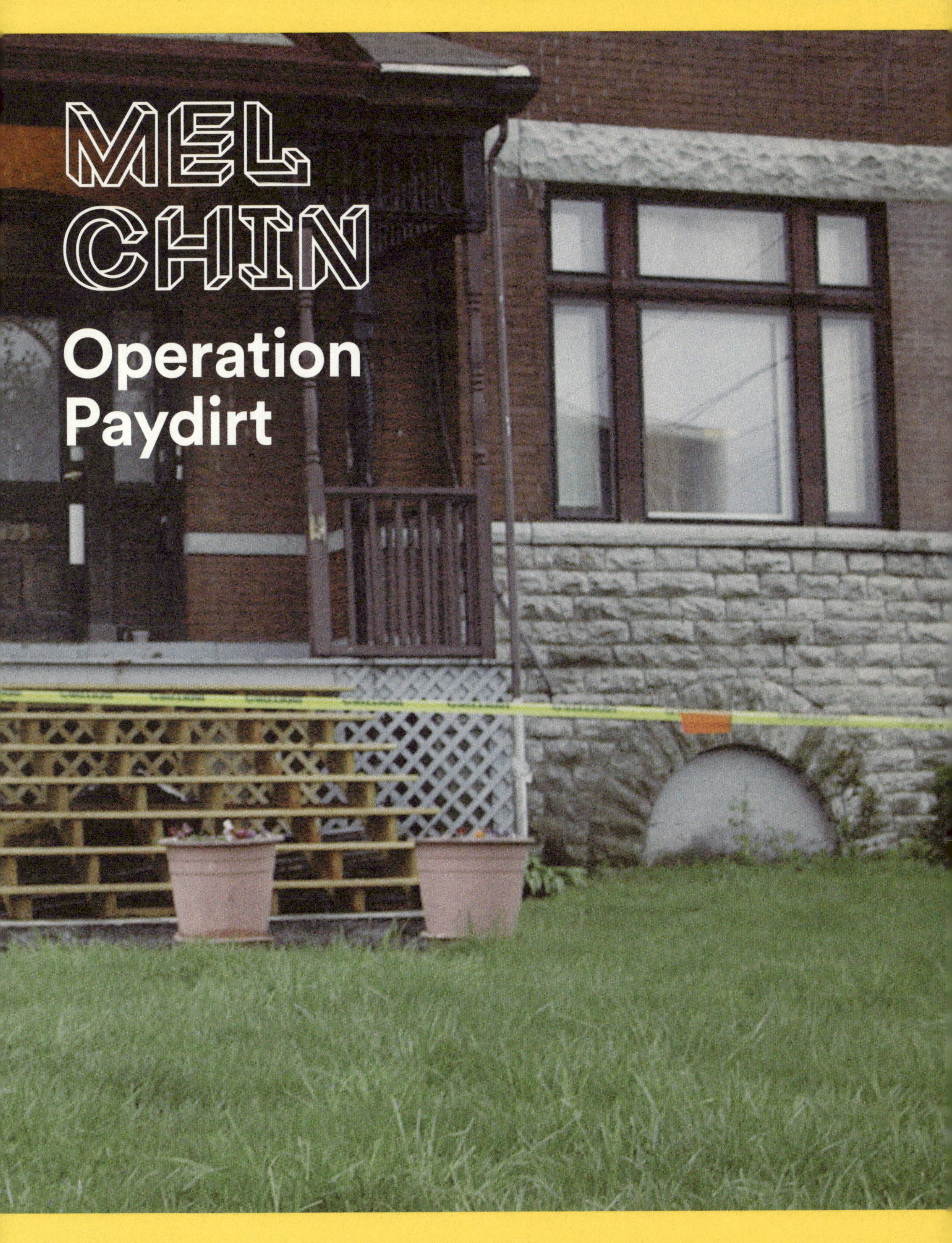
MEL
CHIN
Operation
Paydirt

Lead poisoning is a terrible, evil and pernicious thing, and its effects permeate our society. Victims can suffer from decreased bone and muscle growth, damage to the nervous system and kidneys, hearing impairment, speech and language problems, and developmental delay. They are more likely to suffer poor impulse control, including violent outbursts that can lead to violent crime. Why, then, do we not do more to prevent it?

Operation Paydirt is a project that Mel Chin has pursued since 2007, using art as a vehicle to bring awareness to the largely invisible yet pervasive problem of lead-contaminated environments, and the resulting widespread poisoning of our nation's children. Acknowledging that lead poisoning is completely preventable, Chin has ambitiously sought ways to support efforts to eliminate it through his art practice. The project works as an umbrella for a number of initiatives that function in tandem to educate people and help forge alliances between nonprofits, governments and communities. By bringing the creativity and vision of an artist's approach and working with an array of creative individuals, Chin and his team have found a variety of fresh ways to animate the issue, engage individuals and connect across sectors to address this persistent nationwide health crisis.

The project has pursued different strategies to address the lead problem, including an inexpensive urban soil remediation protocol, TLC (treat-lock-cover), designed by Dr. Andrew Hunt of the University of Texas Arlington and implemented in West Oakland by the United States Environmental Protection Agency. While the initial years of the project focused on soil and lead issues in New Orleans, the project has expanded to more broadly support lead awareness and prevention in communities across the country. Chin and his team, including Amanda Wiles and Mary Rubin, have spent the last couple of years building relationships with individuals and organizations within art, education, and health networks to develop strategies to work with Fundreds as part of an awareness campaign tied to increased

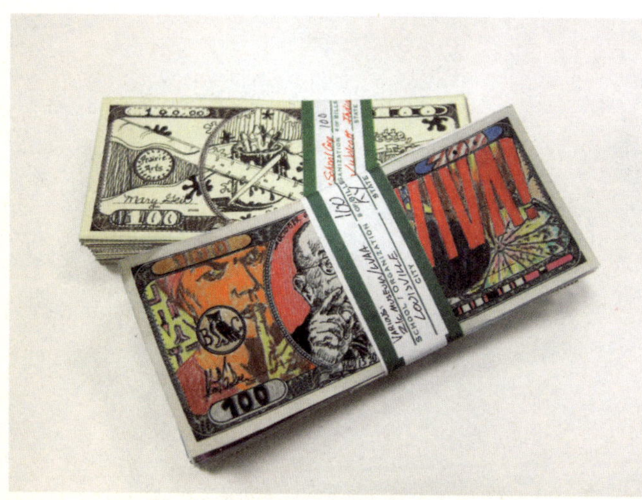

Previous spread: *Operation Paydirt*, Cincinnati, 2015.

Left: *Fundred Dollar Bills* (Kentucky, Indiana), c. 2010.

Opposite page: *Fundred Dollar Bill Project* armored delivery truck.

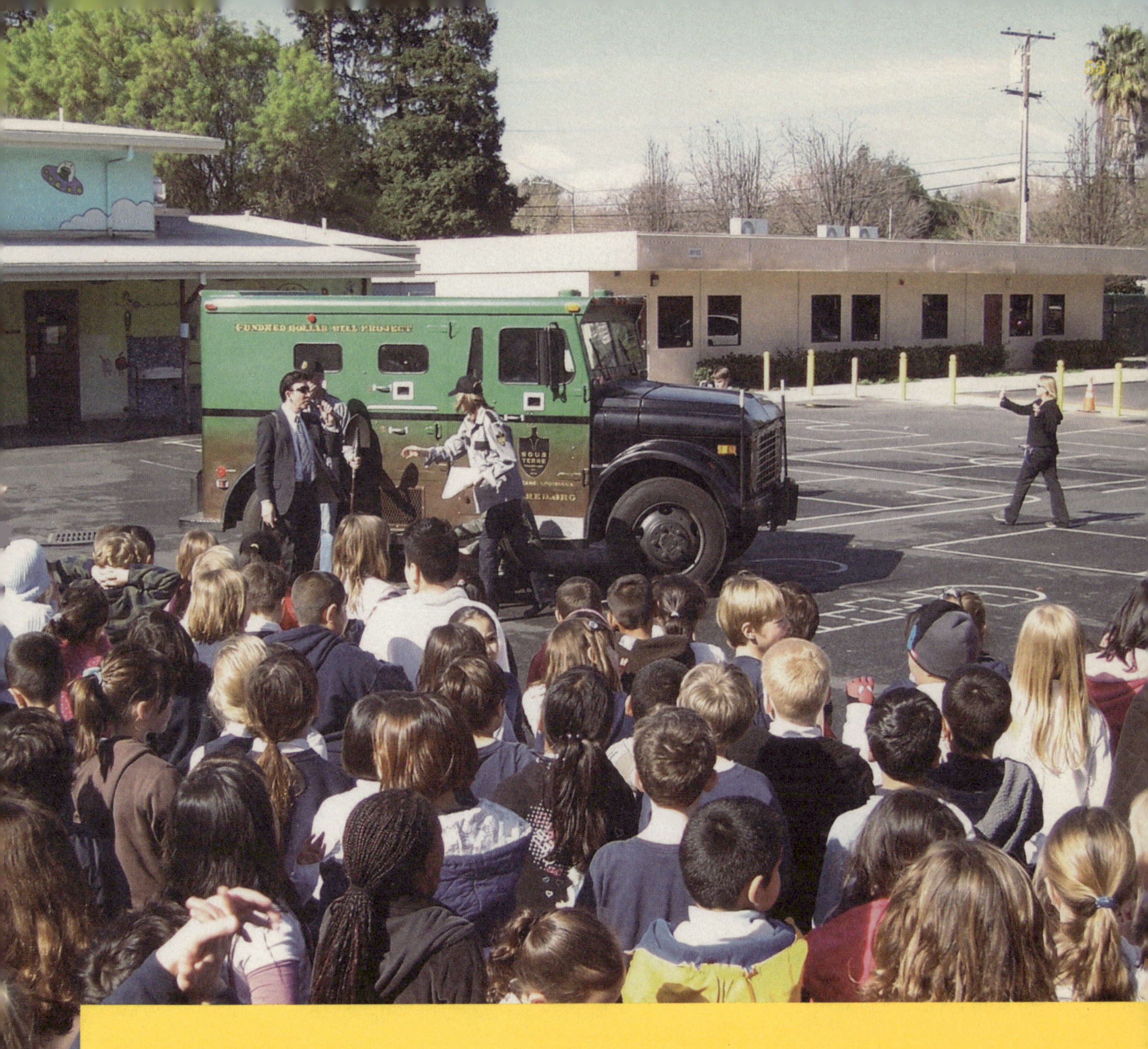

Creating a Socially Engaged Art Curriculum with Mel Chin and Cheryl Maney

Elizabeth M. Grady in conversation with Cheryl Maney
May 23, 2014

Cheryl Maney worked with Mel Chin during his residency at the McColl Center for Visual Art in Charlotte, North Carolina. She helped implement his work into the curriculum at Charlotte-Mecklenburg Schools, and discussed working with students on *Operation Paydirt*.

Elizabeth M. Grady (ABOG)
What prompted you to get involved with Mel's project, *Operation Paydirt*?

Cheryl Maney (CM)
Our district was working with the McColl Center for Visual Art, which was hosting Mel. They asked about our interest in participating. I also had heard from a videographer who was creating a video of Mel, and he thought we might be interested in participating. We piloted the project in the spring of 2013 and then took it district-wide in the fall of 2014.

ABOG
Why was it important to do this project with kids?

CM
In our district we promote personal voice in students' art. We also promote collaboration. Each year as the Curriculum Specialist, I select a visual arts-based, socially engaged project for our teachers

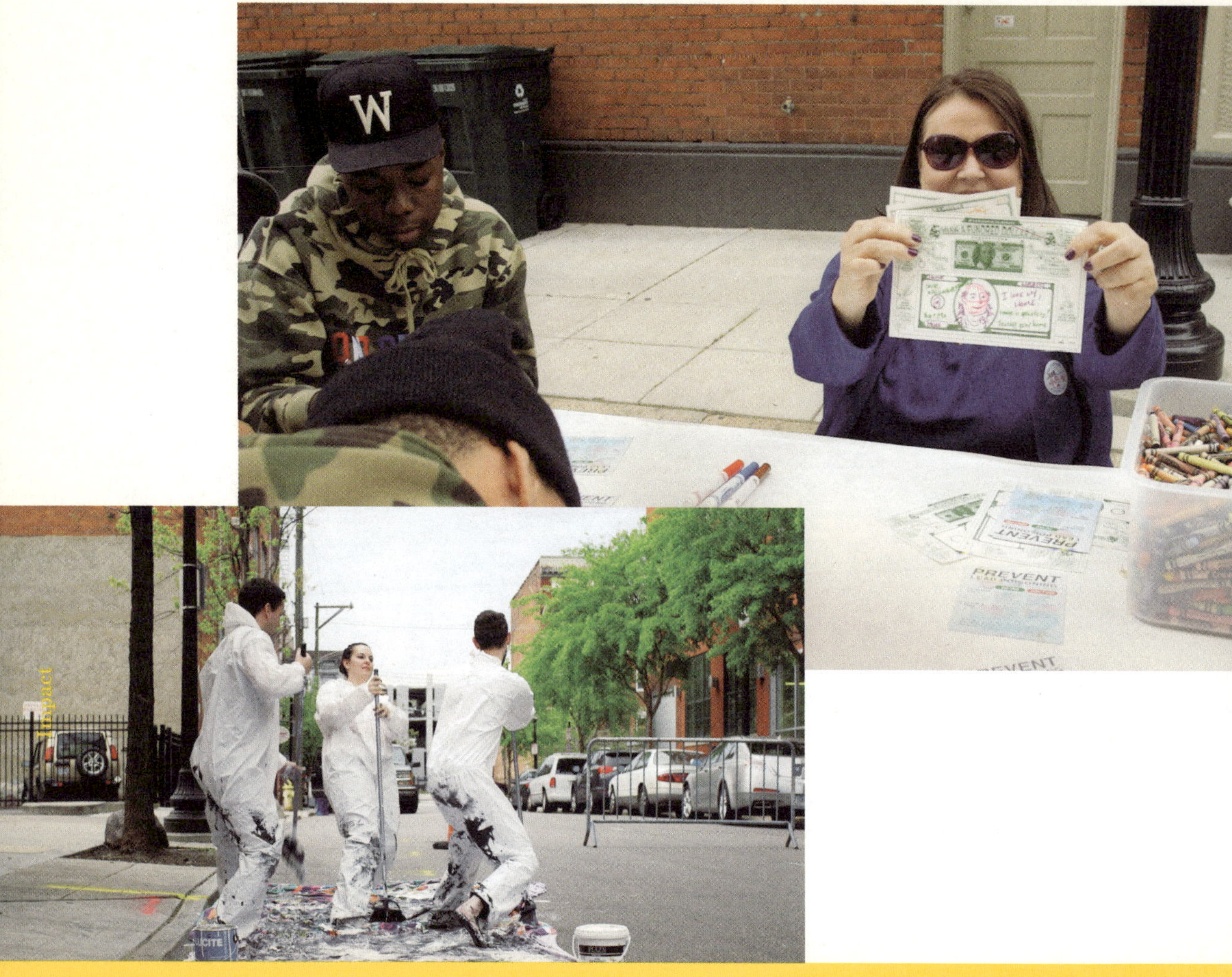

and students to participate in. We want our students to understand the power of art, the ability to express one's voice through art, the effects of collaboration and how art can impact social issues.

ABOG
What was the kids' response to *Operation Paydirt*? Did they understand the connection between what they were doing in the classroom and the problem of childhood lead poisoning?

CM
Yes, on a variety of levels. We implemented this project in classes from kindergarten through 12th grade, so students understood at different levels. Many of the elementary students took it to heart, checking out their own environment. The high school students tended to look at it as more of a global issue, with some of the students investigating other social justice art.

ABOG
Do you feel that the project will help promote social change?

CM
I think elementary students began to understand that art can have an impact. For many, this was their first association with socially engaged art. Middle school students liked the idea of collaboration and working together, so some schools have done other projects to have an impact either in their school or for other causes. The high school students that were introduced to this project began to understand how as an artist Mel Chin developed the concept that has grown out of him to be this 'thing' on its own. Some of them have investigated other conceptual artists that do socially engaged art.

Because we implemented *Operation Paydirt* district-wide in such a large district, we feel it brought some bonding to all of the teachers and students. It was a unique experience to complete lead prevention efforts. Because they approach organizations and individuals as artists rather than lead experts, they are in a unique position to forge new and sometimes unexpected alliances. They have established a steering committee that informs the overall strategy, with an end goal of presenting the citizen voice to policymakers at the city, state and federal levels, to encourage the appropriation of adequate funds to support the elimination of lead poisoning. Ultimately they would like those in power (governmental, non-governmental and private) to take appropriate responsibility. As awareness is one of the keys to address this tenacious problem, it is likely innovative methods of communication by activists and artists will be useful for many years to come and Chin hopes *Operation Paydirt*'s tools and strategies can continue to support the many relevant organizations and agencies in ending lead poisoning in the coming years.

Operation Paydirt originated with Chin working in communities in New Orleans where lead contamination is a serious issue. He wanted to find a way to use art to raise awareness in a way that would appeal to kids since they are the group most vulnerable to the effects of poisoning. He came up with the idea of "Fundreds"—coloring book style templates with outlines resembling hundred dollar bills. Kids and the general public were invited to color them in any way they wished, then "deposit" them with the artist for safe keeping. The Fundreds, as a symbol of money, visually represent individual voices in support of the funding required for lead poisoning prevention and remediation.

Chin is gathering millions of these drawings—over 450,000 so far—which he plans to deliver to lawmakers in Washington, on a pallet, in an armored truck. In 2009–2010 over a hundred schools across the country became regional collection centers for hundreds of thousands of Fundreds. He hopes that this highly visible and dramatic gesture can be "made real," and the Fundreds exchanged for actual funding to be used in the lead poisoning prevention effort. The beauty of this effort is the way that it aligns the grassroots tradition of signing petitions with the idea

a Fundred, knowing that students across the district were doing the same thing. The students really wanted to see what the total impact was.

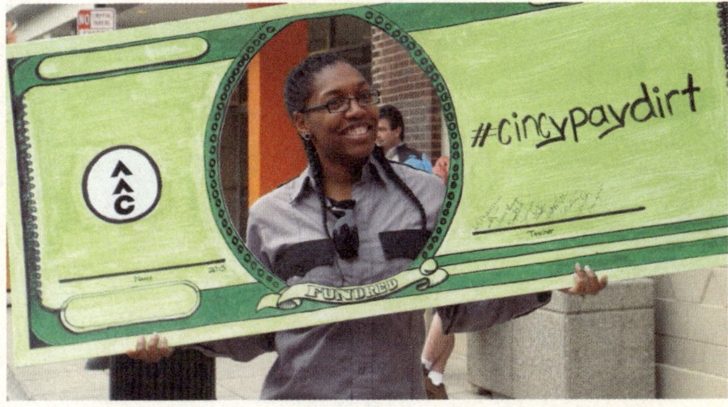

All: *Operation Paydirt*, Cincinnati, 2015.

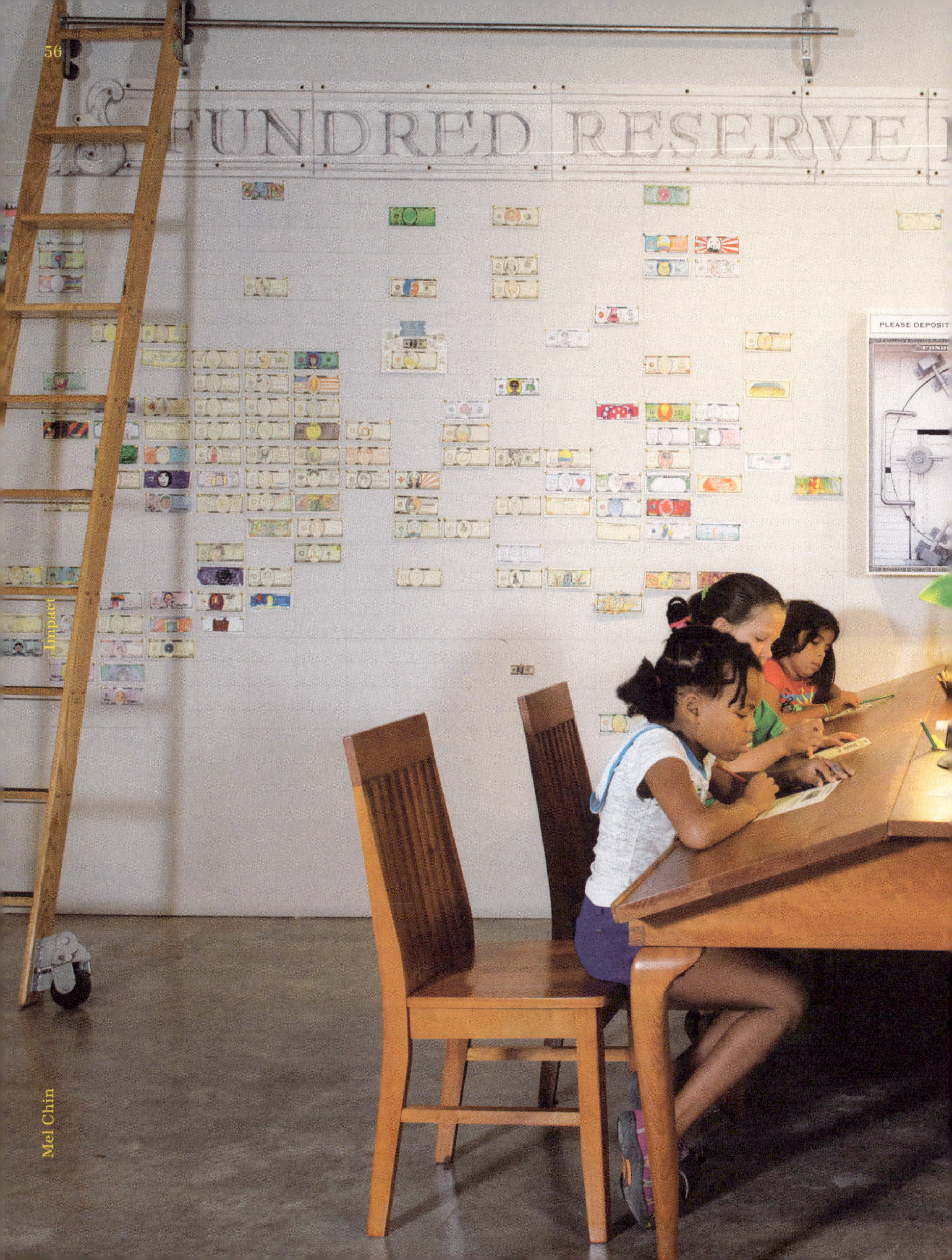
FUNDRED RESERVE
PLEASE DEPOSIT

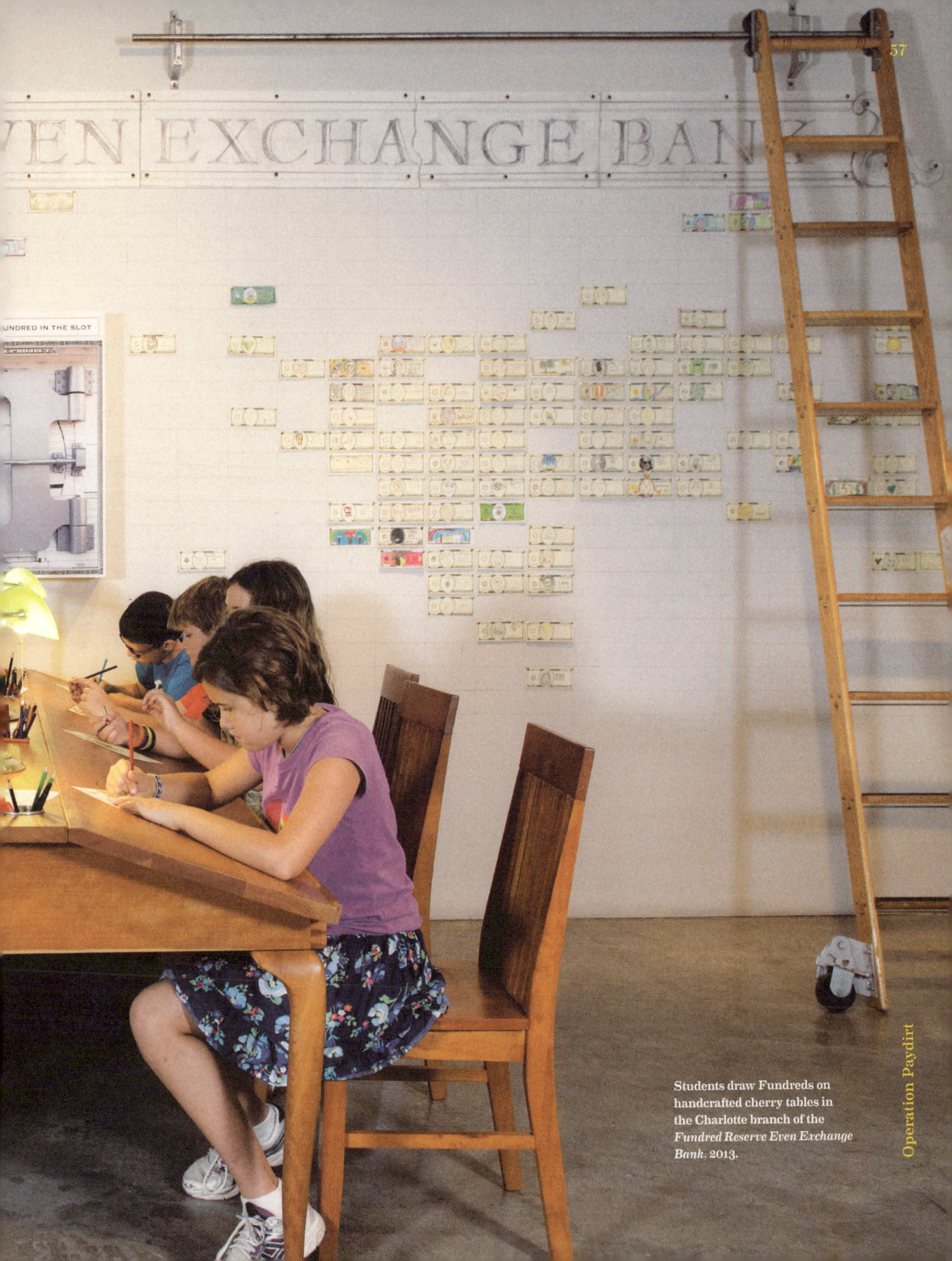

Students draw Fundreds on handcrafted cherry tables in the Charlotte branch of the *Fundred Reserve Even Exchange Bank*, 2013.

of community activism and education, as well as art workshops that are engaging to children and adults alike. The Fundreds become part of a symbolic sculpture representing the support of countless Americans for a nationwide solution. A simple drawing, the plea of a lone voice, is magnified into a chorus of righteous demands that the nation do something substantive and systemic to protect its most vulnerable citizens.

Visionary though the Fundreds project is, still kids are being poisoned every day across the country. In an effort to continue work to ameliorate the problem at a grassroots level even as a nationwide cohesion on awareness strategies is sought, Chin continues to branch out. In addition to New Orleans, he has worked in Charlotte, Grand Rapids, Oakland, Cincinnati, St. Louis and Houston, among other places. Currently, the *Operation Paydirt* team is working on a pilot curriculum that can be taught in schools nationwide, enlisting teams of local partners in each city where they are active to develop teaching tools and put them to work. This will be done in tandem with the efforts of nonprofits and government agencies with the funding and infrastructure to allow people to act on what they learn. Kids still make Fundreds and Chin still collects them, continuing to build momentum in preparation for the final performance in Washington, DC. In addition, he has produced public service announcements and other resources that can be deployed on an as-needed basis wherever the Fundreds capture the public imagination.

As Chin is well aware, to solve the problem of lead will take years, and billions of dollars, so the question is how the project can be sustained over time. As a model is developed and tested to replicate the initiative in multiple cities, can the artist pass its administration on to others? There are precedents for such transitions. Risë Wilson recently stepped down as founding director of The Laundromat Project, turning over its day-to-day functioning to a nonprofit board. Rick Lowe similarly turned *Project Row Houses* over to the community. Both artists remain involved, but are free to pursue other important work. To see whether it is possible, through the Make It Real initiative and the development of curriculum, to pass the torch to a nationwide, grassroots coalition of committed individuals and organizations will be the ultimate test of the reach and impact of this targeted yet expansive work.

Opposite page: *Fundred Dollar Bills* (Atlanta, Nashville, New Orleans), 2007–2010.

LEAD (Pb)

WITH AWARENESS OF THE THREAT...

DRAW

TRIM

SEND

COLLECT

LOAD

DELIVER

PRESENT

EXCHANGE

SUPPORTS A FUTURE FREE OF LEAD POISONING

TRANSFORM

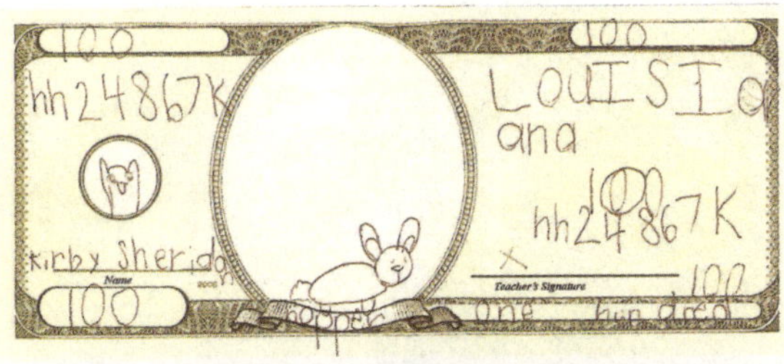

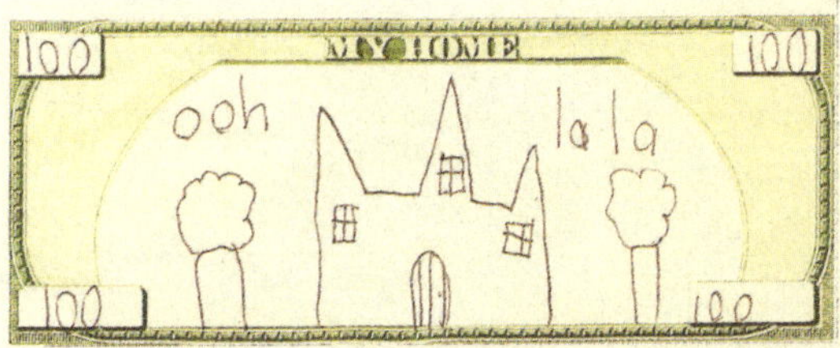

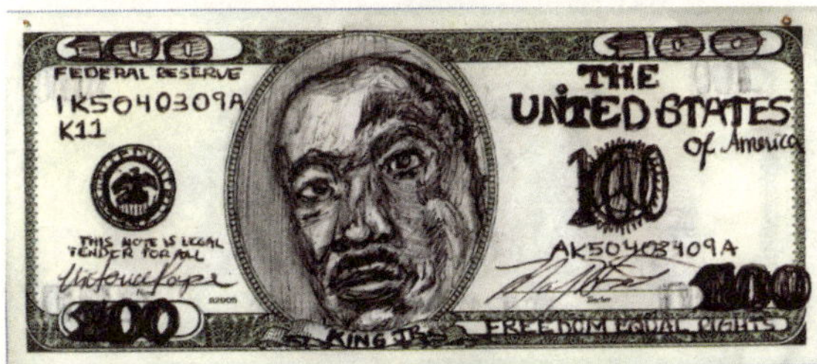

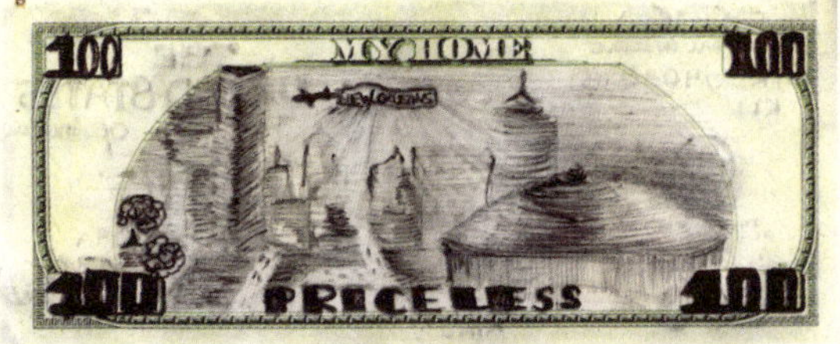

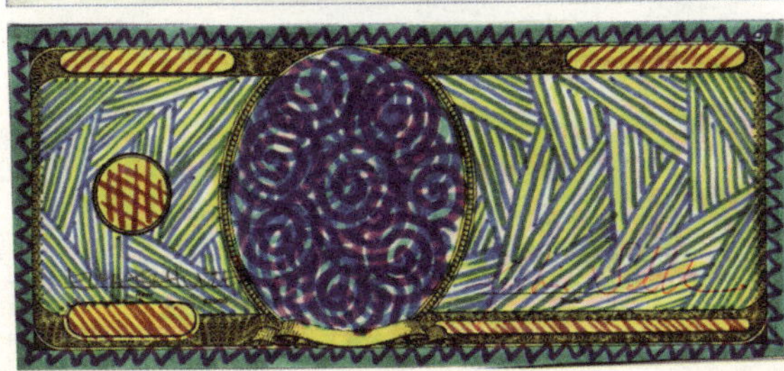

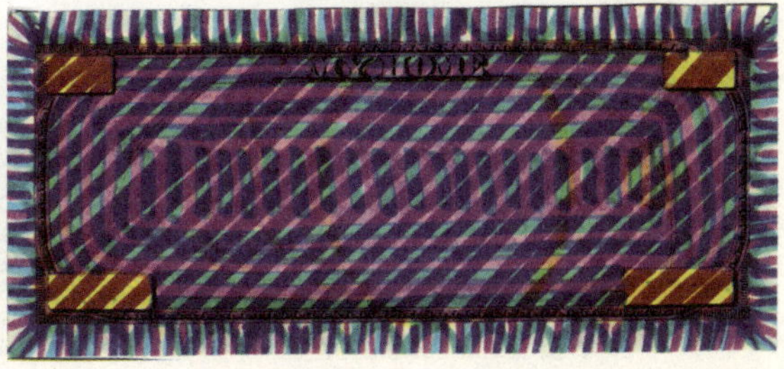

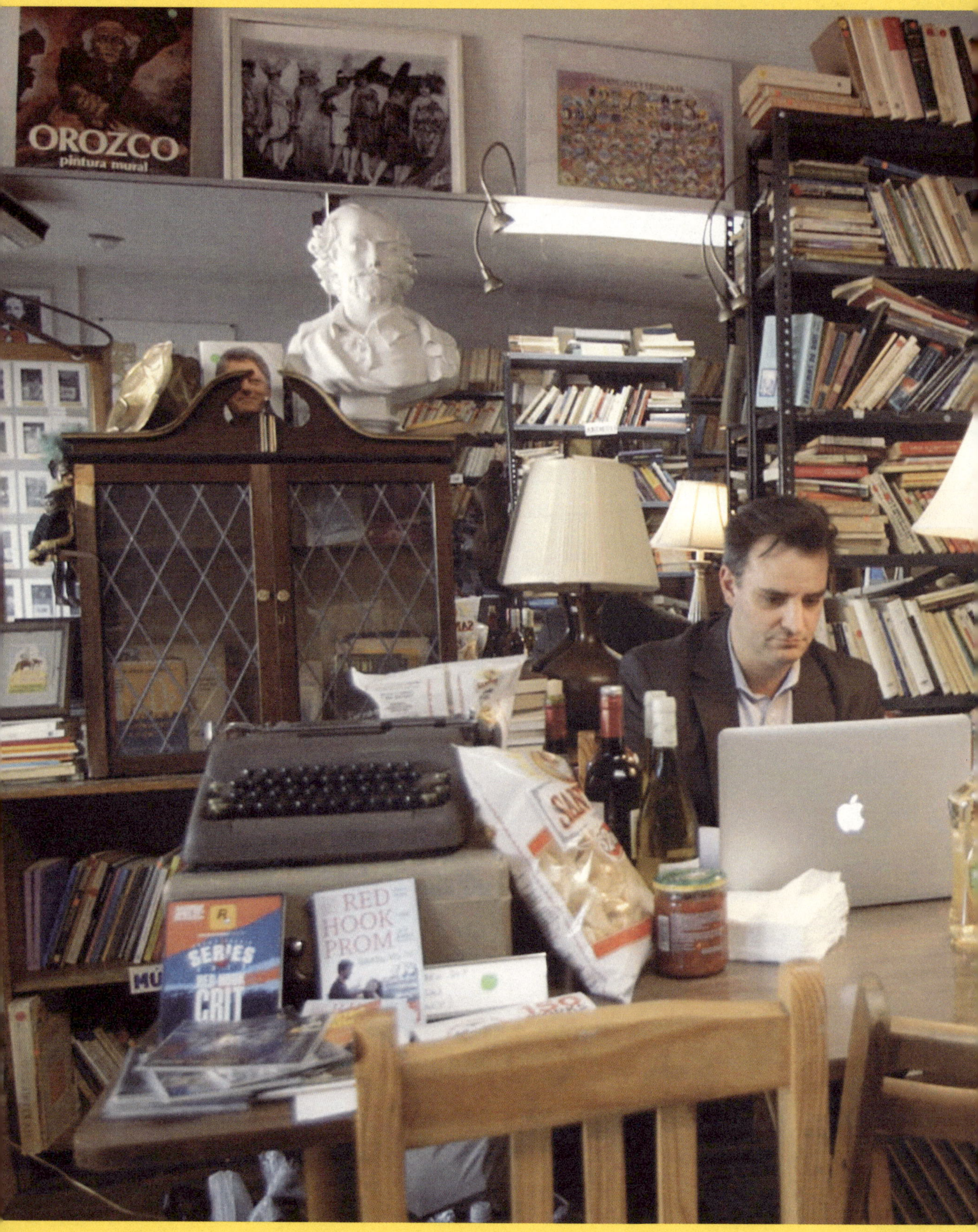
OROZCO
pintura mural
RED
HOOK
PROM
SERIES
CRIT

PABLO HELGUERA

Librería Donceles

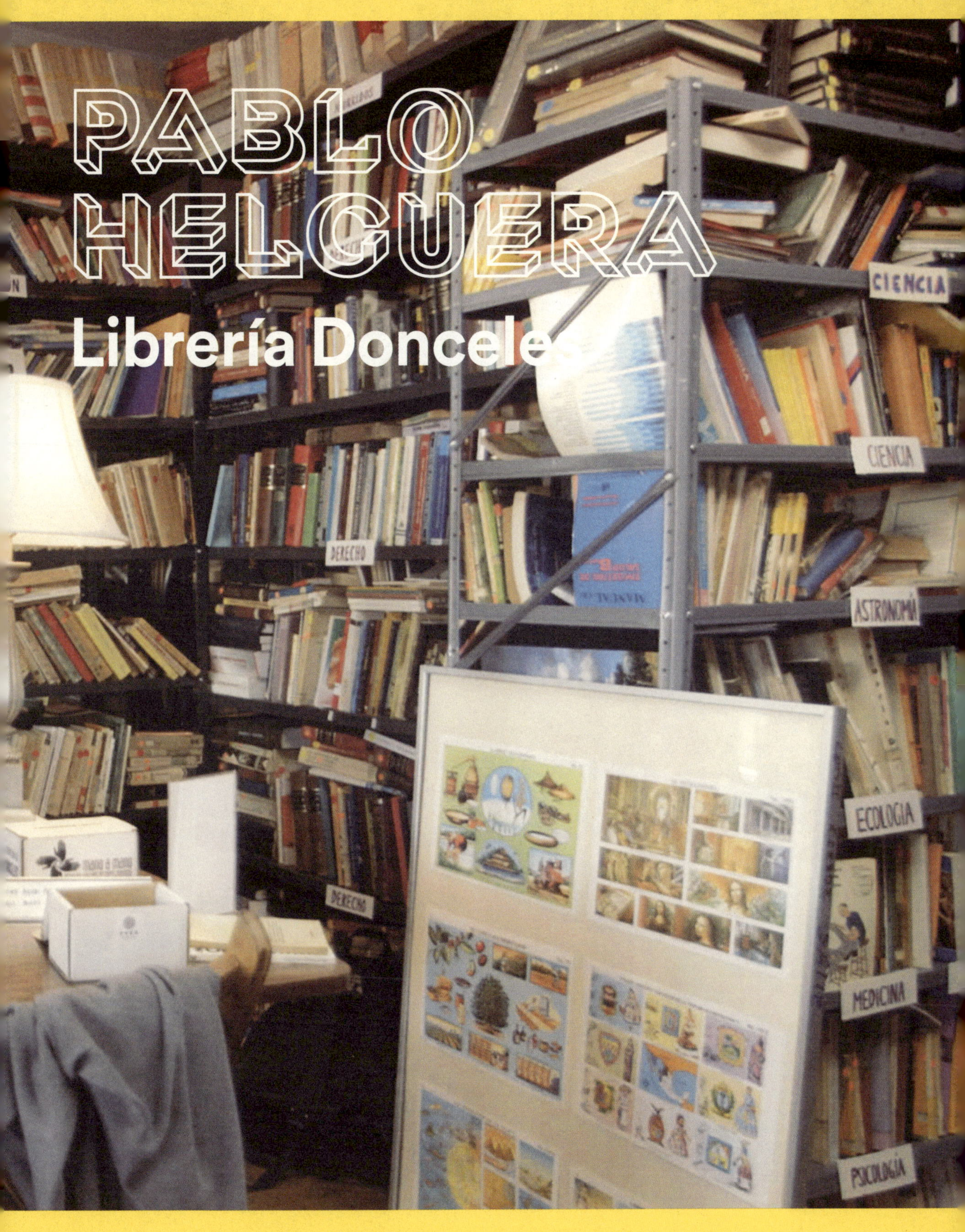

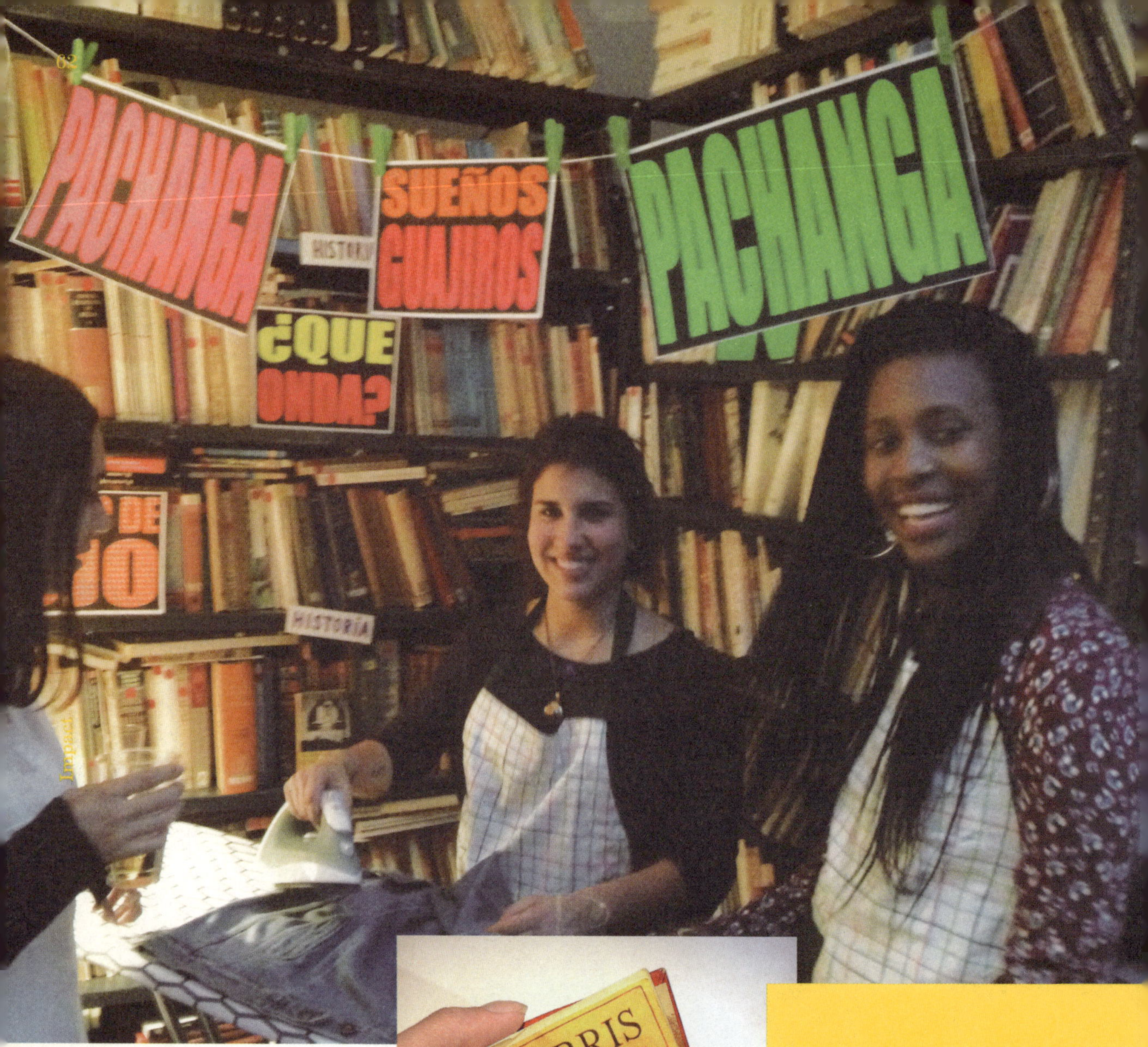

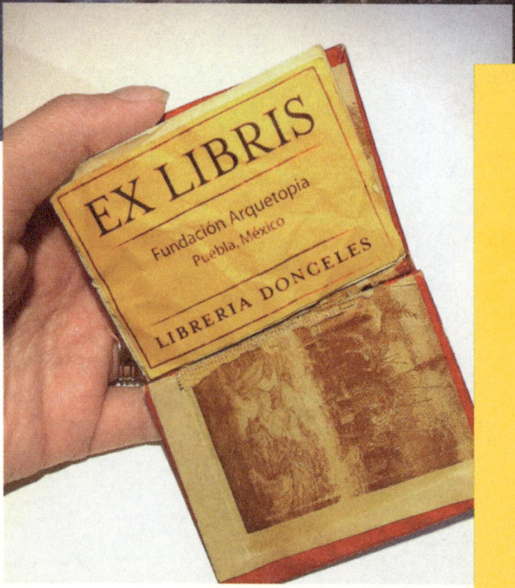

Previous spread: Pablo Helguera seated at the front desk at *Librería Donceles*, Brooklyn, 2015.

This page, top: Martina Hoyos, Camila Capra and Mayan Hennemeyer. *Librería Donceles*, Brooklyn, 2015.

This page, bottom: An *ex libris* from *Librería Donceles*, Brooklyn, 2015.

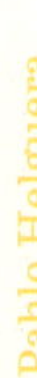

Remembering *Librería Donceles* with Claudia Nuñez de Ibieta

Pablo Helguera in conversation with Claudia Nuñez
November 21, 2014

Strolling down Van Brunt Street in the Red Hook section of Brooklyn in March 2015, you might have seen a little shop that you hadn't noticed before. Oddly, it looked as though it had been there forever. How could you have missed the old-fashioned reverse-painted black and gold lettering on its windows? The odd assortment of books, tchotchkes and children's furniture displayed there?

It was *Librería Donceles*, the brainchild of artist Pablo Helguera. The latest version of his Spanish-language bookstore popped up in Red Hook from March to May 2015, offering an inviting, cozy refuge where visitors could enjoy the kind of publications usually inaccessible to New York shoppers. Like the used bookstores Helguera enjoyed perusing on *Calle de Donceles* (Donceles Street) in Mexico City as a youth, the shop was filled with homey furniture like chairs and rugs, and a remarkable array of odds and ends such as small commemorative busts of authors, photographs, prints, and even games that invited the visitor to linger. All who entered were invited to buy a single book per visit, on a pay-as-you-wish basis. In this way, the wares were accessible to everyone, and the playing field was kept level. Even those with intimate knowledge of first editions, some of which could be found there, were permitted to select only a single treasure to carry home.

The décor was something of a cross between the oddball contents of a typical used bookstore—which is often as much an expression of its owner's personality as a sales vehicle, and apparently an international phenomenon—and Helguera's childhood home. In the comfortably furnished living room of his youth, the artist learned to love books and literature, and the *Librería Donceles* project was inspired in part by a desire to share that love with his adopted community.

One of the peculiar things about living in New York is that although there are nearly two million Spanish speakers, there are almost no Spanish-language bookstores. Those who want to read the language in print must resort primarily to the news outlets *Hoy* and *El Diarío*; surely

I remember the museum's announcement, a few months ago, regarding an installation: an interesting, intriguing invitation. A bookstore as the artwork? As gem, rarity, antiquity? As movie set, as time machine? To open the door of the space and enter *Donceles* for the first time was like entering a home, a warm home built of books, a relaxing space. *Donceles* drew me inside with the sincere embrace of an old, beloved bookshop. I was instantly reassured: books are not the past, even when they're old or worn; they are, still, living art.[1]

And, book lovers are romantic people who vibrate to words and to the music of paper; in *Donceles*, these are in the air, surrounding you, whispering to you. The curator, Julio [Cesar Morales], a warm and charming host, immediately receives you and makes you a part of *Donceles*. The art students, greeting visitors and guests, also welcomed us in ... And this is how our book group was invited to hold one of our monthly conversations in *Donceles*. However, one meeting was not enough: such was our pleasure at gathering in *Donceles* that we wanted to inhabit the space as much as we could.

We celebrated our May and June meetings there; the memory will become part of our history. We call our group *La tertulia de la literatura hispana* (something like "The Hispanic Literature Club"), and, as our name indicates, we read and discuss books in Spanish, choosing from a range of voices and works from around the Spanish-language world, from the verses of Neruda and the worlds of Gabo—Gabriel García Márquez—to the novel voices of Falcones, Dueñas and Allende. We started meeting at our local independent bookstore in Tempe, Arizona, nine years ago, and made it our place. When *Donceles* came to Phoenix, it was as if someone had built a home thinking especially of us.

With all my heart, from our entire group, thank you for bringing this beautiful space, this fabulous idea, to our city; it has allowed so many encounters between important sources of information, but not the kind of literary fare that the artist had eagerly devoured growing up. Helguera recognized that entire generations are coming of age without knowledge of the remarkable complexity of the literature of their native tongue, so he created a real-life version of the ideal bookstore that had formed in his mind's eye, with the aim of encouraging others to view reading and books through the same affectionate lens that he does. His bookstore had the usual sections on history, literature, law, science and religion, and also included "boring" books, "doubtful theories," "rejected books" (tucked between the doorframe and the wall rather than on shelves, but labeled nonetheless) and other categories that revealed a quirky sense of humor.

Like many used bookstores, Helguera's popup served as a community anchor, playing host to meetings, lectures, musical and art performances, discussions, parties and other gatherings. The idea was to give people a sense of what they're missing, and what might be possible if they put a little energy into creating such a space. And so it continues to be, as *Librería Donceles* reappears periodically at various locales, when favorable circumstances materialize.

Other versions of Helguera's bookstore have been presented at Kent Fine Art in New York City, at Arizona State University in Phoenix, and in San Francisco at the Kadist Art Foundation's space. At Kent Fine Art, a commercial gallery, it was viewed primarily as an art installation. In Arizona, a state with contentious attitudes toward immigration and laws that permit police to demand proof of immigration status, the store was an important site of solidarity with the immigrant community. In contrast, it was a popular if temporary community hub at Kadist, located in the Mission District, which has historically been a Latin American quarter.

The Red Hook incarnation holds special significance for Helguera because it was in the artist's own neighborhood, and only the second (after Kadist) in an actual storefront. By fully embedding the work into his own

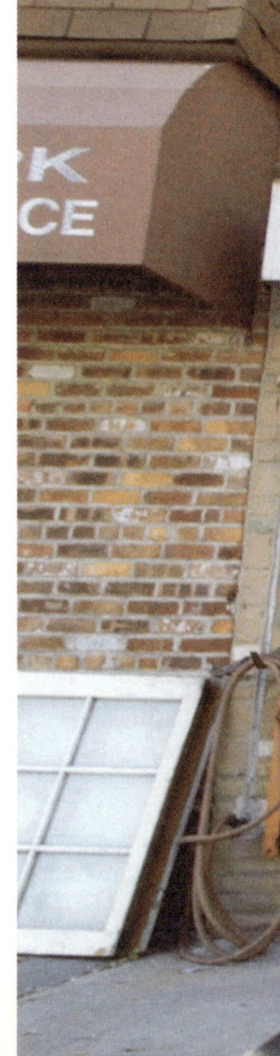

people and words, so many events and moments of dialogue and creativity, so many connections. Personally, I enjoyed not only bringing our group there, but also the other events I was able to attend at *Donceles*. The physical dimensions of the space only strengthened that certain quality of experience—closeness—that is so vital when shared. Whether the event at *Donceles* was a reading or a recital, the voice of the book or other instrument easily filled the space, touching everyone present, causing all to vibrate to the sounds that books inspire.

Endnotes

1 Pablo Helguera had an exhibition at the Arizona State University Art Museum in 2014.

community, he has been able to effectively realize his vision. So why not keep it going? The bookstore is a dream—a perfect world where people engage openly but deeply with friends and strangers alike, suspending cynicism and disbelief, if only for an afternoon or evening. Utopias are notoriously hard to sustain. Rather than go into the used book business, Helguera has chosen to move along, taking his dream on the road, sharing its warmth and beauty with the people of Seattle, Chicago, and beyond, where the work will continue to gain in resonance as it is encountered in new places, by new people, across the United States.

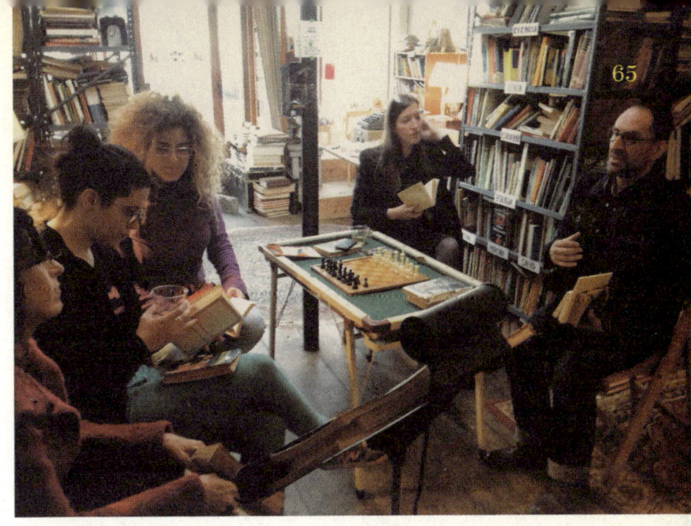

Above: Paco Cao leads a *tertulia* at *Librería Donceles*, Brooklyn, 2015.

Below: Façade, *Librería Donceles*, Brooklyn, 2015.

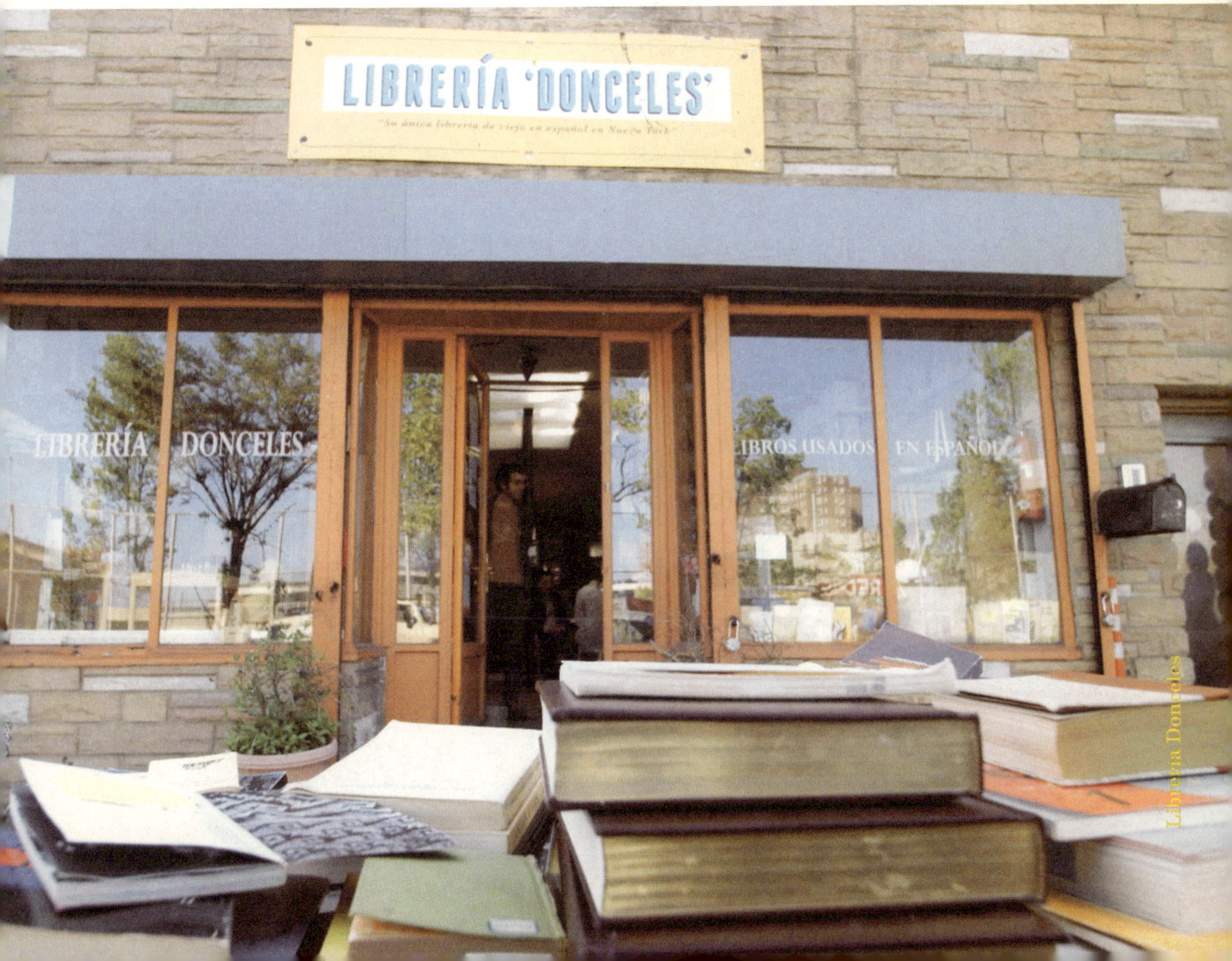

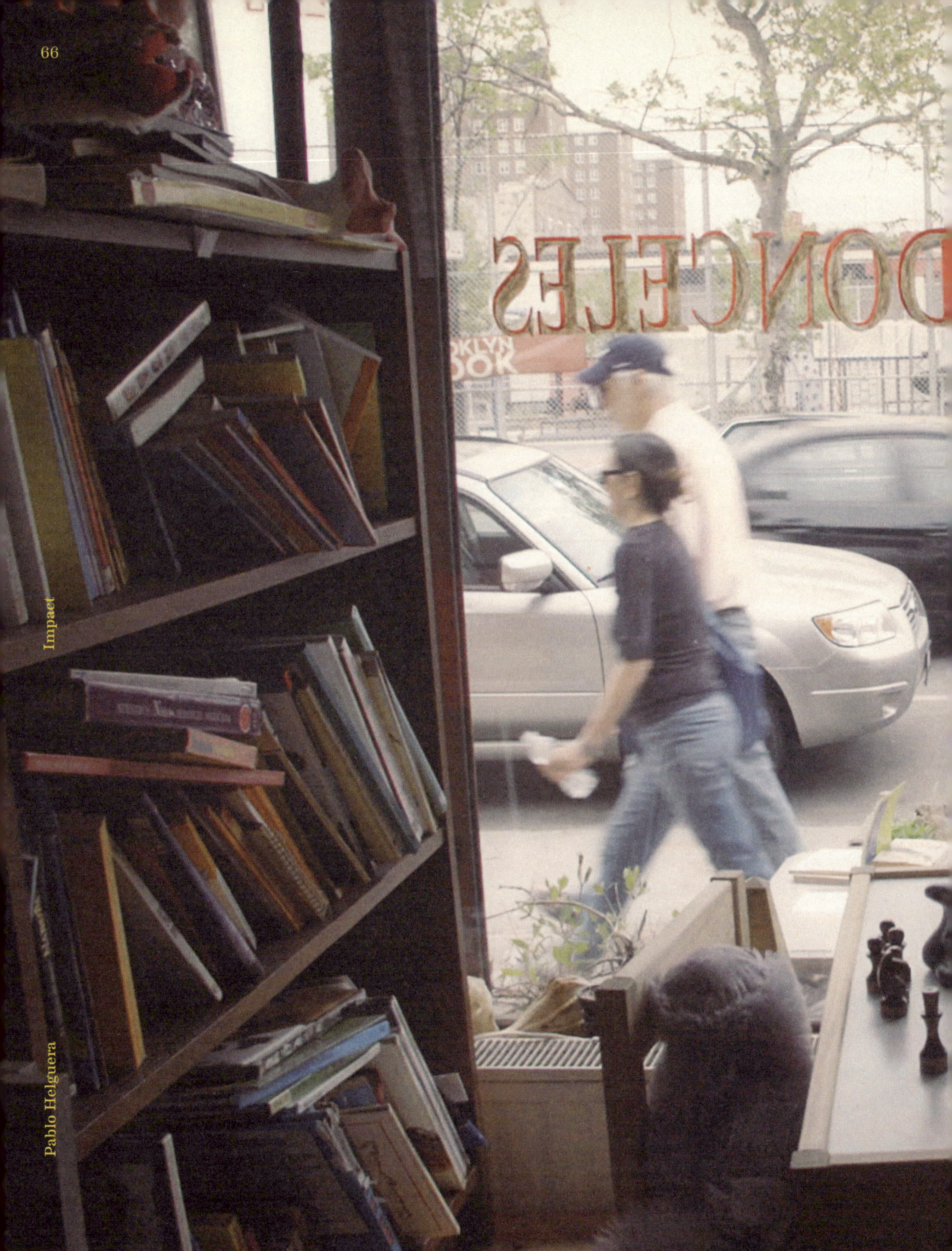

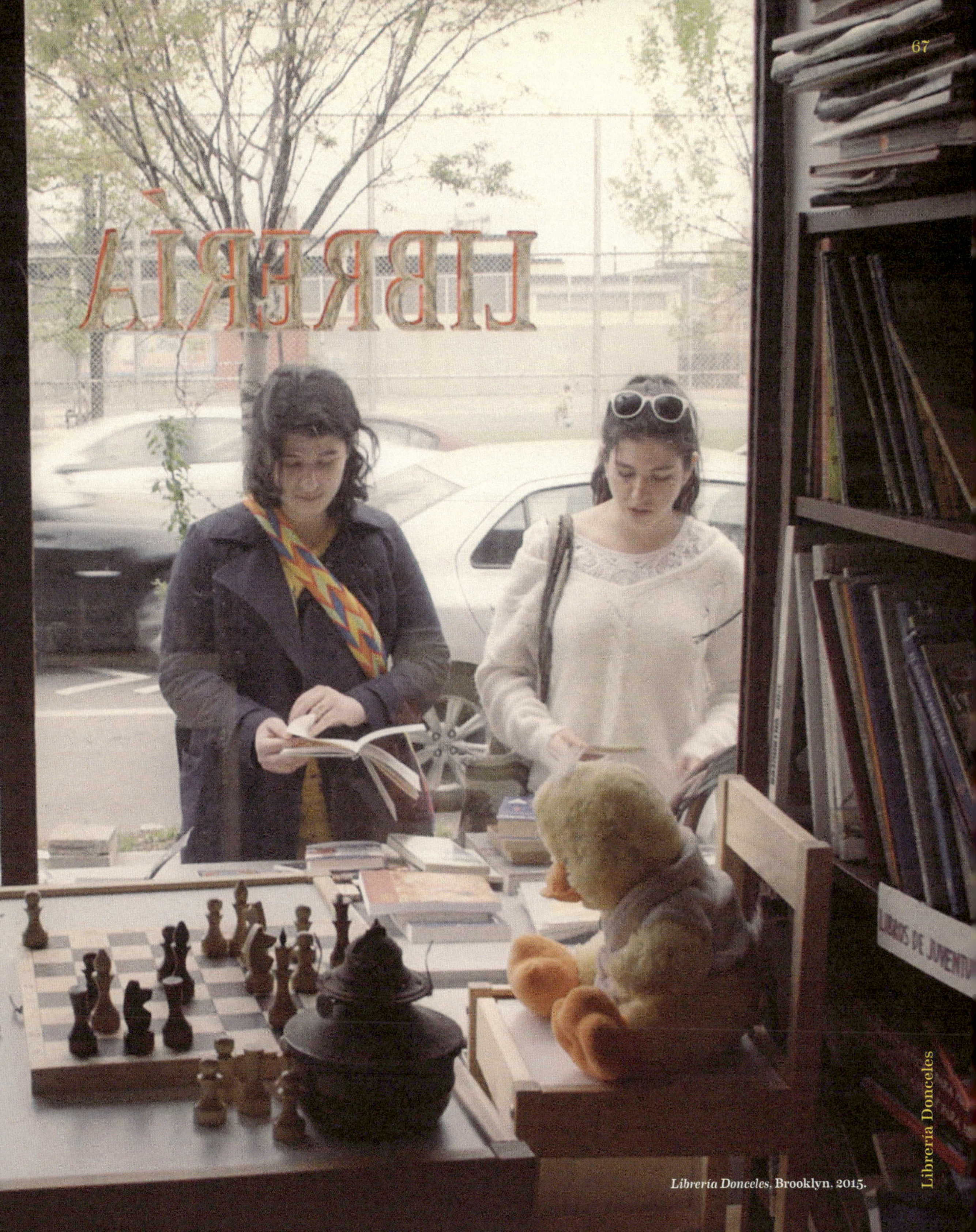

Librería Donceles, Brooklyn, 2015.

Along with being a fully functioning bookstore, *Librería Donceles* also hosted meetings, lectures, musical and art performances, discussions, parties and other gatherings, collectively called *tertulias*.

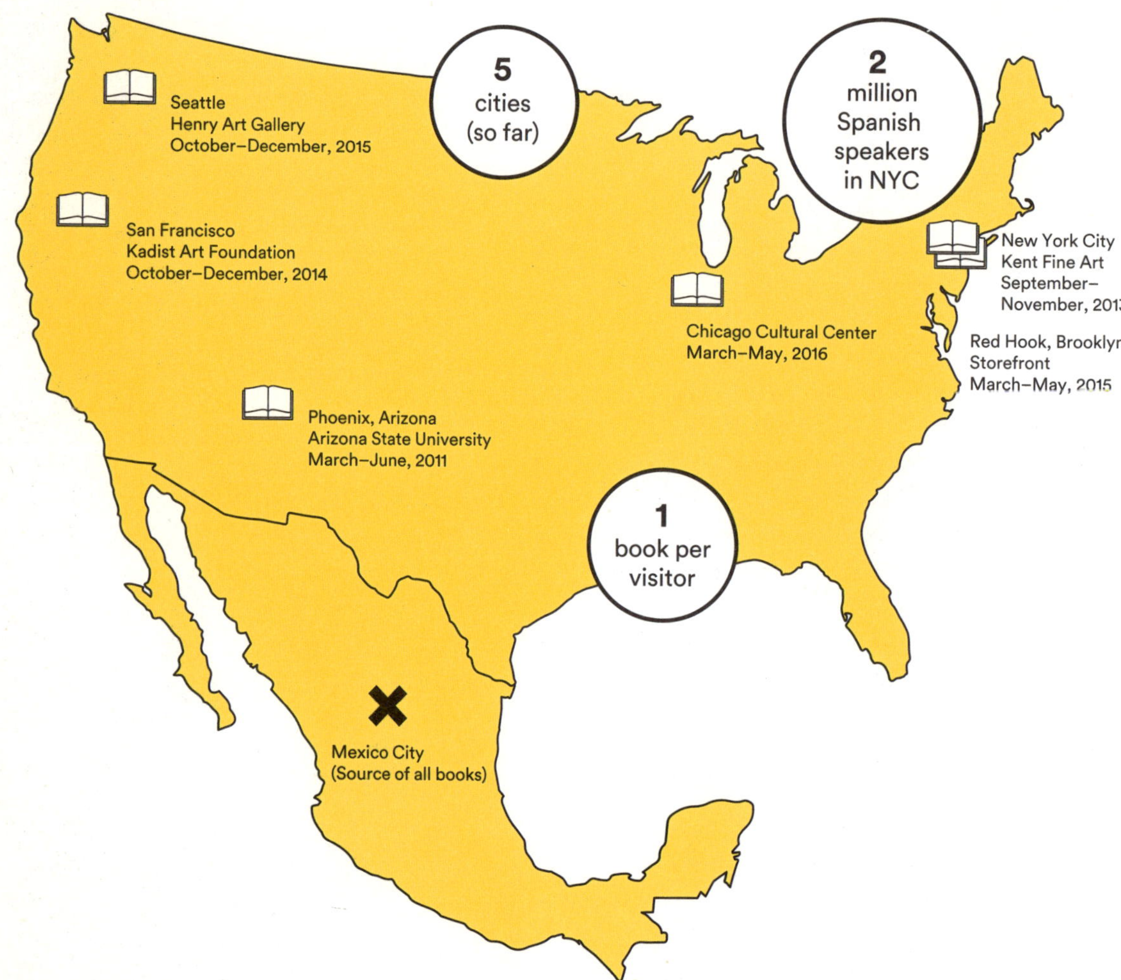

City	Phoenix	Seattle	Chicago	San Francisco	New York City
Total population (5 years and over)	1,385,000	552,000	2,535,000	767,000	7,788,000
Spanish-speaking population	467,000	20,000	628,000	86,000	1,891,000
% of Spanish speakers	34%	4%	25%	11%	24%

¡GRAN INAUGURACION !
GRAND OPENING

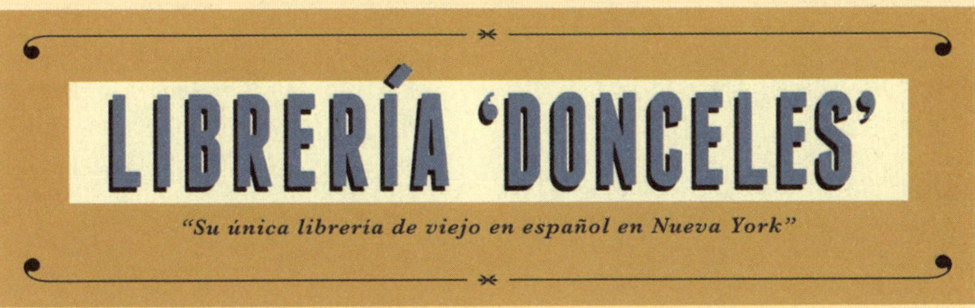

Librería Donceles es la única librería de viejo de libros en español en Nueva York. Por dos meses estaremos abiertos en Red Hook, ofreciéndole nuesto extenso inventario así como varios eventos gratuitos a lo largo de la semana.

Librería Donceles is the only Spanish language used bookstore in New York City. For the next two months we will be open in Red Hook, offering you our extensive inventory of titles along with several free events throughout the week.

Inauguración: Sábado 28 de marzo
Saturday March 28th

4-6pm
360 Van Brunt Street, Red Hook

Música, bebidas, comida, y libros usados en español
Music, drinks, food, and used Spanish books

¡¡Acompáñennos!!

This project is made possible by a generous grant from *A Blade of Grass*

Digital announcement for *Librería Donceles*, Brooklyn, 2015.

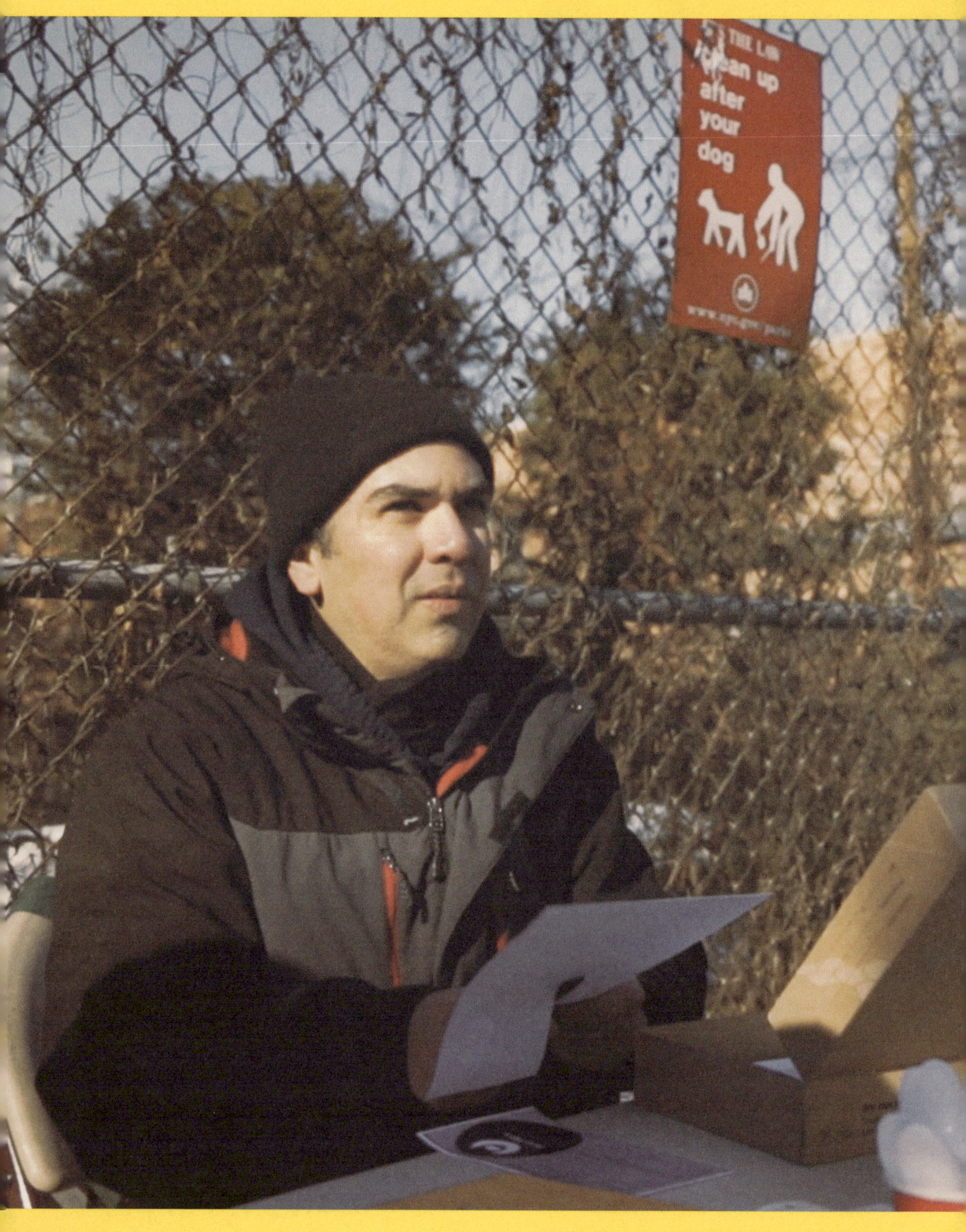
up
after
your
dog

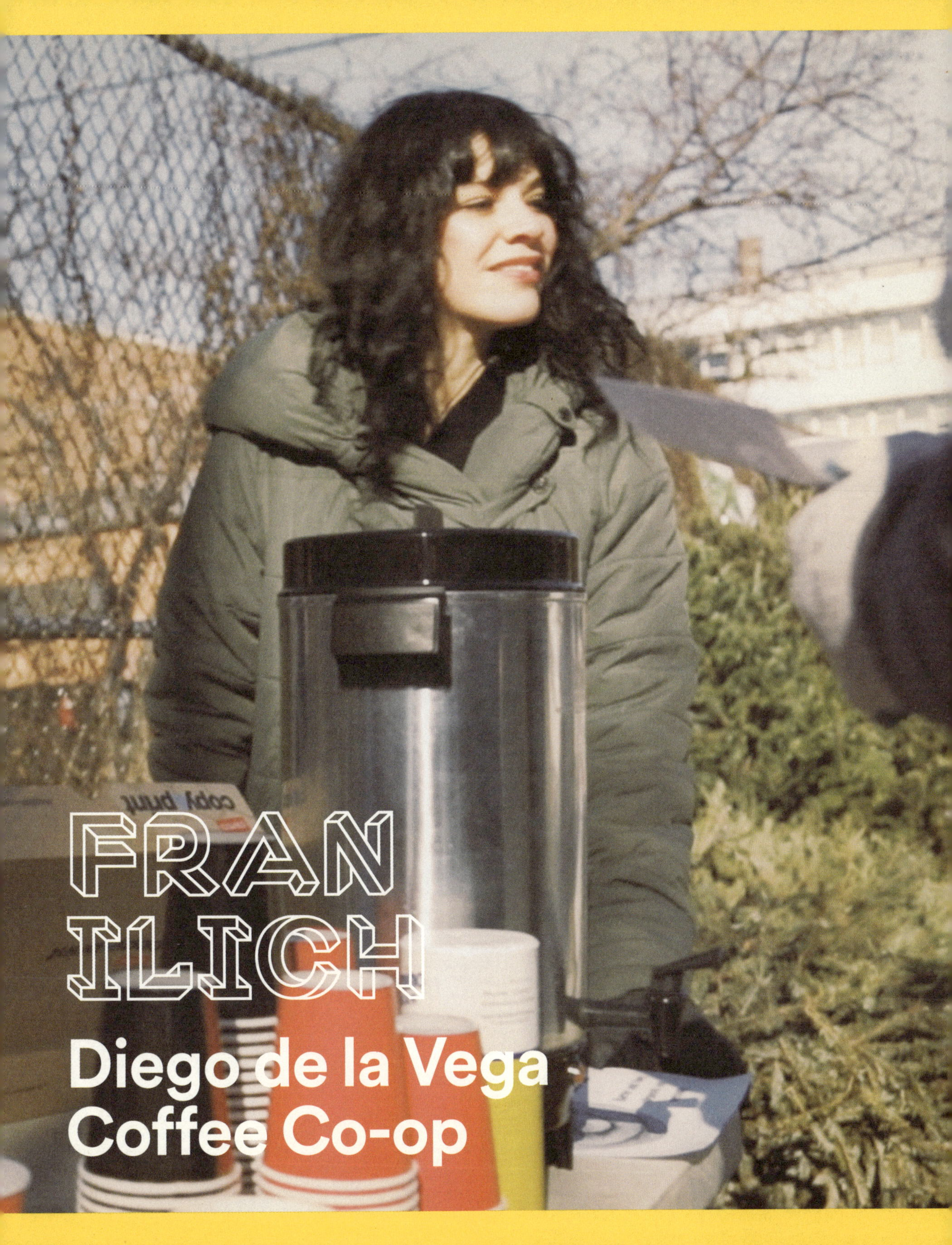

FRAN ILICH

Diego de la Vega Coffee Co-op

Cutting-edge art is often described as revolutionary, but in the case of Fran Ilich's project, the *Diego de la Vega Coffee Co-op*, the label carries more than a metaphorical truth. Ilich works with Zapatista farmers in Chiapas, Mexico to bring their products (especially coffee, of course!) and ideology to activist communities in New York and elsewhere. He creates horizontal relationships between radical social movements through the trade of goods, services and money, and serves the coffee as a way of starting conversations. He hopes that the exchanges will mutually reinforce the economic sustainability and influence of the groups involved. The ultimate aim is to promote localized, small-scale, fully participatory democracy between small groups seeking to build harmony and livelihoods through mutual aid. Because the work Ilich is engaged in has a strongly aesthetic sensibility, it has the potential to reach far beyond its immediate community of impact. As an art project, its job is not to change the face of the world economy, or establish more responsive political systems. Rather, through softly spoken conversations and poetic means, Ilich forges the connections and networks across vast distances that allow people to imagine alternative realities, and are thus the foundation of their aesthetic experience. By performing the kinds of discussions used by the Zapatistas to share knowledge with one another and reach collective decisions, he enacts their political system through his project.

In sympathy with the postcolonial aims of the largely indigenous Maya Zapatistas, Ilich seeks to build bridges between their cause and that of other bottom-up egalitarian social movements. To do so he founded three main initiatives, *Possibleworlds.org*, *Spacebank*, and *Diego de la Vega Coffee Co-op*. These projects operate as real-world economic endeavors, and also in the symbolic space of art. In this way, they make a small contribution to solving immediate challenges faced by the Zapatistas, and represent their ideals to a broader audience. Indeed, by operating through them, Ilich extends the reach of the Zapatistas' ideas by putting them into practice.

Transforming Relationships with Gabriela Ceja

Joelle Te Paske in conversation with Gabriela Ceja
April 19, 2015

2014 ABOG Fellow Fran Ilich's *Diego de la Vega Coffee Co-op* is a collaborative project that aims to connect rural agricultural workers in Mexico's Zapatista communities and service industry laborers in New York City by serving Zapatista-grown coffee at events throughout the city. Joelle Te Paske spoke with artist Gabriela Ceja, a primary collaborator in the project, at Open Engagement, a conference and platform for socially engaged art in Pittsburgh.

Joelle Te Paske (ABOG)
You are a large part of the *Diego de la Vega Coffee Co-op*, and you are also its artist-in-residence. I'm curious about how you got involved in the project.

Gabriela Ceja
I was invited to work and collaborate with the *Coffee Co-op* and in exchange to do a residency in New York City. When I started my project, I was interested in the indigenous people who came to Mexico City to work in construction. I interviewed people who were living in the buildings in which they were working. I started to create relationships with them. That's how I think, as artists, we can really try to change reality, when we try to transform the way we relate.

The opportunity to do the project in New York City was great because I could be involved with workers from all over the world. I could trace what the workers

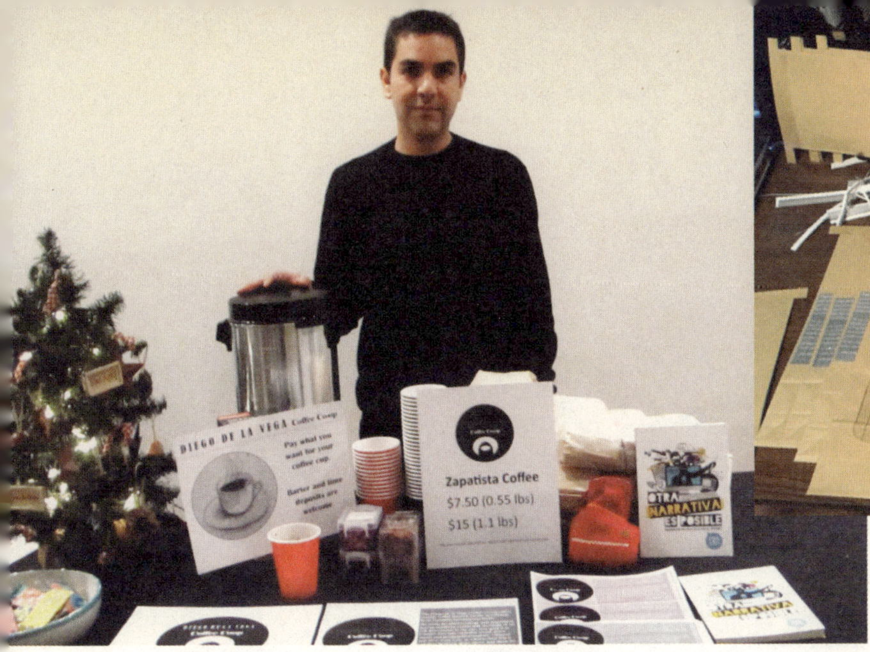

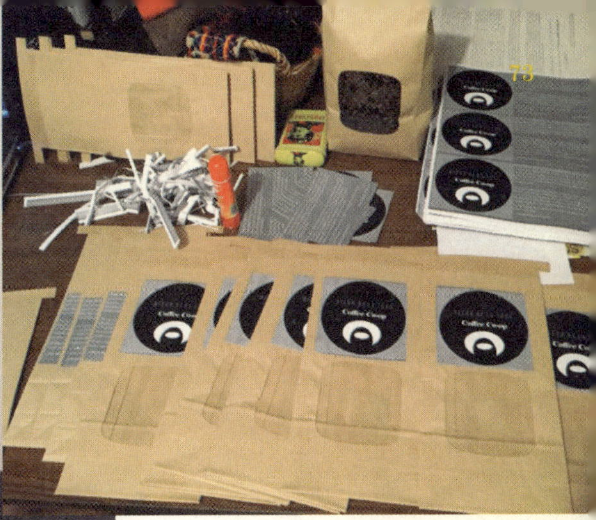

Previous spread: Fran Ilich and Gabriela Ceja serving coffee, 2015.

This page, top left: Fran Ilich serving coffee at the Bronx Museum, 2014.

This page, top right: *Diego de la Vega Coffee Co-op* graphics and branding.

Right: Various currencies and activist literature.

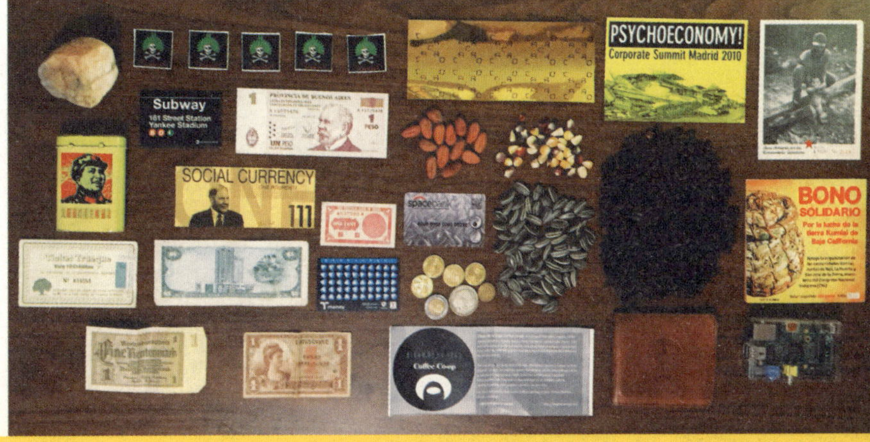

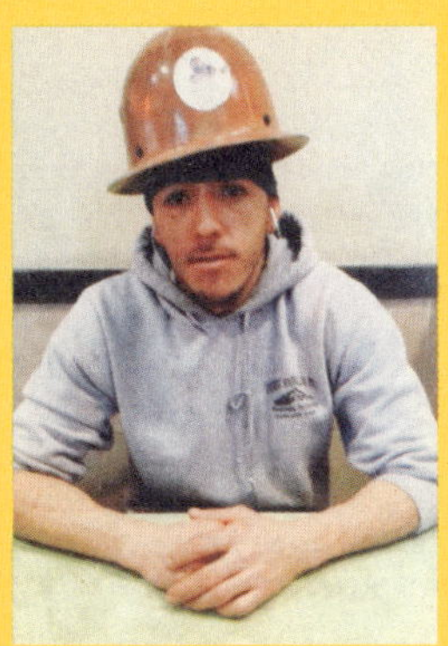

Jesús, a 30-year-old construction worker, has been working in the US since the age of 14.

from my own country were doing there and the conditions that they found. I met this construction worker from a state in Mexico called Michoacán. He worked as a grape picker in California when he was 14. Then he moved to another state, I think it was Georgia, to build roads. After that he moved to New York City and he worked in elevators. He was only 30 years old, and he had worked since he was 14.

I tried to trace their lives and see why they moved into cities. Labor shaped their lives. It gave them the path that they followed from a very young age. At JFK Airport, I met this other guy, he was from Bangladesh and had an MA in social development in his country. He was a very

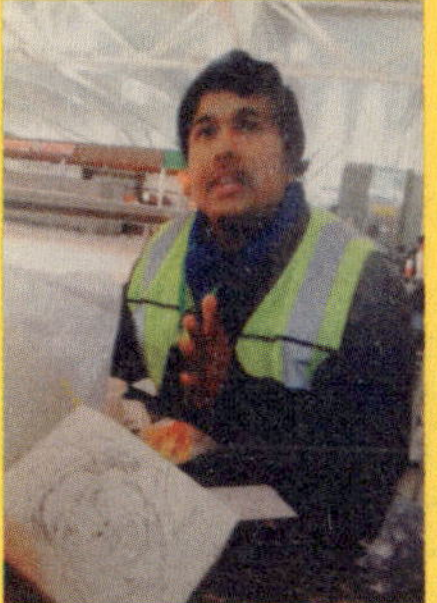

Mishu, who has an MA in social development from the University of Dahka, Bangladesh, works as a janitor at JFK Airport. He tries to work on independent projects every 15 days.

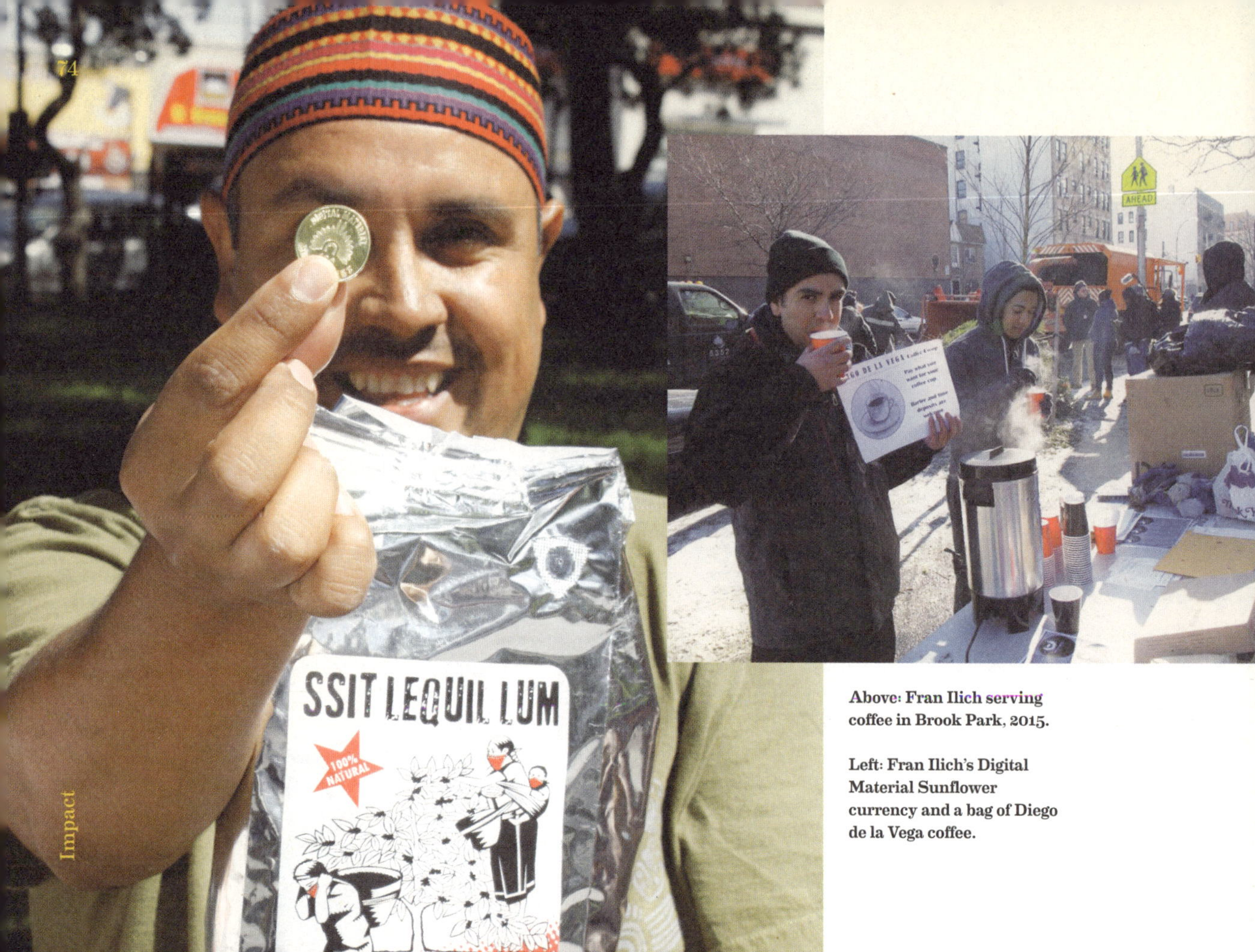

Above: Fran Ilich serving coffee in Brook Park, 2015.

Left: Fran Ilich's Digital Material Sunflower currency and a bag of Diego de la Vega coffee.

smart person who had lots of ideas for projects. He said he was interested in taking photographs of landscapes changing with industrialization, and that he wanted to do a documentary about the careers that were going extinct in his country. But the most surprising thing was that he was working as a janitor at JFK.

In these people, I see all of the problems that the system has. The incoherencies. What is this person doing here? Why does he have to go through these life paths? To have this incoherence in life—that he's so well prepared, and he's working in this place.

ABOG
What has been the most meaningful part of working with the *Diego de la Vega Co-op* thus far?

GC
Everything about the project has to do with constancy and a kind of humble activity, and doing a radical thing with a simple activity, which is serving coffee. The most meaningful part for me is being part of the global economy and actually moving a rebel cause that concerns the indigenous people I care about. I've seen them suffer. My own family is part of that. So through a product we can move an idea. It's very material. What I love about the project is that it materializes into people's bodies and people's minds and real conversations.

ABOG
That makes a lot of sense. It's a beautiful thing, because it's not a grandiose philosophical idea—even though it's connected to those things. At its essence, the coffee is something from the earth that someone grew. You drink it. It gives you sustenance in some ways. It provokes conversation.

GC
I agree with you. The coffee—it's a whole process. We are trying to be coherent in the whole process of ideas and political

The artist has been working with the Zapatistas since the early 2000's, just after Mexico elected its first non-PRI (Institutional Revolutionary Party) President, Vicente Fox, in over seventy years. The Zapatistas had been founded in the mid-1990s, and in 2001 marched on Mexico City to present the case for their independence to Congress. Fox responded with offers of agreements that did not fully meet the Zapatistas' terms, so they created 32 "autonomous municipalities" in Chiapas, thus partially implementing their demands without government support but with some funding from international organizations. The society they seek to build would keep the means of production—in this case, primarily agricultural production—in the hands of the people, who would make decisions beneficial to the community through fully participatory democracy. This approach is a response to NAFTA, the North American Free Trade Agreement, which had the result of aligning Mexico's economy more integrally with the global economy, and resulted in the increasing dependence, marginalization and poverty of small-scale agricultural producers.

The project grew out of Ilich identifying key logistical needs that social movements were faced with, and working to find ways of addressing those needs using mechanisms that would not compromise their ideals. The key was to provide services through conduits as autonomous as the Zapatistas themselves. He began with *Possibleworlds.org*, an independent Internet server launched in 2005 that offers web hosting to social movements in Mexico. Ilich determined that a fundamental requirement for such movements is to have reliable Internet access and an online network for communication. The proceeds from this web hosting service are reinvested into the social movements themselves through *Spacebank*, a community investment bank.

Spacebank is essentially run by Ilich on an Excel spreadsheet, but remarkably has (limited) capacity to loan money, exchange currency, and engage in other basic financial transactions. Its

things, which are so important in our country right now. We think about the Zapatistas and what they're trying to do, and what social movements try to do. We think about these communities who are actually living differently and being autonomous. The way we can help is by distributing the coffee they sell. Sometimes we can be very, very idealistic and think we can change the world, but if we try to do it by ourselves, we can only make very local changes. Those are important, of course. But if we contribute to a cause that is actually working [*laughs*], that is a little bit more realistic.

Maybe the Zapatistas are out there working in the fields, but they do not have distribution means that normal coffee companies have. They cannot distribute their product the same way. For that, there's a voluntary network of people, including us, who will help them. Then we can also have this other alternative economy that helps us produce other materials, such as narratives and maybe artwork.

ABOG
It also helps people to see an alternative. I think it is refreshing to see a different sort of economy working. It is important to know that there are alternatives, even if just as models.

GC
We worried a lot about that part. We really wanted it to work, but then it is a model. When is the model going to become reality? It needs a lot of work and concentration.

ABOG
You can take this question however you'd like to, but where is the art part of it for you?

GC
The art part comes in with this change in reality we are trying to create. Look, there is a performance every time we serve coffee. It's a very poetic idea, no? The coffee is what awakens your

main purpose is to serve as a vehicle for investing small sums in social causes like that of the Zapatistas in Chiapas. There are over two hundred investors, who have committed approximately $1000 each. *Spacebank's* assets are available to its investors through a variety of vehicles, including dollars, pesos, Bitcoins, precious metals, gems, land, and the bank's own currency, the Digital Material Sunflower. Because it is simultaneously a real bank and a performative symbolic system invented by an artist, *Spacebank* operates with a degree of fluidity that one does not expect from a bank. For example, if an investor cannot pay back a loan in the form in which it was lent (for example, pesos), *Spacebank* can choose to accept alternate items of value, such as bonds or even comic book collections, as payment. As long as there is real value and real mutual benefit, in-kind payments are seen as equivalent to cash ones. Like any other bank, it is in the interest of *Spacebank* to invest in ventures in line with its mission and goals. The distinction is that *Spacebank's* goals are less about making money for investors, and more about supporting sustainability for, and spreading the ideas of, social movements.

Diego de la Vega Coffee Co-op was founded as a *Spacebank* venture. It offers organic coffee that the artist often personally sources at great risk from farms in the autonomous regions of Chiapas, offering farmers things of value, including currency, that they may need to acquire items beyond what they are able to grow on their own land. He brings the coffee to New York and San Diego, where the coffee is served by the artist and his collaborators at various art spaces and grassroots political meetings. He accepts bartered items, like Bitcoins or meals, in exchange for the coffee, in addition to also occasionally accepting money for the service. While serving the coffee, he shares the ideas of the kind of participatory democracy that is practiced in the autonomous zones in Mexico, hoping to continue to find affinities across cultural and national barriers and to disseminate and cross-pollinate political ideas about how a more egalitarian political and

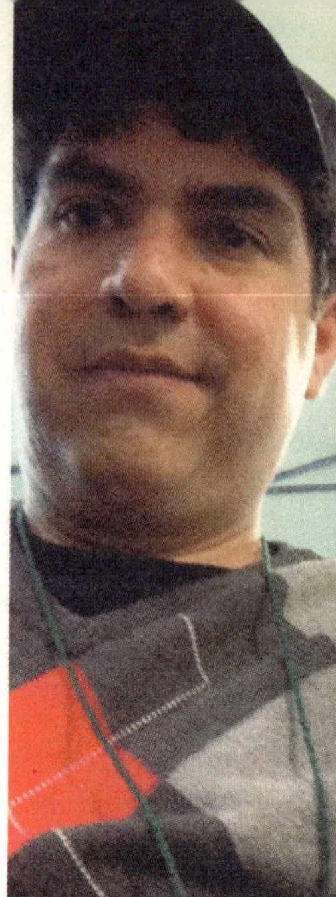

awareness. It symbolizes conversation. It stimulates intelligence, whether you're alone or whether you're with people. The poetic aspects of coffee and its historical symbolism are political. We thought about making packages and selling them, and making some prints, but the whole thing about serving the coffee as waiters is an important aspect of our statement, because we are always aware of the service position that so many Mexicans have in the United States. It is an ironic way to present this project.

ABOG
Yes, and reclaim it a little. I do see a lot of performance in what you do. You *could* package it up—but no, you don't want *Diego de la Vega Coffee Co-op* at Whole Foods, with a little screen-print [*laughs*].

GC
[*Laughs*] Do we want that? We were wondering. We were actually really wondering—maybe that will work better, though? Distributing it to stores so that normal people can consume it. But it didn't make sense with the Zapatista movement, because they share it only with people who have ideas in common with them.

ABOG
Now I'm curious—how do you think that would change the art part?

GC
I don't think it would change. It would change the way it is delivered, but it would still be art because we are transforming relationships. We are reinventing economic relationships. We are using the imagination of the artist to reinvent reality. That's the power we can get, because we are not economists. We are people—creative people—who want to intervene in reality.

ABOG
I feel like you decided the performance part of it was the best way to be a part of those relationships, or change those relationships in the way you wanted to.

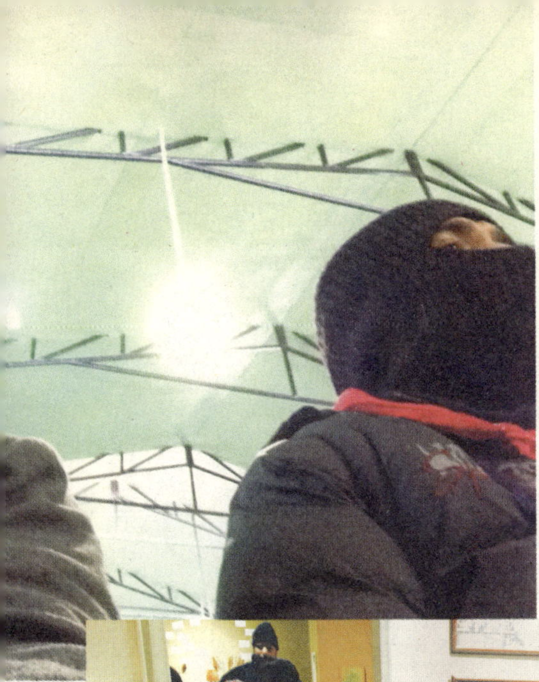

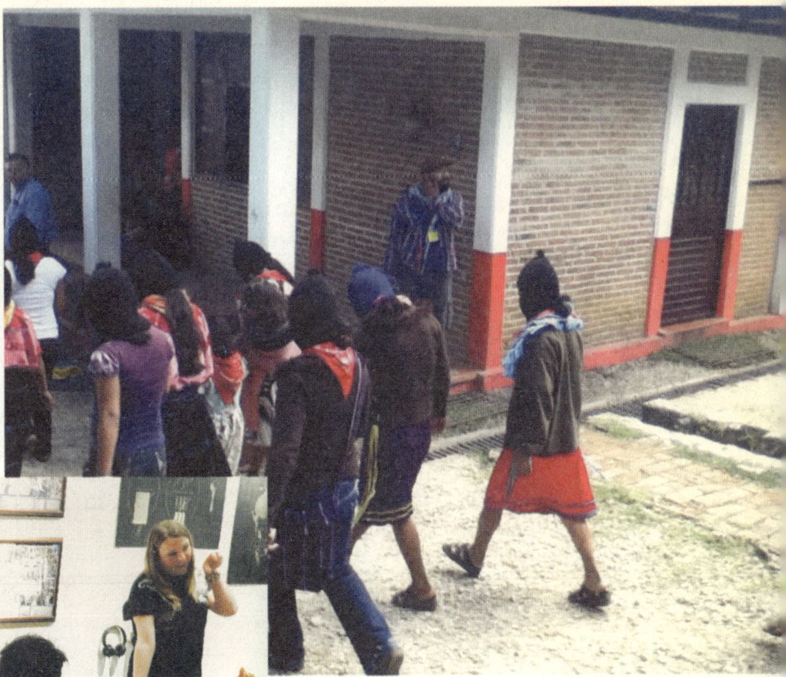

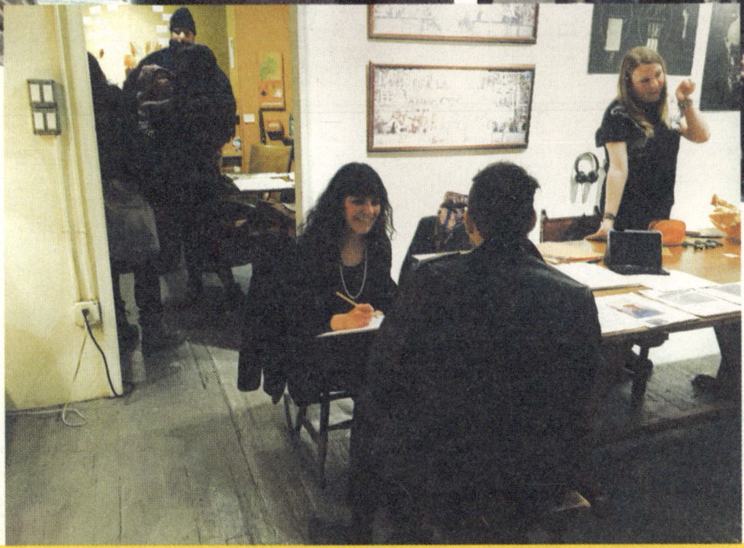

Clockwise from top left: Fran Ilich at Escuelita Zapatista, 2013.

One of Ilich's visits to Chiapas, Mexico.

***Diego de la Vega Coffee Co-op* at Proteus Gowanus, Brooklyn, 2015.**

GC
Well, I don't know if it was the best way to change relationships. Yes, it was a way to communicate with other movements, just by being part of them. And we don't know if it was the best way to have the coffee distributed as well. But it was the most joyful, maybe.

The performance is like a service, and in a way it is like a ritual. It is so many things that involve presence. It's great because we force ourselves to be part of things. Ordinarily, your attention span is such that you consume whatever you can at events, and then leave. But we were at events from the beginning and we would meet people in a different way. Like, "Where are you organizing? How am I going to serve the coffee?" We were there when they were closing, so everything became different.

ABOG
You became part of their whole process. You were there when they started; you were there when they finished.

GC
Yes. And you would have a different conversation. You would become familiar to people in your own way.

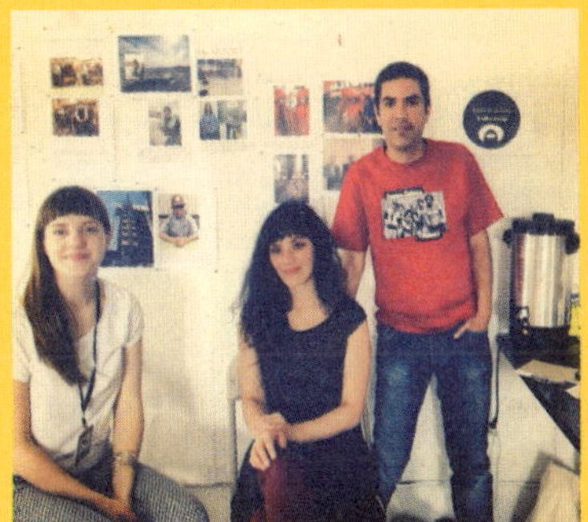

Joelle Te Paske, Gabriela Ceja, Fran Ilich at the Open Engagement Conference, Carnegie Mellon University, Pittsburgh, 2015.

economic system might function. The co-op is named for the alter ego of Zorro, the son of a Spanish-descended hacienda owner who fights for the rights of the indigenous workers. Likewise, Ilich—a well-regarded writer and media artist—seeks to use his access and education to serve a noble cause.

By founding autonomous mechanisms of support for social movements, Ilich experiments with answering the question, What if the world really worked in thc ways that the Zapatistas are calling for? What if true, grassroots, person-to-person participatory democracy were activated on a broader scale? Ilich's work is a real-world exploration of a deeply utopian vision for what the future might look like, if we just give it a chance.

This text was written using contributions from Deborah Fisher, Felix Salmon and Joelle Te Paske.

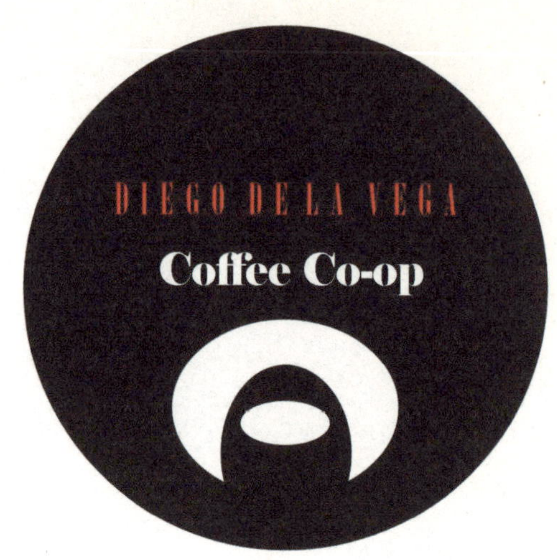

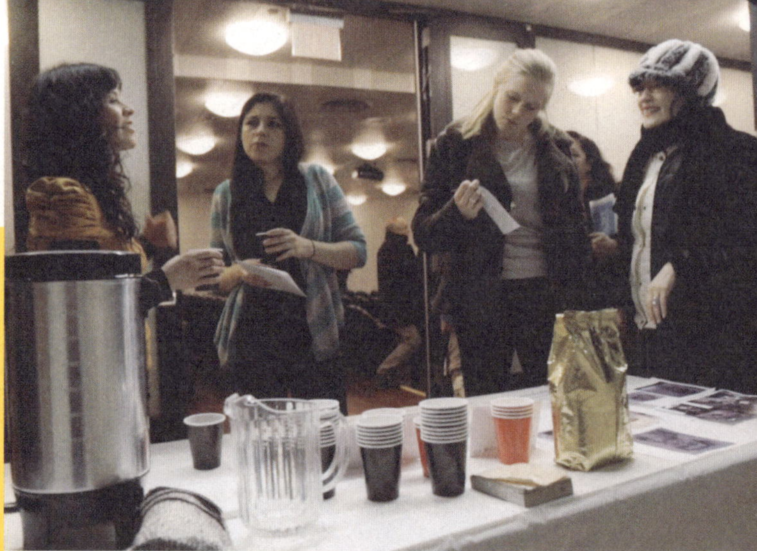

ABOG
What are your hopes for how the project continues?

GC
Many! [*Laughs*] I believe this was just a beginning. It helped us really organize ourselves to see how it would work. I think that the idea of having the catering service is great. It is practical because we can just decide the dates when we were going to serve the coffee, rather than have a coffee shop and be there all the time, expecting people to come. We go to the people and we go to the events.

Top: ***Diego de la Vega Coffee Co-op*** **logo, 2015.**

Bottom: Gabriela Ceja, left, serving coffee, 2015.

possibleworlds.org

An independent internet server launched in 2005 that offers web hosting to social movements in Mexico.

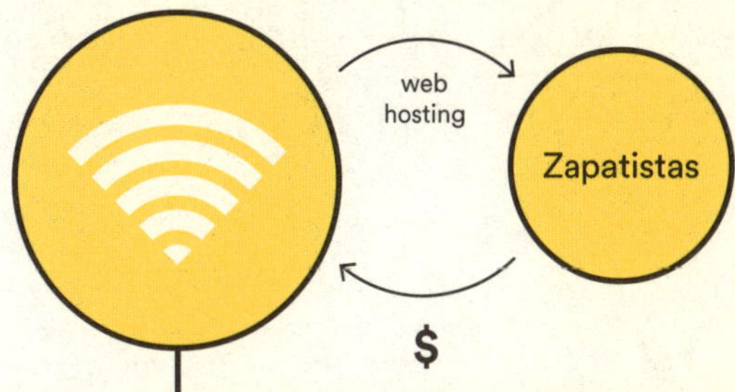

Spacebank

A community investment bank dedicated to serve as a vehicle for investing small sums in social causes.

over 200 investors!

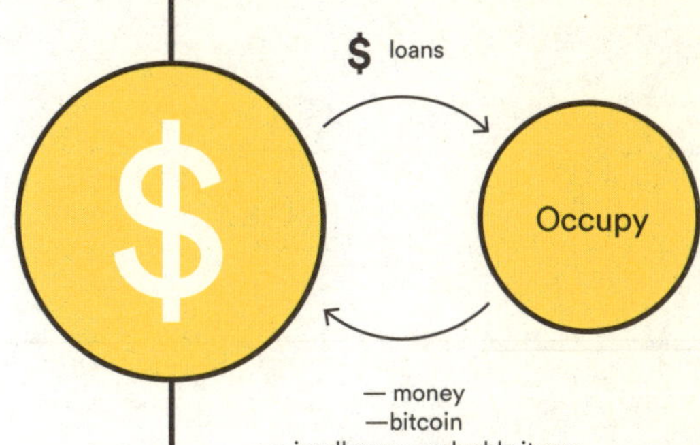

Diego de la Vega Coffee Co-op

A project working with the Zapatista farmers in Chiapas, Mexico to bring their products and ideology to activist communities in New York and elsewhere.

Diego de la Vega was founded as a Spacebank venture.

While sharing the coffee, Ilich shares the ideas of the kind of participatory democracy that is practiced in the autonomous zones in Mexico to create a dialogue.

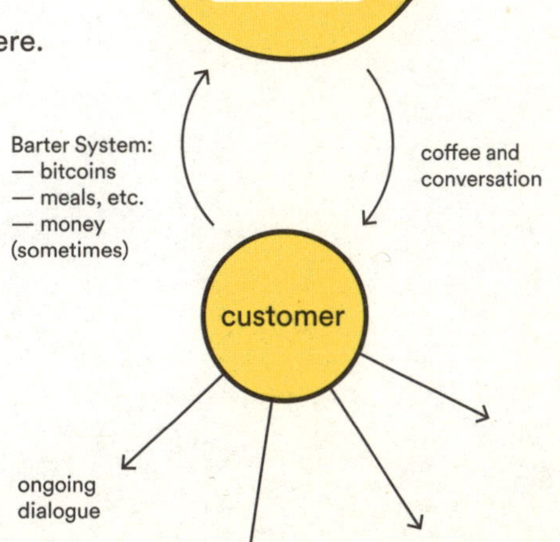

PART TWO

ETHICS

Doing Good: The Ethics of Engagement

As part of the ongoing Growing Dialogue conversation that was generated in response to an article by Ben Davis, that became the first one published in ABOG's online DISCUSS forum, the question of the ethics of working with communities arose. This question can serve as a framework for thinking about some of the projects ABOG supported, as well as the organization's web content. It leads one to ask, is socially engaged art necessarily progressive? What is its overall purpose or goal? Here, Rick Lowe, Elizabeth M. Grady, Deborah Fisher, and Nato Thompson weigh in.

Rick Lowe
In my work, I'm concerned with both the symbolic (aesthetic) and the practical (outcome) and don't have a problem explaining to housing funders the outcome of our housing work, i.e., economic impact. I just don't think that art funders should have the same assessment criteria as housing funders. Is there an assessment model that can honor the full range of artistic contribution without neglecting the outcomes that are expected in political and sociological terms?

Elizabeth M. Grady
There is a range of models for addressing community impact, aesthetic value, and metrics of the sort that housing funders and others outside the artsphere need to see in order to feel comfortable sharing their resources to promote change. A good start would be a multifaceted approach that allows for the voices (and often conflicting perceptions) of multiple stakeholders (artists, community leaders, partner organizations) to be heard, with parallel statistics about participation and community makeup. This approach combines theories of change with ethnographic methods of evaluation and dialogic approaches like collaborative action research, and participatory action research.

Rick Lowe
To me, determining when art has a negative effect or when it uses communities (social, political, etc.) for the simple purpose of social or financial capital is one of the most important challenges for the emerging field of SEA. This is no easy task, mainly because of the diversity of practices and motivations for engaging in such work.

I like to think of my work as "progressive" in that it seeks some form of justice for working-class and underserved communities. But I rarely speak of the desired "justice" outcome of the work because it can be seen as risky in a society that has basically dropped the notion of working-class justice as a concern. This appears to be relevant to the conversation about the effect of SEA. Is SEA inherently progressive? Does SEA work aim at some form of justice? Can SEA make such a claim [to promoting justice] when the field of practice and motivations [of artists] are so diverse?

A Blade of Grass states on its website that "activism is important to socially engaged art because it is inherent to the principles of this art practice." Are artists inherently activists by practicing SEA? I know that there are many like myself who consider themselves both artists and activists. Some have no desire to be considered activists because they do work that is socially or community engaged. There are some who may not consider themselves activists, but share the goals of activism, so they try to connect their work to activists or movements.

If the SEA movement does not seek a progressive identity, and is a field of a wide range of work by artists experimenting in social and community spaces, will it become a field that does not support any ethical responsibility in the work? This question reminds me of a conversation I had with a friend about how the ethical responsibility of working with working-class communities differs from the ethical responsibilities of working in the art world. In my opinion, you can talk bullshit in the art world. In fact, it's not only allowed but expected on some level. When the bullshit in the art world begins to stink, it's swept out the door to make room for what's new. But when the bullshit starts to stink in underserved communities, the artist can move on, while folks in the community have to live with the negative impact. So is it possible for SEA to not adopt an ethical agenda?

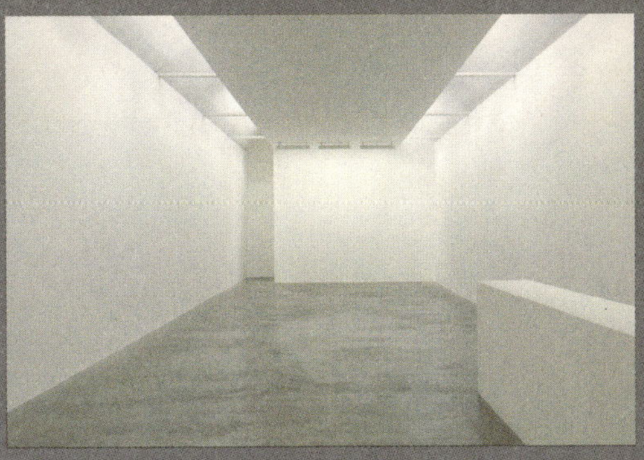

Empty gallery. Kerlin Gallery, Dublin. 2007.

Deborah Fisher

Rick, you point directly to the tension between the art world's tendency to encourage bullshit, and the potential SEA has to be a movement, with a progressive agenda and maybe even shared goals. This is work that, as Nato says, has the potential to reshape power. This reimagining of power is some of the most important cultural work that we can do right now. We live in a world in which power feels uniquely fixed and monolithic, and these seemingly omnipotent *Powers That Be* are wreaking all sorts of havoc!

So, in response to the art world allowing for bullshit, I would ask if instead it is trying to preserve the magical paradox and multiplicity that we want out of art? Is this bullshit acting as fertilizer in some way? It feels really tough to ask an artist to come up with something that is a little bit magical because it preserves and expands paradox, and is also rigorously accountable to others. I don't know whether this is *why* the art world is organized around avoiding accountability, or if I perceive this toughness *because* the art world is organized around avoiding accountability. Either way, it feels important to recognize that SEA exists in a larger context in which the art world tries to suspend reality for artists by creating faux-contextless white cubes, institutional structures that handle artists, curators whose role is to protect ideas and so forth. The art world is a value-creation engine in which artists are allowed, literally, to do whatever they want except value their own work. In order for SEA projects to achieve maximum potential, we need to think about them in terms of their uneasy relationship to the existing art world, which creates its own reality.

I am focusing on this bullshit aspect because I have been thinking so much about what parts of the existing art world must be imported into our organizational structure in order to preserve the creative latitude, integrity and freedom that makes these projects work. Like Rick, I have been thinking a lot about what actually happens in the communities where this work is being done, and whether it's harming or helping, or simply being tolerated. One of the most peculiar features of the current landscape is how dependent we are on oral history and the artist's documentation, or interpretation of what's happening on the ground. This creates a persistent question about what is actually happening in these communities, who owns the story, and whether that story is being told in an accountable fashion. This, to me, is where the rubber meets the road.

I want to create a structure in which artists can define their social change agenda however their brains need to in order to make, expand and preserve multiplicity and paradox. This is why we are using the softer, more vague language of *social change* as opposed to *social justice*. This is also why we don't currently declare that we have a specifically progressive agenda, although we might revisit this.

Nato Thompson

To have a catch-all phrase or not to have a catch-all phrase, that is the question. It strikes me that Ben Davis's response has a simple solution. We can either accept that SEA is a term that encapsulates a form of culture making that has no direct link to social justice or we can limit SEA to those ways of working that we feel are more productive in terms of social justice. It strikes me that when looking at such a stark picture, the answer to what must constitute SEA will have to remain ethically opaque. It is, in a sense, a formal term with no ethical prescription. For now, it seems, the term SEA continues to focus on cultural projects produced within the infrastructure of contemporary art. If so much of contemporary political and social action shares the formal qualities of an expanded notion of SEA (could we call it Socially Engaged Culture?), then where does one find the political stakes? How we benefit in expanding the notion of SEA towards broader cultural life is that we can finally grapple with the powerful effects of cultural production as a way of being in the world.

Charles Esche

I Am Not Interested in UTOPIA Today

I am not interested in UTOPIA today. There are times when the pure imagination is vital but not now. Today, I want to take account of the here and now, not the nowhere and nowhen of the "no place."[1] In any case, as an artistic device UTOPIA is more than exhausted. The one-size-fits-all, free market project of *Utopia Station* in the Venice Biennale of 2003 did away with any possibility to use it meaningfully in art for the coming decades. *Utopia Station* was curated by Molly Nesbit, Hans Ulrich Obrist and Rirkrit Tiravanija, and included a wide array of artworks and performances by dozens of artists that created a temporary utopian environment, while also exploring the idea of utopia. It was the end of the line, at least symbolically, though the end had happened earlier in fact. By invoking the convenient placelessness of UTOPIA, the art world excused itself from every responsibility to the here and now. From then on, it could celebrate the glory of its impotence in the face of neoliberalism's notorious claims to have ended history. In its place, for a while, art was able to give itself permission to embrace the role of critical decor for the 1%. In return, those superrich increased their depredations on society at large while upping the price of art to untrammeled heights.

So enough with UTOPIA, let's start somewhere else instead. For the sake of argument, let's say we begin in 2015. The state of European cultural politics has rarely looked bleaker. The *ancien régime* of social democracy is on its uppers, neoliberalism has turned suicidal, and communism was buried long ago. Xenophobia and social constriction are in the dark shadows looming behind the coattails of them all. There is probably now only a small chance that they will not step out into the light. If and when they do, we can choose to be ready. These are the urgencies we face and there are indeed few reasons to be

1 This is a phrase used in the original press release for *Utopia Station*.

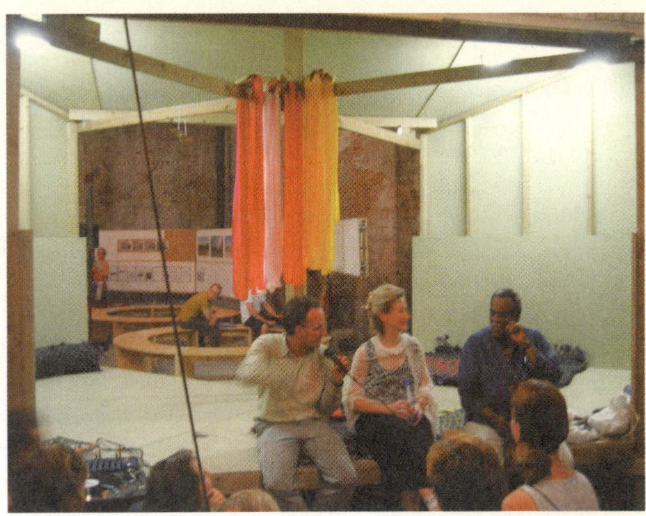

cheerful. Yet there are many positive reasons to be attentive, cooperative and constructive in our analysis and action. If it really wants to, the art world can play a real part, small but perhaps crucial, in making a difference to what that famous concept "history" (that never did go away) will tell to the future about our time and place today.

Having demolished UTOPIA, however, I don't want to leave empty-handed. The word has other potentialities, at least if we make a small orthographic change. It's an addition that has already been suggested by other art writers since UTOPIA first grabbed the art world's attention in the 1990s. Let's just add an "E," they say, and suddenly UTOPIA (no place) becomes EUTOPIA (a good place) and in doing so it takes on the contours of something I can talk about. Once "good place" replaces the "no place" we are back on more solid ground, where the ethics of behavior and choice flow back into the discussion and we can talk about what living the good life might be like today.

Hans Ulrich Obrist, Edouard Glissant and Molly Nesbit in a public conversation during opening weekend at "Utopia Station," Venice Biennale, 2003. On view: *Sonic House* by Karl Holmqvist and Uglycute, seating by Liam Gillick, and an installation by Manfred Pernice and Sean Snyder.

In 2001, I was invited by Tilo Schultz to write a text for a poster campaign called "The Return of Display" that he was about to launch in San Sebastian. He asked four writers to produce short texts that he then designed and fly-posted in the city. Seven years later, the project was repeated in Leipzig. I haven't returned to this text for some time, but in thinking about EUTOPIA and what I might be able to contribute to it, it seemed relevant.

28th August 2030,
Instead of a revolution

After it had happened, no one could really find a convincing explanation for it all. Why did a local art museum issue its call and suddenly open its doors to all the city's asylum seekers? How did such a small, local action then connect to all sorts of gatherings across the European continent? And why did the corporations of the day not see it coming? After all, consumer intelligence was their speciality, and this was nothing if not a free choice revolt. Each person seemed to join by themselves, perhaps out of some unfathomable herd instinct, but nevertheless as individuals. And it wasn't really true that they joined anything anyway. They just went to the museums, kunsthallen, artist spaces—art venues of all sorts and in every major city. They sat, looked around, slowly started to speak to each other and enjoyed it all enough to keep coming back. Soon, the museums started to respond—organizing meetings and commissioning short-term projects as a result, inviting the press and asking artists and others to turn the tables on cynical journalists. The art mausoleums that had slumbered for so long suddenly started to live. Impromptu activities were welcomed and the rules of engagement with art were changed whenever necessary. Museum workers even started to talk about the need for unconditional hospitality and visitors responded.

Strangely, the action spread across central Europe. For once, our disempowered citizens seem to shrug off their apathy and find a voice beyond the reach of administrative control. Of course, everything relied on action at the local level and there were different reactions, but a new spark was ignited almost daily and every week a new city fell into line. The speed of the change produced problems, most of which we still have today. When people failed to turn up for work, production initially fell by over 70%. But gradually provisional solutions were found, priorities were changed and people drifted back to work for two or three days a week anyway, just to make enough money to carry on. The corporations issued threats, sackings, even appealed for military action but there were no laws against public cultural attendance and the smart entrepreneurs quickly adjusted to the new lower level economy.

Now, it simply goes on like this. The museums are the new public forums, the remaining party politicians try to go there to make their point but the lower level of production and distribution is taken care of locally, administered by the few who understand the necessity or still take some pleasure in the regularity of work. The purpose of meeting seems to be changing. No longer about protest, it's now about something closer to the old, perhaps mythical, idea of the agora. Exchange simply happens for its own sake and for the pleasure of the result.

Maybe we could say everyone's an artist now, except hardly anybody uses that term, preferring other words, usually adapted from local slang still surviving in our international patois. Why did it all happen? If you ask me it's pretty straightforward. It happened because there wasn't anything else to do. We'd exhausted every other option and this was the one place left worth trying. Funny, I guess, but I don't know why we never thought of it before.

At the time I wrote this in 2001, I thought a nearly 30-year time frame was still a bit risky. There was no way the collapse would happen so quickly. Now in 2015 it doesn't read so preposterously anymore. There's even a chance something like it might happen sooner.

Though my old text completely avoids dealing with the practicalities of life and survival, its proposal raises some even more urgent objections, or perhaps, hidden questions. To what extent is the huge social, political and economic change that any eutopian formation might shape actually worth the struggle, the destruction and the suffering that it will cause? Am I right to suggest that the museum must give up its cherished role as bastion of cultural heritage and defender of the objects that lend us a sense of history in order to respond to demands on the street? These issues pervade all discussion of EUTOPIAS—small or large—because there is no way to change without leaving many dear things behind. To respond to them, I need to go to the root of the "good" in the first part of the EUTOPIA of a good place. If the place we create after the change is objectively, demonstrably "good" for the users and people involved then the change is valid. If not, we would all agree that we are in big trouble. This "goodness" is, however, a very slippery concept, one that relates to the perception of the individual, his/her history and hopes for the future and the nature of a society that welcomes the good into its midst. How does criticality survive in the effort to strive for the good? How does development take place when such a seemingly absolute and fixed value is at stake?

We might start to deal with the good by relating it to another word, "small." A "small good place" sounds persuasive. It suggests a site limited in some way by geography, climate, culture or context so that it could be separated from and compared with a bigger outside. It would not need to be inclusive, let alone universalist, in its claims to ethical rectitude because it would be a place of difference as well as goodness. So far, so good—but if we each can have our own private idea of the good life, are we not back to the relativist, laissez-faire approach that measures success in terms of popularity and not ethical value at all? The good becomes the desired and in the end that doesn't much differ from the well-intentioned UTOPIAN option in which real decisions are postponed into the far, unproblematic future and a sort of loose permissiveness prevails in the art world alongside the hardest logic of the superrich hegemony.

So, an effective "small good place" needs to be more than a choice amongst other less good places. It has to be small only in terms of its size and not in terms of its claims or aspirations. If we can create and sustain small EUTOPIAS in art, they have to hold true for longer than the lifecycle of a single new fashion trend.

To escape from the bonds of small-scale relativism, we need to get specific. Let's take a work like *Aktiengesellschaft*[2] (2002) by Maria Eichhorn. It sets itself up rather beautifully for a dispute about its quality and purpose, its goodness and narrowness. At first glance, its materiality and subject do not belong to what is traditionally considered the ethics of art. Wooden benches, perhaps modelled on examples from the 1930s, as well as a number of copies of a book, separate a series of precisely defined hidden light boxes that contain administrative documents connected to the establishment of a public company. The form is precise but dispersed; the content, bureaucratic. The backlit documents, beautiful in their plainness, set out the purpose of the public limited company that Eichhorn established. This is a normal company except that its goal is uniquely to preserve its initial capital of €50,000 intact and unchanged for as long as the company exists. To achieve this, the company itself must own all its shares, thus never allowing the objectives of others to interfere with its given goal. In doing this, the company becomes a separate entity responsible to itself. In this state it can define its own goodness because nothing outside itself seems to be at stake—a utopian system in the worst sense, but not yet eutopian.

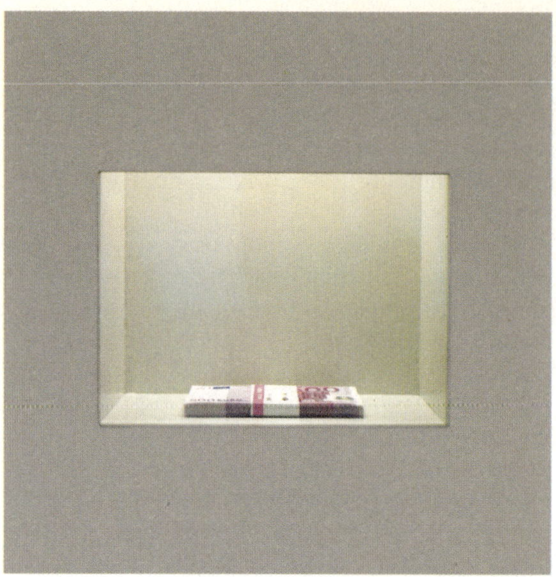

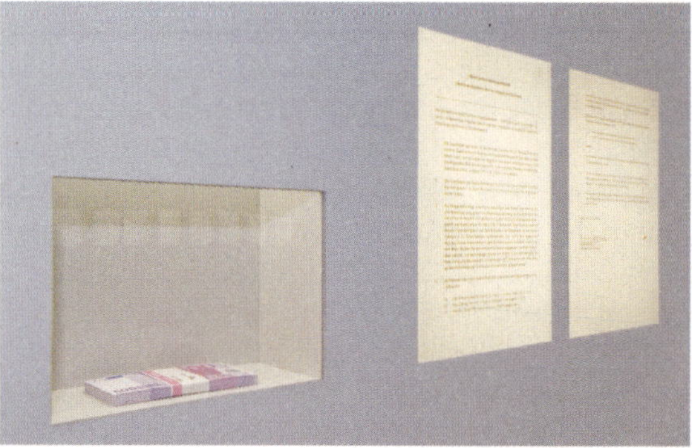

Top and bottom: Maria Eichhorn, *Maria Eichhorn Aktiengesellschaft*, 2002. Collection Van Abbemuseum, Eindhoven, The Netherlands.

To take that step to the small good place, the work needs to inhale the intense free market capitalism of the economic system by which it is surrounded in the early 21st century. This is an economic belief system that treats public limited companies as legal subjects akin to human beings. They are autonomous entities that can, as we know from the banks since 2008, behave with the utmost disregard for others without any consequences falling on themselves. Instead it is the often meager capital of real human beings, requisitioned by the state in taxes, that ensures the continuity of the neoliberal system by impoverishing the people. This status of a human-like entity is guaranteed by the nation state through the full range of its legal and disciplinary power, visualized in *Aktiengesellschaft* by the almost endless official documentation reproduced in the book and on the wall.

2 The title translates as *Joint-stock company*.

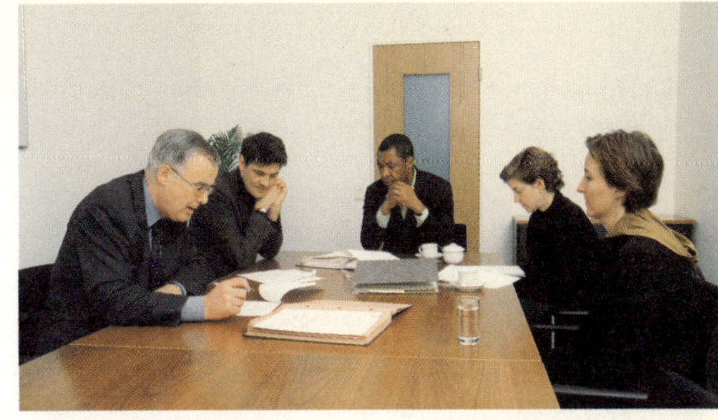

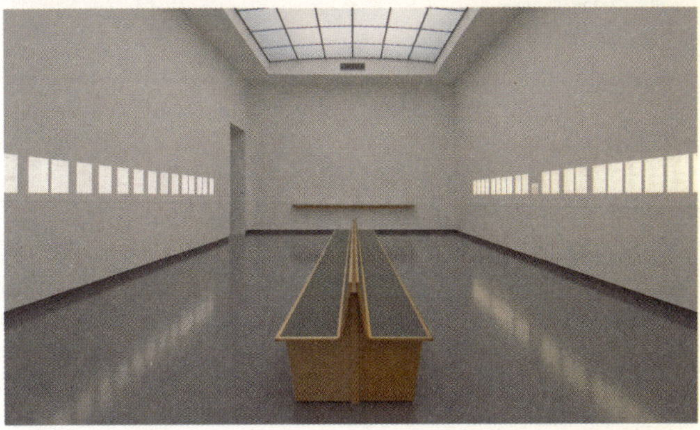

Top and bottom: Maria Eichhorn, *Maria Eichhorn Aktiengesellschaft*, 2002. Collection Van Abbemuseum, Eindhoven, The Netherlands.

But this jewel of capitalist propaganda does not fulfil the most basic condition of the free market because it produces no profit. The small good place that she creates between the transparencies, book and benches is both small and good because it is particular, and because it challenges the iron rule of growth and profitability that has come to control and overwhelm almost all human transactions of whatever kind, from love to death. Its goodness lies in its exceptionalism to this rule, its space apart in a universe of no growth and de-growth that might be, on the margins, beginning to take root in our consciousness.

To make a real case for the possibility of a EUTOPIAN art, we need more examples. These examples will be less conscious of their status as art, or at least as art that roots itself in modernist originality. To escape the UTOPIAN desire for the unreachable horizon, EUTOPIAN artworks may often find their place within the warp and weft of art history, pulling out loose strands that might point to certain specific, small moments of possibility.

The *Raum der Gegenwart* (*Room of the Present,* or *Contemporary Room*) was first planned as the final room in the permanent display of the Landesmuseum in Hannover and was commissioned from László Moholy-Nagy by the institution's director, Alexander Dorner. Dorner was one of the earliest museum curators to see the possibility of the exhibition as a three-dimensional narrative. His displays in Hannover ran from prehistory to the present and sought to tell a total story of art. The intention of the *Raum der Gegenwart* was to be a changing display of the latest technological inventions in the reproduction of the image. Photography, film, slideshows and moving elements including Moholy-Nagy's own *Licht Raum Modulator* (*Light Space Modulator*) were included in the plan. In many senses, one could read in this room the end of the art that was shown in the museum up to this point. No longer was art to be a precious object for an elite few, but the mechanical image would depict and shape contemporary life directly through literal reproduction in different frames and contexts. Movement was key, with the room effectively combining elements of both realism and abstraction in film, giant scrolling light boxes, slide presentations and rolling screens.

However, this room was never built. The early success of the local NSDAP[3] in Hannover ensured that Moholy-Nagy was decommissioned, and eventually Dorner himself was forced to resign and leave Germany. Only in 2007 did the room come alive again, as a copy without original interpreted and constructed by Kai-Uwe Hemken and Jan Gerber and bought by the Van Abbemuseum. Thus, the practical realization took place long after the first impulse, displacing the work both in time and place to such an extent that its avant-garde and therefore largely utopian content is replaced alternately by nostalgia and confusion. Its status as an artwork was questionable from the beginning, when it was both a Moholy-Nagy proposal and a space for the presentation of images that were (not yet quite) art. By 2007, given the history of reproductive media, this reproduction without an original starts spinning around itself. So, what makes this small room into a small, good (eutopian) room? In this case, good would mean a clear critical understanding for the potential viewer of the processes that went into (re)producing the work, as well as an ethical relationship between the maker, designer, historian and future artists who might come to influence and occupy it. In the context of 2015, it is precisely in the confusion of origin and purpose, authorship and copyright, that a capacity for this good might be released. Already as a drawn proposal, the *Raum der Gegenwart* foreshadowed the end of modernity—an end that we have spent most of the last 80 years repeating across all human activities from warfare to economics. If modernity, as Guy Debord would argue in his *Society of the Spectacle*, was "separation perfected" then *Raum der Gegenwart* already offered a different image in 1930. Today, in the coming world of global equivalences, its awkward status as copy without original makes it into an even more forceful experience of fluidity and synthesis. How can we represent difference and sameness? How can we copy ethically? How can we move and stay still all at once? The (re)construction of the *Raum der Gegenwart* provides answers to these questions and presents us with a small eutopia—much more so now than back in 1930.

The final example is perhaps the most complex. The Museum of American Art, Berlin has existed for some twenty years. It manifests itself in different installations of the history of exhibitions and their host institutions, all the time foreswearing a claim of authorship of artworks and replacing that with a claim to curatorial (even janitorial) analysis. One project within the greater project is the "Museum of Antiquities," in which two

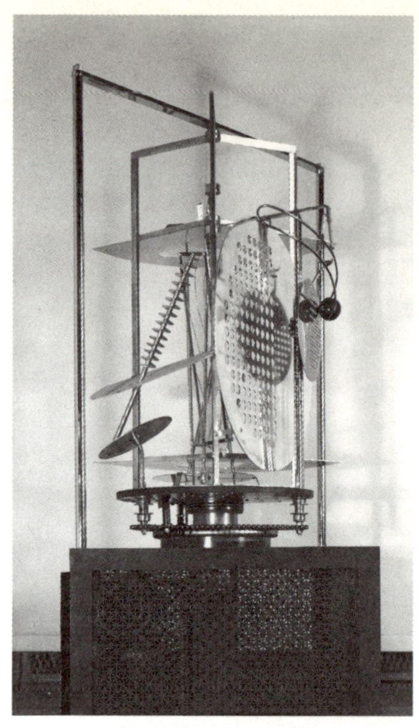

László Moholy-Nagy, *Light Prop for an Electric Stage (Light-Space Modulator)*, 1930. Harvard Art Museums/Busch-Reisinger Museum, Gift of Sibyl Moholy-Nagy, BR56.5

3 *The Nationalsozialistische Deutsche Arbeiterpartei*. In English, the National Socialist German Workers Party, informally called the Nazi Party.

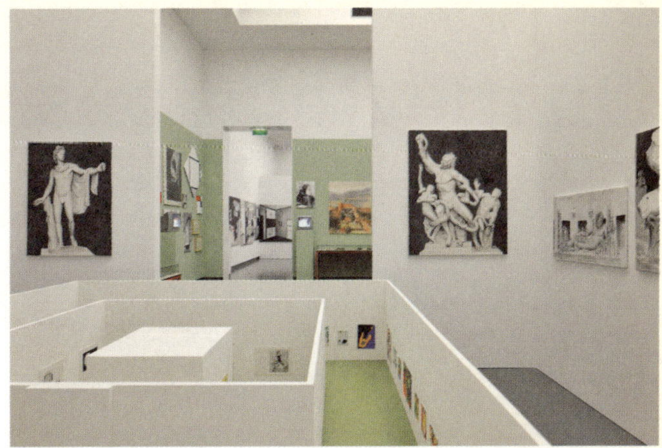

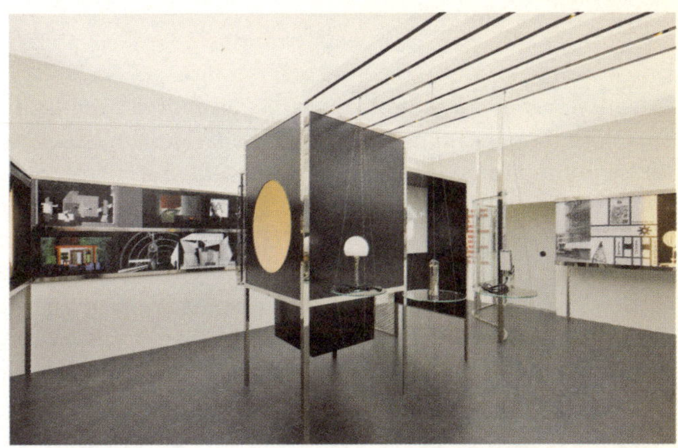

crucial moments in the public consumption of art are compared. The first, around 1503, marks the effective foundation of the Vatican art collections by Pope Julius II. The second, in 1936, marks the exhibition "Cubism and Abstract Art" at the new Museum of Modern Art, New York, founded by Alfred Barr. Julius and Barr make quite strange bedfellows but that separation of four hundred years and a continent they nevertheless come to represent the alpha and omega of modern art and its histories. Julius is not only posited as the founder of the museum but also of non-Christian history, which allowed both past and future time to begin rolling. This gave papal license both the archaeology and the linear developmental narratives inherent to modernity. In "Museum of Antiquities," it is clear that Barr ends what Julius begins. By drawing up his famous table of modernist movements and putting it on the cover of the *Cubism and Abstract Art* catalogue, Barr claims ownership over the future of modernity's arrow just as Julius did of the past. In both cases they lost control and new sets of conditions slowly emerged.

The Museum of American Art, Berlin sets up this confrontation in order to release the grip of modernity over so much of the contemporary world. The complexity of the argument is reduced at this moment to the simplicity of a gesture of liberation by saying that the modern past is really done while absolutely refusing to forget about our contemporary accountability to it. This is, for me, an extraordinary double gesture in which remembering and forgetting are combined and a space is created for a departure accompanied by the full weight of history. This is nothing if not specific and nothing if not ethical—a precise, small and wondrous EUTOPIA.

Top: Museum of American Art, Berlin; Sites of Modernity (collection of the Museum of Antiquities) (1502–2010), 2010, Collection Van Abbemuseum, Eindhoven, The Netherlands.

Bottom: László Moholy-Nagy and Alexander Dorner, *Raum der Gegenwart*, (1930) 2009 1:1 scale, Collection Van Abbemuseum, Eindhoven, The Netherlands.

This essay was first published in The Small Utopia: Ars Multiplicata *(Milan: Progetto Prada Arte, 2012) 221–229, and is reprinted here in edited form with permission from Fondazione Prada.*

Grant Kester

On the Relationship between Theory and Practice in Socially Engaged Art

Recent debates around socially engaged art have focused on the spatial and temporal nature of social change (the relationship, for example, between an ephemeral event and the more lasting transformation of a given social structure, or between local or situational action and global, or geographically extensive, forms of organized resistance). More specifically, these debates ask how the local, situational or "ad hoc" actions often encountered in socially engaged art practices are related to systematic forms of domination.[1] A typical reproach directed at projects of this nature is that they function as little more than window dressing for a fundamentally corrupt system. The only way to produce real, meaningful change is to engage in the direct overthrow of the capitalist economy in its entirety. This criticism is necessary but not sufficient. The problem with this approach, of course, is that it relies on a hyperbolic model of capitalism (as an entirely impenetrable and fixed system of domination) while also assuming that artists today actually have the option of aligning themselves with an existing revolutionary movement, poised to launch an all-out assault on neoliberal capitalism, and have simply refrained from doing so. The conventional avant-garde resolution to this impasse is to withdraw from any direct engagement with the social or political world in order to embody a pure principle of radical negation, assaulting all existing values and systems of meaning. Not surprisingly, these gestures have become almost entirely routinized within the protocols of international exhibitions and biennials (often serving as the necessary scandal that demonstrates the openness of a system predicated on hierarchy and wealth). In most cases they simply allow artists to pose as incendiary critics of capitalism while securing a comfortable living from the investment habits of the 1%, to whom they sell their work.

1 See, for example, ABOG, "Future Imperfect" (theme for 2014–15), http://www.abladeofgrass.org/discuss/themes/ (July 14, 2015): "Social change often challenges 'the system'. Sometimes the system is visible—the prison system, the health care system, the education system. Sometimes, the system is a habit of thought or internal 'cop in the head' (hat tip to Augusto Boal) that polices our behavior and governs the way we see ourselves in the world. Perhaps the failures of our governmental, economic and social systems can be seen as a failure of the imagination. If so, what happens when art, an act of imagination, is used to creatively address these failures? What happens when instead of 'fighting the man,' artists become involved in reimagining the way things work? A Blade of Grass' 2014 Fellows for Socially Engaged Art and Organizational Grantees address this notion in different ways. By creating and expanding on ad hoc solutions to seemingly unsolvable problems, the artists' projects we are working with this year visualize ways of addressing, changing, getting around and otherwise confounding 'the system' to foster greater freedom and equity in our society."

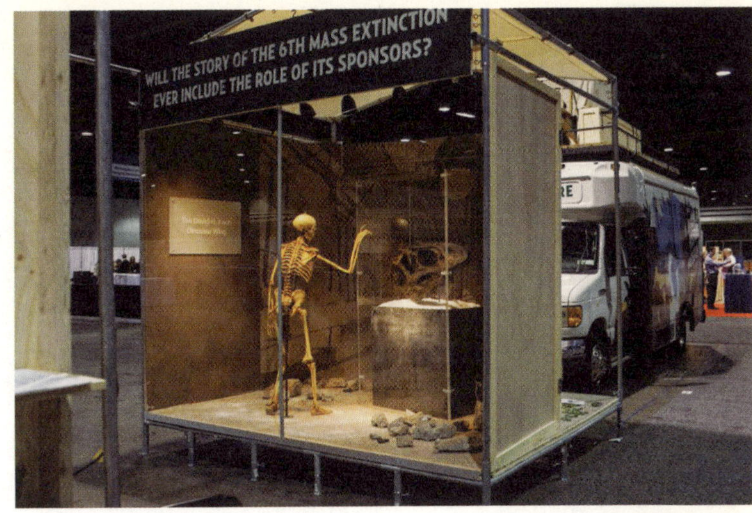

Not An Alternative, *The Natural History Museum*, installation view, 2015.

The residues of this larger belief system continue to inform art criticism. We can identify two related assumptions that have been especially problematic when directed at the analysis of socially engaged art.

— The assumption that any form of art practice that produces some concrete change in the world or is developed in alliance with specific social movements (via the creation or preservation of a park, the generation of new, prefigurative collective forms, shifts in the disposition of power in a given community, etc.) is entirely pragmatic and has no critical or conceptually creative capacity.[2] Or, alternately, that such projects, by suggesting that some meaningful change is possible within existing social and political structures, do nothing more than forestall the necessary, but inevitably deferred, revolution.

— The assumption that any given art project is *either* radically disruptive or naïvely ameliorative (trafficking in "good times, affirmative feelings and positive outcomes" as a typical blog posting describes it).[3] This is paired with the failure of many critics to understand that durational art practices, and forms of activism, always move through moments of *both* provisional consensus or solidarity-formation *and* conflict and disruption.

This isn't to say that there aren't numerous "social art" projects that are based on simplistic, de-politicized concepts of community. However, if these projects are problematic it's not because they seek to engage in a concrete manner with the world outside the gallery or museum, or rely on processes of consensually-based action. It's because they have a naïve or non-existent understanding of power and the nature of resistance. The most damaging of these assumptions, for a theory of socially engaged art practice, involves the failure of critics to grasp the generative capacity of practice itself—it's ability to produce new, counter-normative insights into the constitution of power and subjectivity.

2 The concept of "prefigurative" modes of social organization, developed in sociological accounts of new social movements, is concerned with the ways in which specific forms of collective action and decision-making (deliberative democracy, horizontality, etc.) have practical value while also serving as potential models for future social systems. See, for example, Ana Cecilia Dinerstein, *The Politics of Autonomy in Latin America: The Art of Organizing Hope* (New York: Palgrave Macmillan, 2015).

3 Amy Spiers, "Is there a place for disruption/reaction/antagonism in social practice art?," *100 Questions*, Open Engagement blog, http://openengagement.info/69-amy-spiers/ (March 9, 2014).

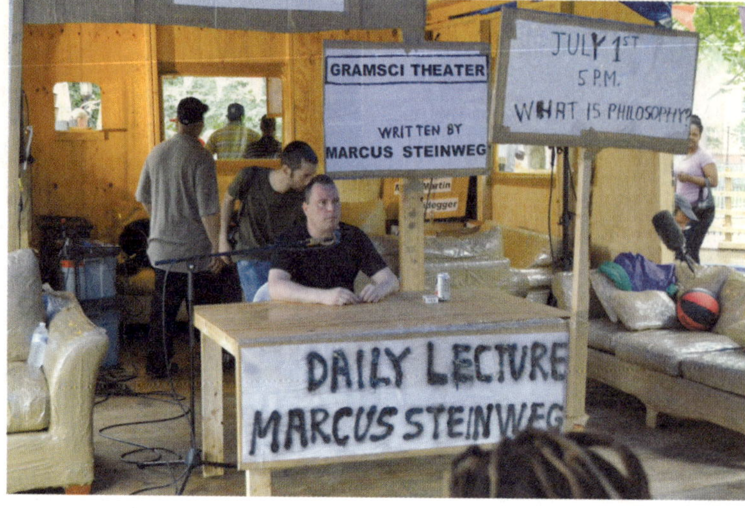

Thomas Hirschhorn, *Gramsci Monument*, Forest Houses, Bronx, NY 2015.

Is there another way for us to understand the transformative nature of socially engaged art practice? This complex question is made more difficult by the accumulated weight of past art theory and criticism. Conventional forms of artistic practice (installation, painting, sculpture, time-based media, and more traditional, actor-centered modes of performance art) raise a very different set of questions that are, in many cases, not applicable to socially engaged art projects. Here the "practice" entails the artist devising a particular set of forms, events or objects that are presented to a viewer. In this case the primary generative moment, the moment when decisive choices are made regarding the formal, material and discursive constitution of the work as a unified, apprehensible object, occurs prior to the arrival of the viewer. The situation is, of course, quite different with many socially engaged art projects. Here the act of production ("practice" in the conventional sense) and reception are coincident. Moreover, artistic practice at this level becomes "transgradient" (to use one of Bakhtin's favorite concepts) with other, non-artistic, forms of cultural production, from participatory planning to environmental activism to radical pedagogy. Thus, we have a form of art production that requires us to reconceptualize our understanding of both the "viewer" and the act of reception, and that also exhibits a promiscuous relationship to other modes of cultural action.

This promiscuity opens up an important line of analysis that connects socially engaged art with a larger set of debates over the more general interrelationship between theory and practice. We might recall here the dramatic transformation that occurs in the ambitions of the Frankfurt School between the moment of its founding in the early 1930s and the period during and after WWII. As Horkheimer outlines in his inaugural lecture ("The Present Situation of Social Philosophy and the Tasks for an Institute of Social Research") in 1931, the goal of a properly "critical" theory was to challenge the abstraction and pseudo-transcendence of traditional theory by integrating theoretical production with the empirical analysis of, and practical engagement with, actual social movements. The Frankfurt School was thus organized around a transdisciplinary approach that would unite scholars in the fields of sociology, psychology, political economy and philosophy with the goal of producing an exhaustive analysis of the nature of capitalist domination and the most effective mechanisms for challenging it. The reciprocal interconnection between theoretical reflection and political action was central to the definition of a "critical" theory. By the mid-1940s the mission of the Frankfurt School had been dramatically curtailed, leading to an often sterile functionalism. Confronted with the failure of the proletariat to unite in opposition to fascism and the emergence of a "totalized domination" that made the capitalist, fascist and communist state systems virtually indistinguishable (at least to Adorno and Horkheimer), the germ of an authentic revolutionary drive had been transferred to the sequestered realm of fine art, where it would be held in trust until a more fortuitous historical moment called for its reactualization.

The key effect of this shift was to uncouple theory from any relationship to the specific, empirically verifiable, effects of social and political resistance. Under the monolithic power of a "totally administered society" outlined in *The Dialectic of Enlightenment*, virtually every other cultural form except art, and every other intellectual discipline, except a very specific mode of self-reflexive philosophy, had been irredeemably contaminated by the instrumentalizing drive of capitalist rationality. If no real change was possible here and now, then there was no point in cultivating a set of analytic tools for understanding the nature of contemporary political resistance. And if art could only preserve its new role as singular bastion of revolutionary truth by abjuring any direct involvement with the social or political world, there was no reason to reflect on the potential relationship between art, or theory, and practical resistance. Here we encounter two key beliefs that remain a persistent feature of much contemporary art criticism. First, that the artist (or artist qua theorist) possesses a uniquely privileged capacity to comprehend the totality of capitalist domination, standing in for a proletariat that has remained stubbornly indifferent to its historical destiny (Adorno uses the metaphor of the artist as a "deputy"). And second, that art can preserve this remarkable prescience only by refusing to debase itself through any direct involvement with social resistance or activism. This is the foundation for Adorno's famous attack on what he viewed as the naïve "actionism" of student protestors during the late 1960s.[4]

We can observe here a symptomatic ideological and discursive transference, in which the conventional principle of aesthetic autonomy is infused with a new, revolutionary, rationale (the very

4 See Grant Kester, "The Noisy Optimism of Immediate Action: Theory, Practice and Pedagogy in Contemporary Art," *Art Journal* (Summer 2012). 86–99.

distance that art takes up from quotidian life provides it with a privileged vantage point from which to diagnose the overdetermination of this life by economic imperatives). This transformed concept of aesthetic autonomy is evident across a range of contemporary art practices, most recently in Thomas Hirschhorn's crude opposition between "pure art" (the foundation of his own practice) and "social work." In his widely publicized *Gramsci Monument* project, Hirschhorn was able to provide an extraordinary level of economic support (including summer art classes and a computer center for children, as well as comparatively well-paying jobs) to the residents of the Forest Houses complex, located in a chronically under-resourced working class neighborhood in the Bronx. He was able to retain his "purity" precisely by refusing to take any responsibility for the disappointment, frustration or disillusionment of those residents when, after eleven weeks, these resources, and the accompanying outpouring of public concern that the neighborhood had enjoyed, were abruptly withdrawn. The lesson, for the residents of Forest Houses, was that in the absence of the artist's charismatic personality (and funding sources), "art" as such is no longer sustainable.[5] For Hirschhorn, the practices and methods of creative transformation necessary to produce more sustainable or meaningful change in Forest Houses are dismissed as intrinsically uncreative "social work."

I would suggest that, far from violating the purity of the aesthetic, socially engaged art practices often represent a compelling re-articulation of it, involving as they do many of the key features we have come to associate with aesthetic experience, including the suspension or disruption of habitual forms of thought, the cultivation of an openness to our own intersubjective vulnerability, and a recognition of our own agency in generating normative values. In order to develop a more substantive theoretical analysis of socially engaged art, however, I do believe it's necessary to challenge the singular privilege we've been taught to assign to art and the personality of the artist, and to acknowledge that art exists along a continuum with a range of other cultural practices that hold the potential to produce disruptive or counter-normative insight. Artistic practice certainly carries its own specific methods, protocols and capacities, generated through its extremely complex history, but it also shares points of productive coincidence with other practices. I would also suggest that we need to reconsider the specific ways in which the relationship between the pure and the impure, theory and practice, and art and life, have been configured in existing art criticism. Too often each of these is treated as a synchronically fixed, *a priori* entity, when the space between them is always, potentially,

5 See Whitney Kimball, "How Do People Feel About the *Gramsci Monument* One Year Later?", *Artfcity*. http://artfcity.com/2014/08/20/how-do-people-feel-about-the-gramsci-monument-one-year-later/ (August 20, 2014).

semipermeable. Certainly "life," if fully comprehended, is not the realm of simpleminded habitual blindness that is so often evoked by the canon of critical theory, and art, in its actual effects, is not always its opposite. Autonomy, or the space of autonomy, is produced diachronically, through the tactical shifting of certain material frames and discursive and institutional systems. And in these spaces it's possible to engage in both "practical" action and the generative, distanced reflection that we have come to associate with theory. Action, as such, always contains both a practical moment (in its orientation to concrete change and in the pragmatic feedback loop that must always exist between this change and self-reflection) and a utopian or prefigurative one, expressing in embryo forms of the social that might be reactualized in another space or time.

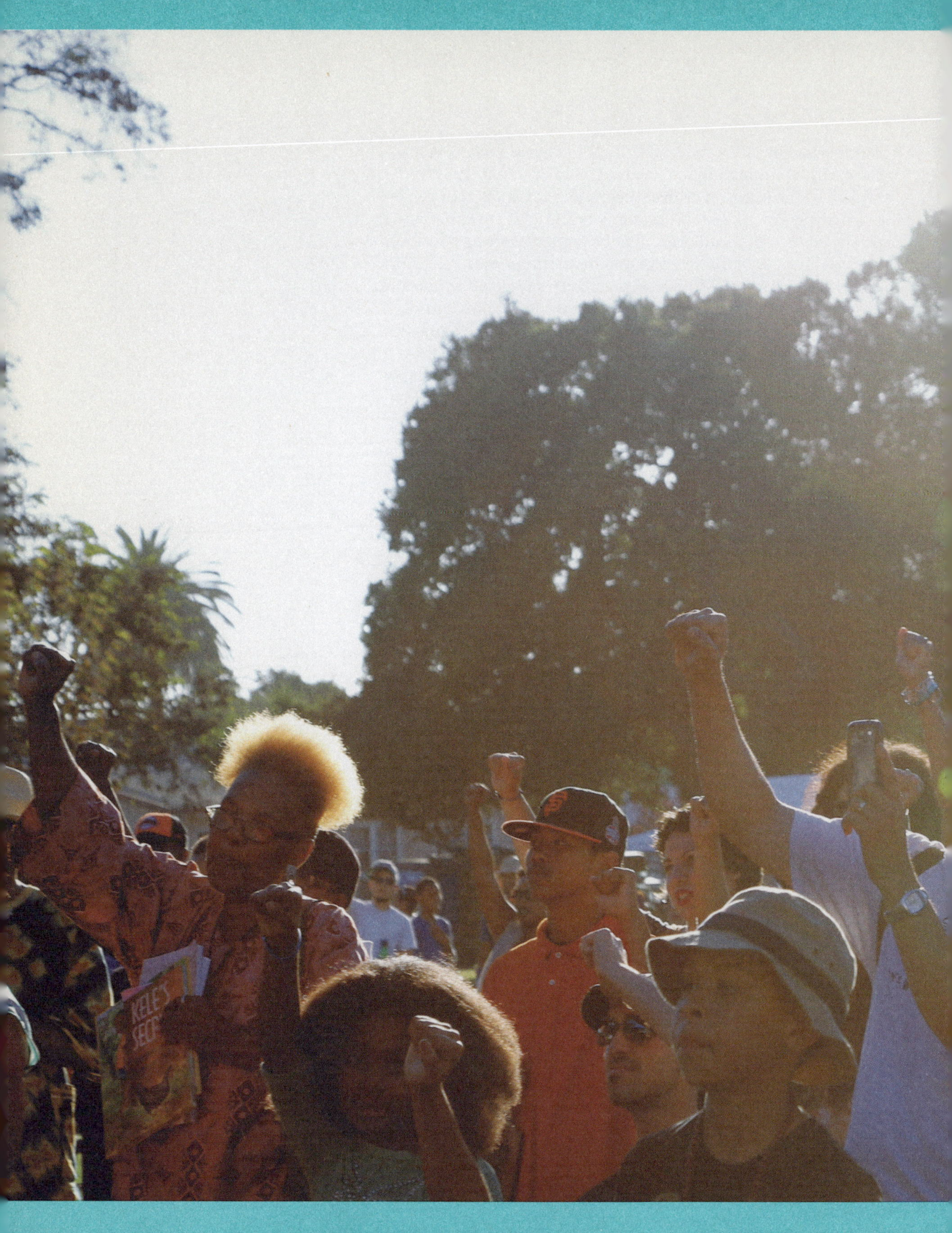
KELE'S

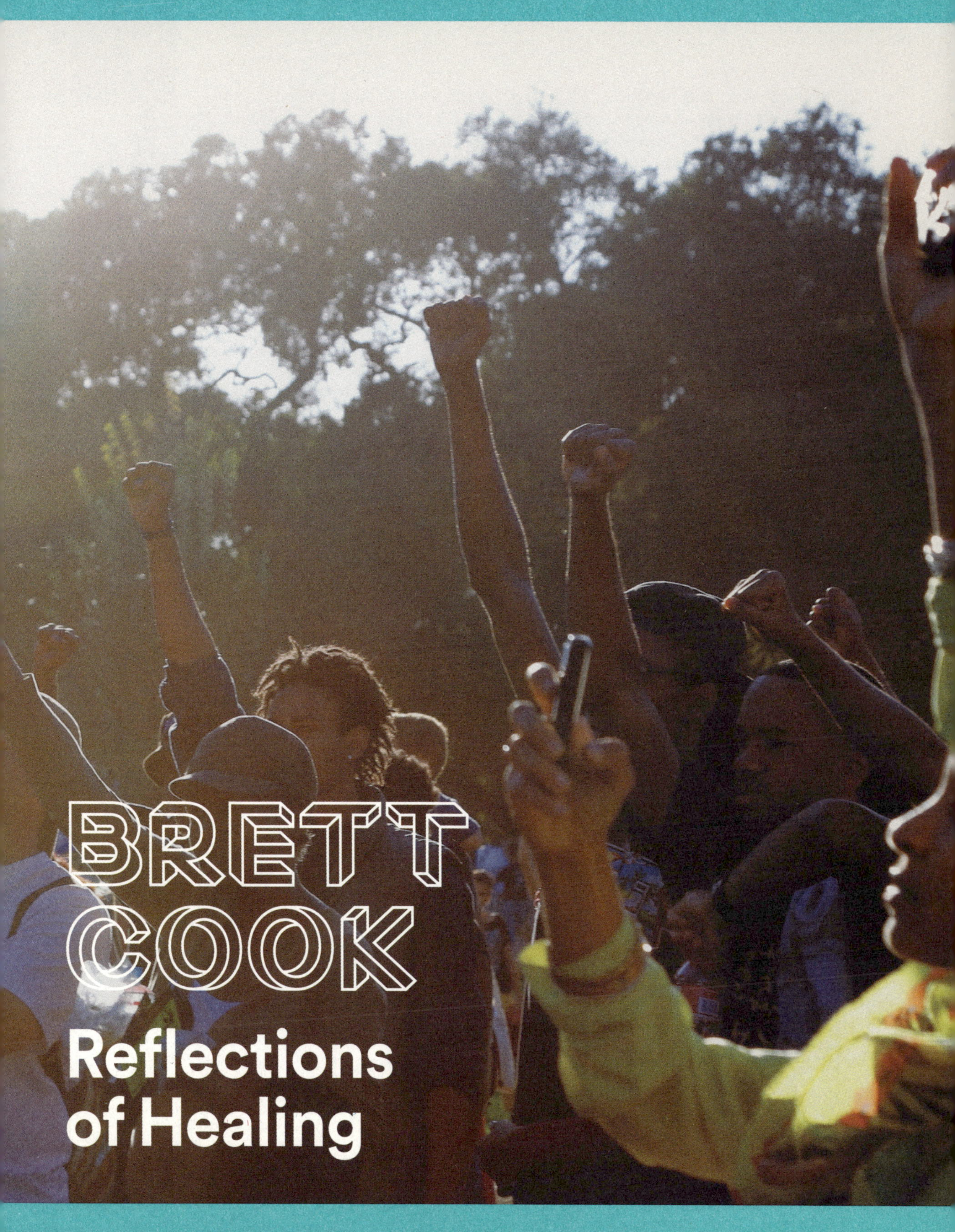
BRETT
COOK
Reflections
of Healing

Brett Cook works actively through *Reflections of Healing* to help heal people in his West Oakland community, while revealing the potential for healing in all of us. The iteration of the project that he did during the ABOG Fellowship year was a process of engaging with healers, and collaboratively making large portrait paintings in acrylic, paint pen, metallic paint and spray enamel on panel. The works were shown at a public festival, Life Is Living, which included a free wellness clinic. *Reflections of Healing* grew out of Cook's recognition that his neighborhood was filled with people who did healing work, often without realizing it or identifying it as such. Over the course of several years, he has been reaching out locally, soliciting suggestions, and seeking out those who serve as inspiration to youth and who nurture their neighbors. For this installment of the project, he engaged with a range of people, including a choreographer/dancer (Traci Bartlow), a public health nurse (Kathy Ahoy), an education advocate (Oscar Wright), a public health administrator (Tyler Norris) and an artist (Melanie Cervantes).

Once he identified individuals and named them healers, Cook engaged them in conversation to draw out the healing aspects of their practices. From each, he requested a photo taken in their youth, to use as a basis for a collaboratively made portrait. The portraits were taken from self-selected images of the healers in their youth because by depicting healers this way, Cook was indicating an open space of possibility: their future, which has come to pass. Using the photos as a basis, his method for making portraits was a participatory process that involved projecting a drawing he prepared in advance onto a canvas in a community-friendly space—in this case, DeFremery Park. He invited the subject and community to share in making the image by drawing in the projected outline. During each drawing workshop the healer had the opportunity to self-reflect while participants inquired, learned and listened as they created a shared vision. Together they imagined an intangible vision of healing as well as the literal vision of the portrait. Following this process is part of the act of envisioning

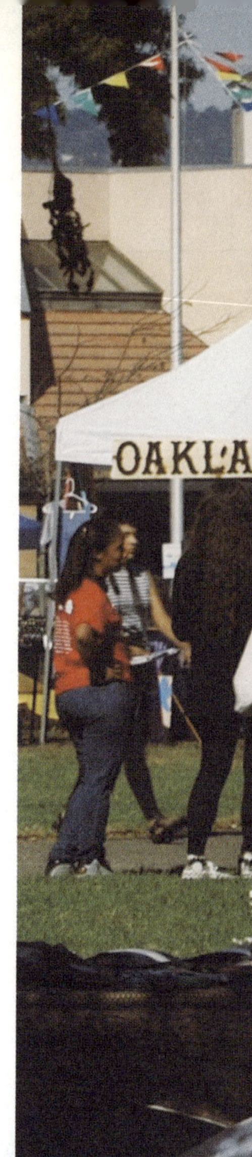

Previous spread: Morning gathering in DeFremery Park for the Life Is Living festival, 2015.

Opposite: *Traci Bartlow*, spray enamel, paint pen, and acrylic on panel, 2014–15. On display at the Life Is Living festival.

Meet the Healers from *Reflections of Healing*: Tyler Norris

Joelle Te Paske in conversation with Tyler Norris
December 19, 2014

In ABOG Fellow Brett Cook's *Reflections of Healing* project, nine prominent Oakland-based healers were selected with help from community organizations to be honored in large-scale participatory portraits by Brett and community collaborators.

As a model for the final paintings, each participant was asked to provide an image of him or herself as a young person to symbolize the collective potential of youth. The finished portraits, along with captions translated into languages local to Alameda County, chalkboards for community reflection, and free health and wellness services, debuted at the Life Is Living festival in DeFremery Park, Oakland, on October 11, 2014, and became part of a yearlong public

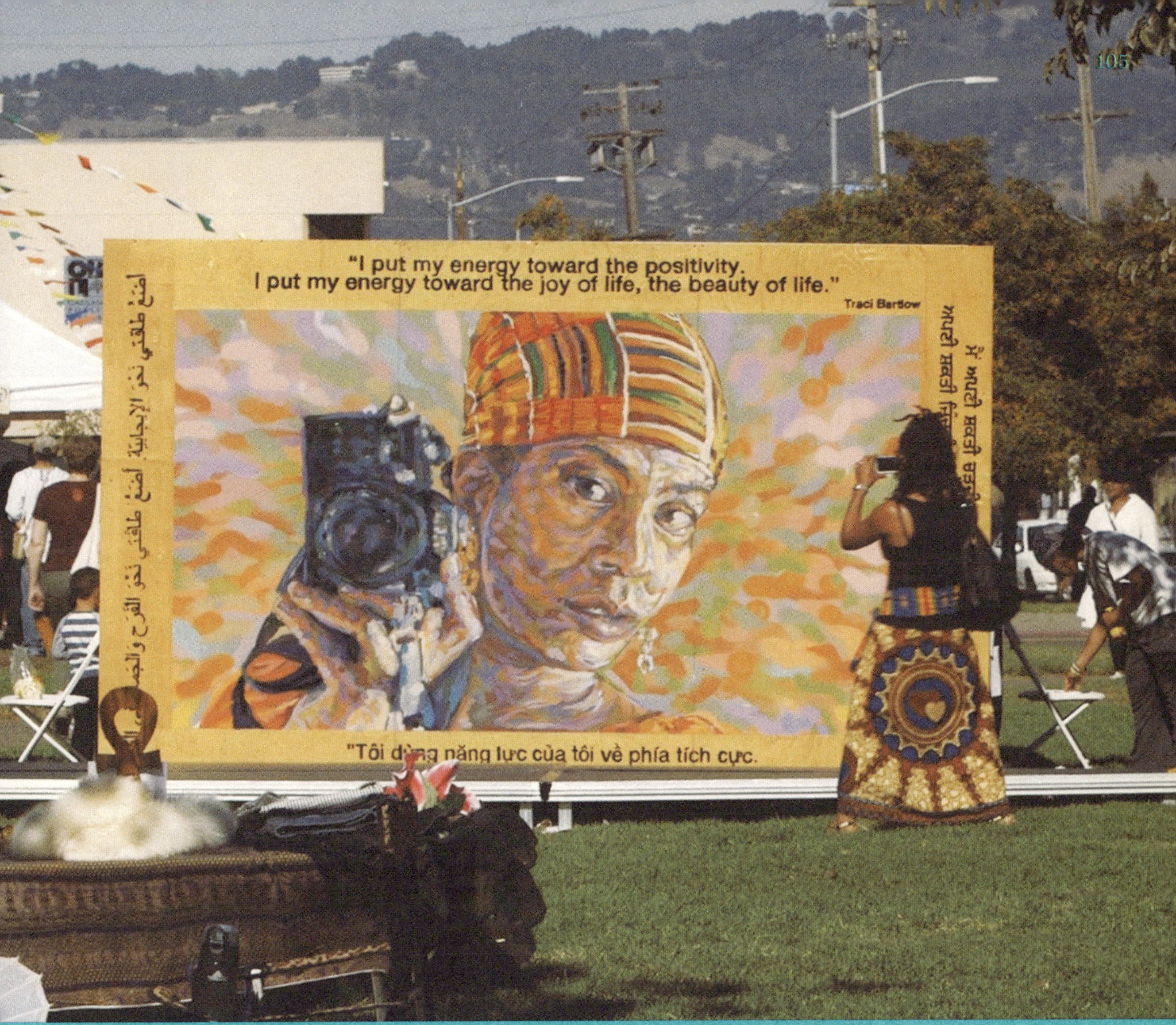

installation at the Oakland Museum of California.

In this report we feature Tyler Norris, Vice President of Total Health Partnerships at Kaiser Permanente and health care consultant. Joelle Te Paske spoke with Tyler in late 2014.

Joelle Te Paske (ABOG)
Thanks so much for taking the time to speak with me. I guess the best place to start is your context. Did you know Brett before participating in *Reflections of Healing*? Had you worked with him, or with other artists, leading up to the project?

Tyler Norris
I was first introduced to Brett by the Downtown Oakland YMCA. I had done a fair amount of work with the Y nationally over the last decade, and locally over the past year, and that's where we first were introduced.

Over the last couple decades I've had the opportunity to work on community visioning and mobilization projects in over 400 communities, that have engaged people from all walks of life, across every line you can imagine, to tell a shared story of a possible future. We've often used graphic artists, and even musicians and theatre to do so—to bring words to life through story, drama, and song.

I've found art to bring essential dimension to people's lives. Art allows people to feel spiritually, emotionally, and physically alive. It can give ideas, feelings, and experiences weight.

ABOG
Definitely, and that's very much in line with Brett's work, too. In the initial interview he did with you, what was your favorite question that he asked?

TN
There was a moment where I was talking about my current work with Kaiser Permanente, and I think I was answering in a typical way, about my role in the

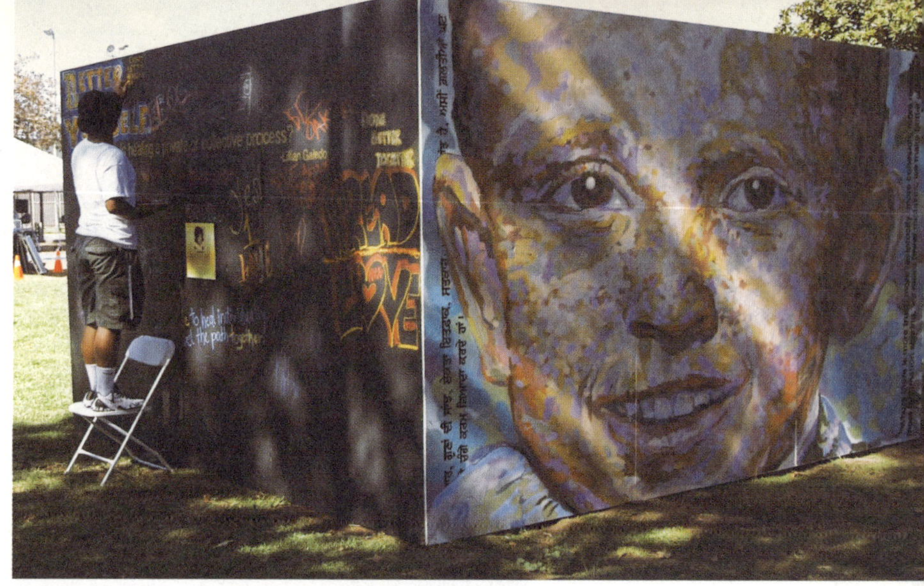

Right: *Tyler Norris*, spray enamel, paint pen, and acrylic on panel, 2014–15, and community wall on display at the Life Is Living festival, 2015.

Below: Group meditation, Life Is Living festival, 2015.

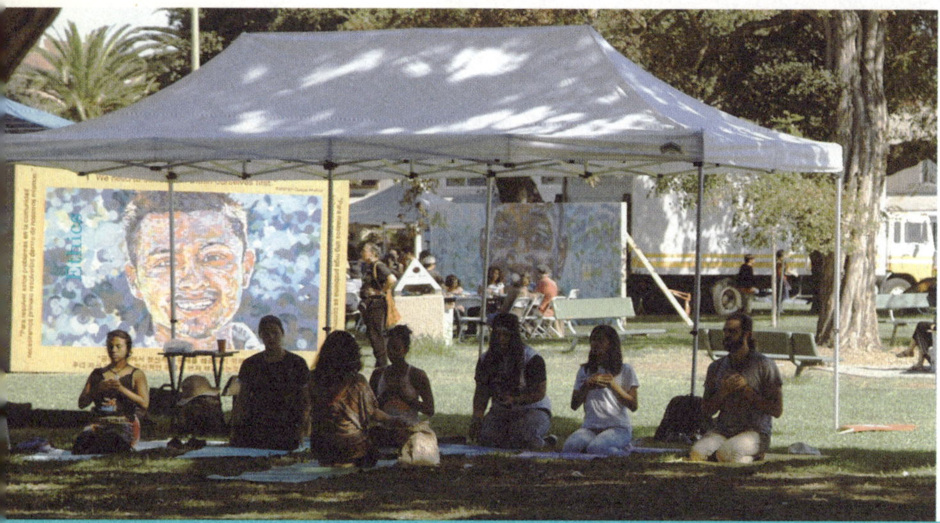

organization, and Brett cocked his head and asked, "But Tyler, why do you really do that work?" It was provocative, and an emotional moment for me. It got me thinking outside of my organizational mindset, to center in on what health and healing is really about.

ABOG

Those moments are so important—I have them too, definitely. Thinking about that, what was it like to see people respond to your portrait and quotations at Life Is Living? Did you have a chance to attend the festival?

TN

I was able to go to DeFremery Park late in the day as it was wrapping up. There was a woman from the neighborhood visiting the festival with a group of kids. Talking with her she said, "I love this park, I love this place, and I love these stories. I will tell these stories to my kids, and to my grandchildren." It was great to feel that the stories in the park were a bridge for her to tell something to the group of kids she was looking after. And this was all while I was incognito, as she did not know I was featured. I felt like a bit of a voyeur in that moment, seeing the goodness of the project from the outside. When I got back on my bike to ride home, it just felt great. I experienced the power of Brett's big idea. She now had something she could point her children to, to stories of the good people in West Oakland, which is not always an easy place.

It was also beautiful at the museum [Oakland Museum of California]. My picture is right on the corner off of Lake Merritt, and my coworkers often comment on it. I'm quite young in the photo, five years old—I might have misunderstood when I sent the picture! In the past, I have to admit to not always being present enough to look at every five-year-old as someone having an impact on the community. What a mistake! Shame on me! This mural makes that vital bridge with every a more just future together. Since we already know the positive future of those depicted, the youthful portraits showed a path of hope and transformation. Just as performing the creative act opens the possibility that an ideal can become real, a focus on a youthful image of an accomplished healer demonstrates the distance between their former and present selves, and the achievability of a personal and collective road that can lead to individual and social justice and wellness.

Once the portraits had been finished in Cook's studio, they were ready for public presentation as part of the Life Is Living festival. The festival is an annual gathering founded by Marc Bamuthi Joseph and co-created by Cook, Hodari Davis and the West Oakland community. It activates historic DeFremery Park, a place where the Black Panthers also offered a safe haven for celebration in the past. Local performers come together each year to celebrate the creativity and vision of inhabitants, and it serves as a significant draw for families and people of all ages. The organizers describe Life Is Living as:

> ... a free celebration of urban life through hip hop, intergenerational health, and environmental action. Life Is Living establishes a new model for partnerships between diverse and under-resourced communities, green action agencies, and the contemporary arts world.

For the festival, Cook mounted the healer portraits on kiosks painted with blackboard paint, and included quotations from the healers in several languages spoken within the West Oakland community. Visitors were invited to comment on the portraits and respond to the quotes, writing their thoughts in colored chalk on the kiosks. In this way, Cook added a new layer of dialogue and participation to his project, and offered an opportunity for collective visioning.

The kiosks were presented alongside a wellness clinic that Cook organized as part of Life Is Living to reinforce the healing message, and also provide free access to much-needed health and wellness services that are often hard to find in the area. Not only

five-year-old child, being at the heart of healing the community. If community is not of, by and for our kids, we are building a hollow shell. We must make that bridge, every day, every encounter, every girl and boy. These recent weeks out on the streets walking with community during the protests, calling for Black Lives Matter, the grieving, the righteous calls for justice for all ... remind me how essential it is to make sure we're paying close attention to every single five-year-old. Whoever's child they are, they are all our children. We need to embrace them now, and assure that their fullest potential is realized on their future life trajectory, holding up their current and future contributions. Brett's portrait reminds me of this, and should remind all of us. Let us be present to that.

ABOG
That's a really interesting way of thinking about it. As something nostalgic but something more, too, as kind of a springboard for thinking about the future. With that in mind, how do you find art and healing to be related?

TN
I've thought about this a lot with my own children. Health is wholeness. The word health comes from the word hale or hælth in Middle English, which means whole.

When we allow ourselves to express ourselves fully—with our spirits, minds, bodies, emotions—that's health and wholeness. When we have the courage to face a blank canvas, a lump of clay, or a stage when you don't know what you're going to say in the moment—that's health and wholeness. If we can bring that wholeness to our voice, to our expressions, that's health in the first place. The ability to express who we are as human beings, in our beauty, and in our humanity—the wholeness of ourselves—that's health.

Art is generous—it's an offering of creation—which is a form of well-being. I often think about well-being as being four things: purpose and meaning; belonging

and community; allowing the experience of gratitude and blessing; and then generosity, giving back through service. Well, that's all part of the arts! In that moment of creation, when we're connecting with others, art is health. Art is radical inclusion and true voice.

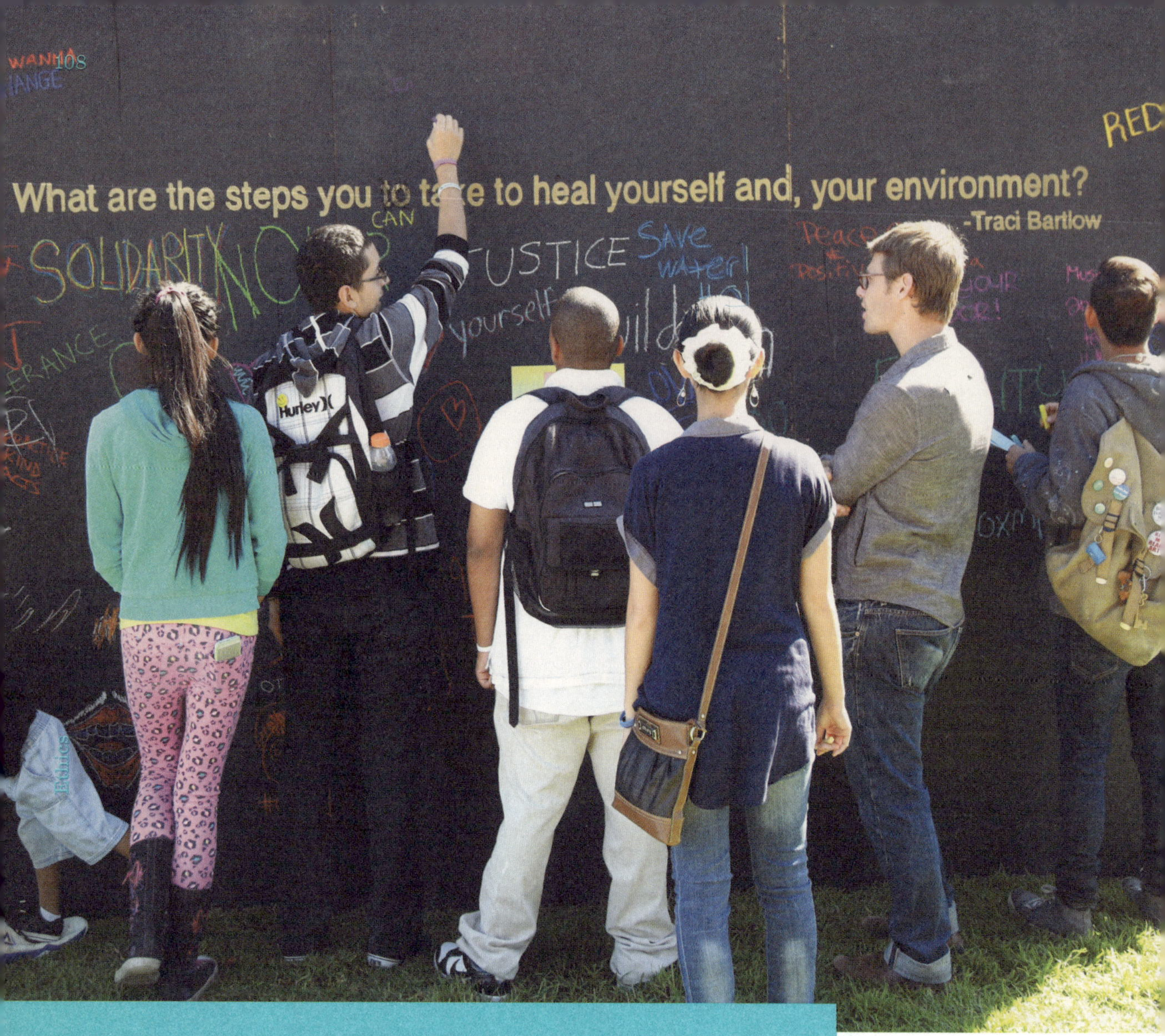

ABOG

That's a great way of thinking about it, as wholeness. If you did have to choose just one moment from your participation in the project that was the most meaningful to you, or you felt most deeply, which would you choose?

TN

I'd have to say my experience with the woman I met in DeFremery Park. She was a caregiver—a mom, or maybe an aunt—to this group of kids, and she was looking at the murals as something that went beyond that one day. This project gave her stories of a healthier future to talk about with her kids. The project is for our children, but also an invitation to our children. This is your community; shape it, speak it, paint it, love it, be it.

Brett Cook, *Reflections of Healing*, 2014, community response wall.

standard medicine, but alternative and holistic treatments were offered, including chiropractic, massage, yoga, acupuncture and spiritual cleansings called limpias. By acting together to talk about and participate in healing, over seven thousand community members collectively modeled the possibility of creating a more equitable health care system. Similarly, the clinic was an opportunity to educate people about the many treatment options that might exist for them. The project was a stunning success, with a resoundingly positive response.

The ideal that Cook hopes to see realized is the use of universal access to healing as a social justice tool. By creating a space not only for performing his ethical position but participating in the exercise of justice—in this case, through the service provided by the wellness clinic—Cook has ensured that the work becomes an aesthetic act of collective imagination. This collective act is not about coming up with the ultimate solution to a single intractable problem. It's about the broader possibilities that can be found across a whole range of problems by using art as a tool for imagining a better future. By imagining it, Cook opens up the possibility that the ideal could become real. By sharing authorship, he creates a space in which people can share and understand his vision, while building their own actions in daily life on the same ethical foundation as his work as an artist. By performing a collective and collaborative act of justice, he has brought reality one step closer to the ideal. Like a stone dropped in the water, this central act will radiate ripples for some time to come.

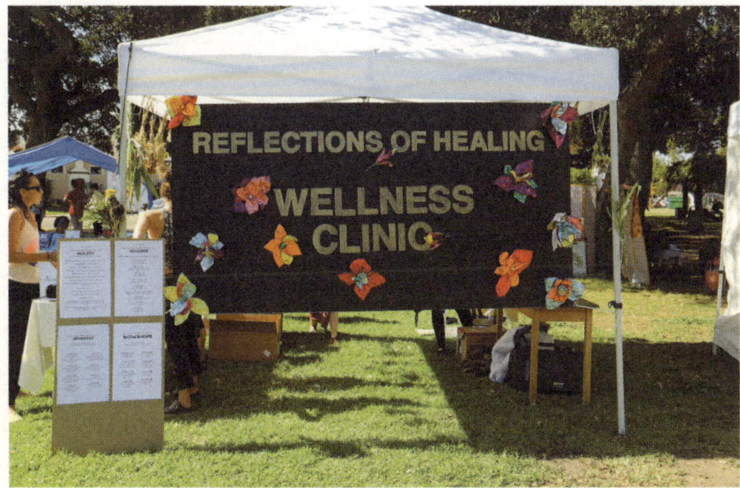

***Reflections of Healing* sign, Life Is Living festival, 2015.**

Following page: Community response wall, Life Is Living festival, 2015.

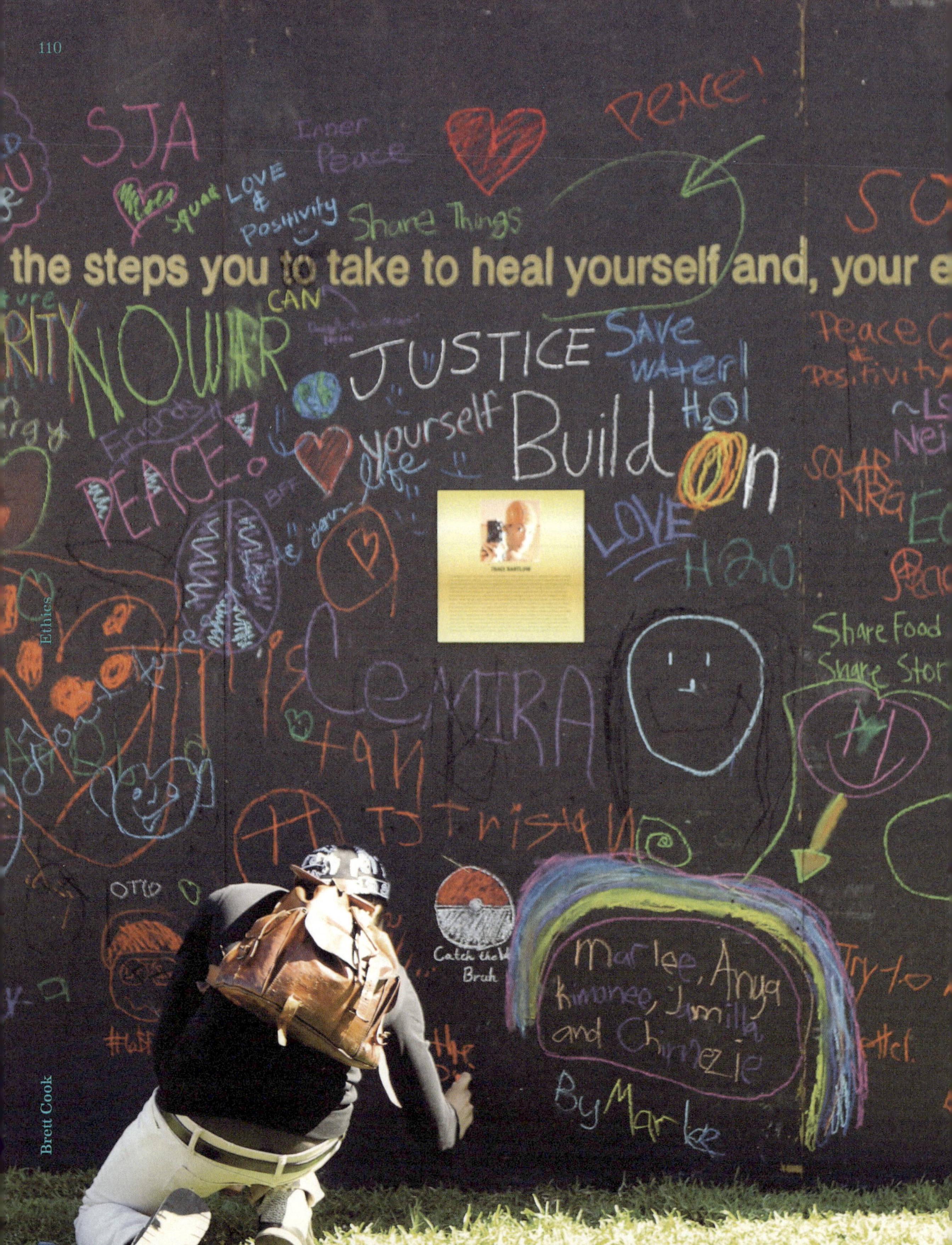

the steps you to take to heal yourself and, your e
PEACE!
SJA
Inner Peace
LOVE & Positivity
Share Things
JUSTICE
Save water!
Build On
LOVE
H2O
Peace & Positivity
SOLAR NRG
Share Food
Catch the
Bruh
Marlee, Anya Kimonee, Jamilla and Chimezie
By Marlee

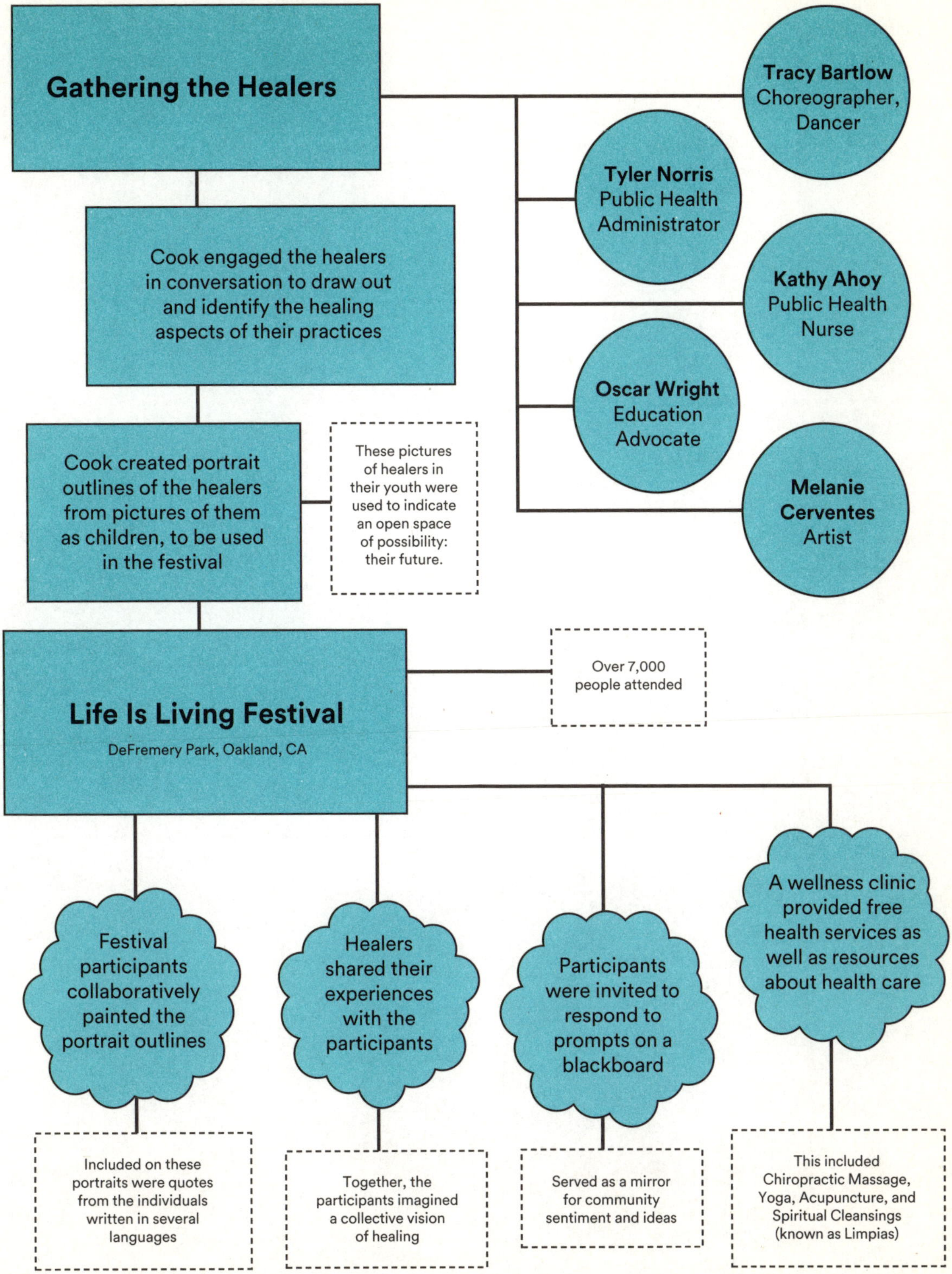

Gathering the Healers

Tracy Bartlow
Choreographer, Dancer

Tyler Norris
Public Health Administrator

Kathy Ahoy
Public Health Nurse

Oscar Wright
Education Advocate

Melanie Cerventes
Artist

Cook engaged the healers in conversation to draw out and identify the healing aspects of their practices

Cook created portrait outlines of the healers from pictures of them as children, to be used in the festival

These pictures of healers in their youth were used to indicate an open space of possibility: their future.

Life Is Living Festival

DeFremery Park, Oakland, CA

Over 7,000 people attended

Festival participants collaboratively painted the portrait outlines

Included on these portraits were quotes from the individuals written in several languages

Healers shared their experiences with the participants

Together, the participants imagined a collective vision of healing

Participants were invited to respond to prompts on a blackboard

Served as a mirror for community sentiment and ideas

A wellness clinic provided free health services as well as resources about health care

This included Chiropractic Massage, Yoga, Acupuncture, and Spiritual Cleansings (known as Limpias)

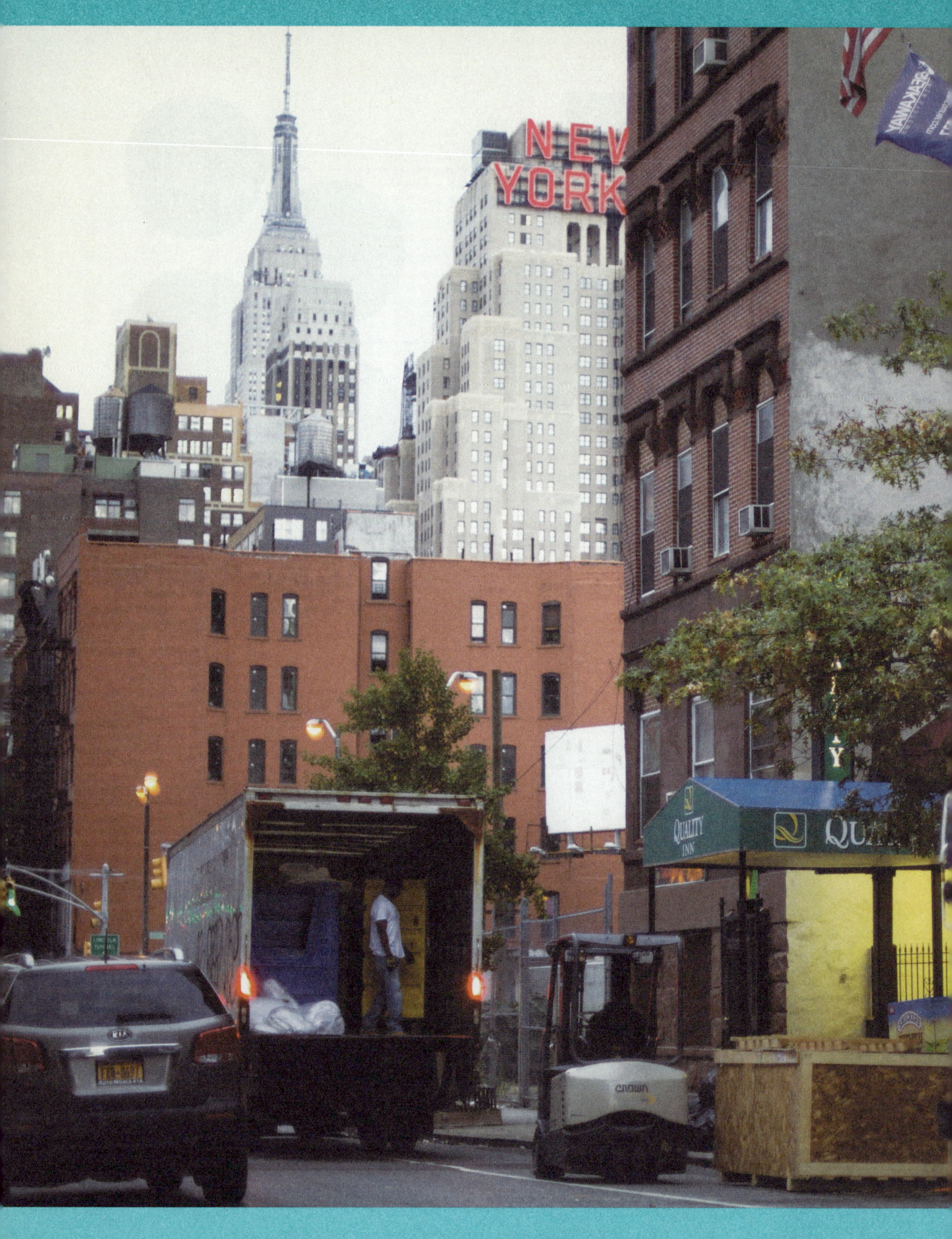
NEV
YORK
QUALITY
INN
QUA
crown

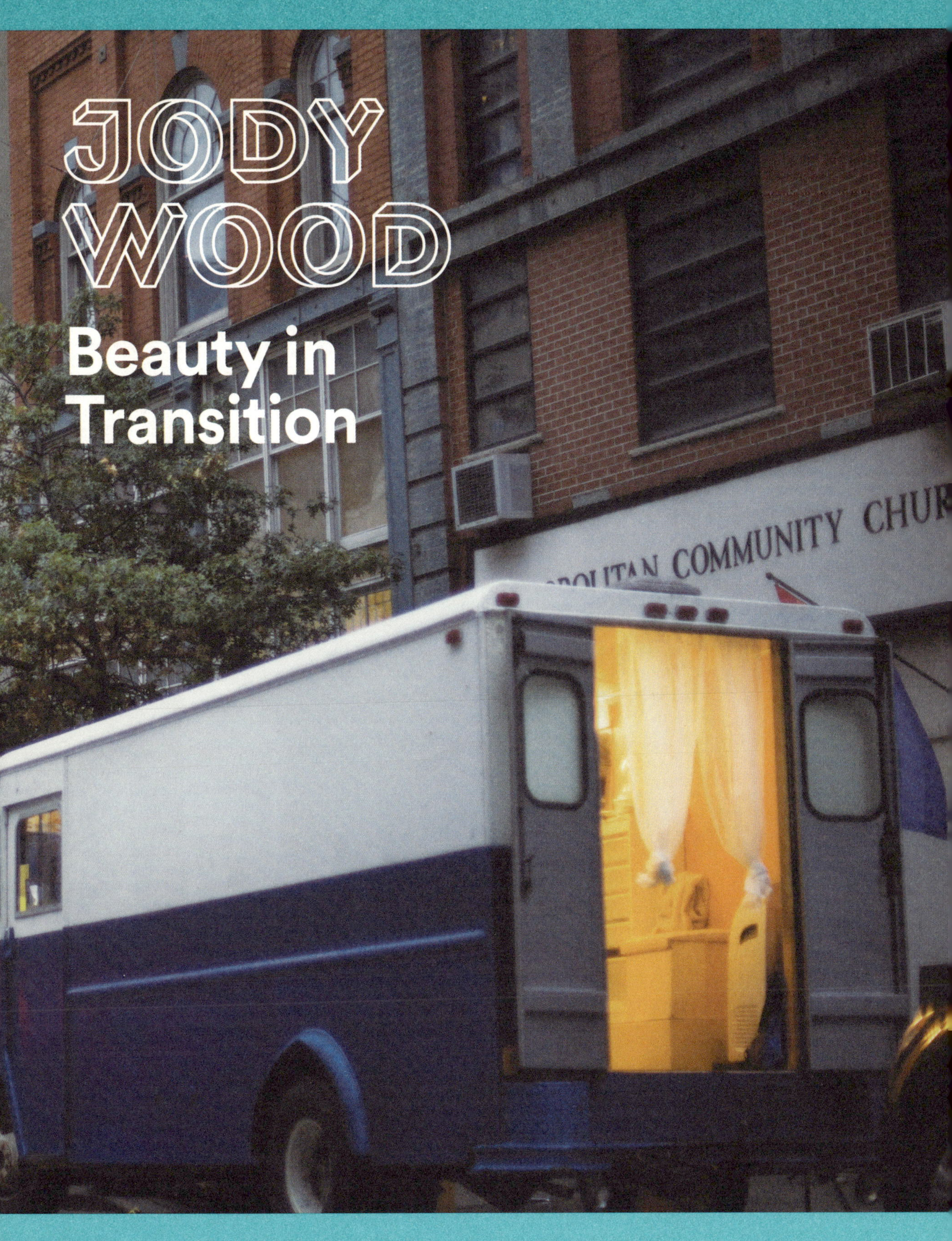

JODY WOOD

Beauty in Transition

When was the last time you passed a homeless person on the street and did something as simple as smile and greet her? One of the toughest parts about being homeless is the label itself. It treats people as a category—a generally temporary state of being (homelessness) becomes a noun (the homeless) that is used in place of a person's name. In her project *Beauty in Transition*, Jody Wood offers a chance for people experiencing homelessness to reclaim their identities and, rather than having their images dictated by circumstances, present themselves as they would have others see them.

Beauty in Transition is a mobile salon housed in a box truck that sets up shop outside homeless shelters and offers free salon services to residents. Unlike many social agencies, which seek to provide the most inexpensive services possible to the greatest number of people, Wood offers the highest level of care to just a few. The unsuspecting passerby is surprised as she comes around the side of what looks like an ordinary delivery truck to find a salon inside, painted a warm and inviting pink, with potted plants, large mirrors, and comfortable salon chairs. The working sinks and hair dryers complete the bewildering but picture-perfect image. Shelter clients are invited to sign up for whatever services they like, including a wash, cut, color, style, and sometimes makeup. Far from the basic services one might expect in an institutional environment like a shelter, Wood's mobile salon is full-service, allowing each client an individualized experience that may last up to two hours.

Wood works closely with shelter staff to determine a schedule that suits the institution's needs, as well as those of its residents. During the fellowship year she worked with a total of nine shelters, in all of New York's boroughs, building on a project that she began in Denver and will continue in Philadelphia. While she needs to partner with shelters in order to reach the people she wants to serve, her project turns the usual shelter experience on its head. Like many social-service-oriented nonprofits, shelters often operate with a mentality of

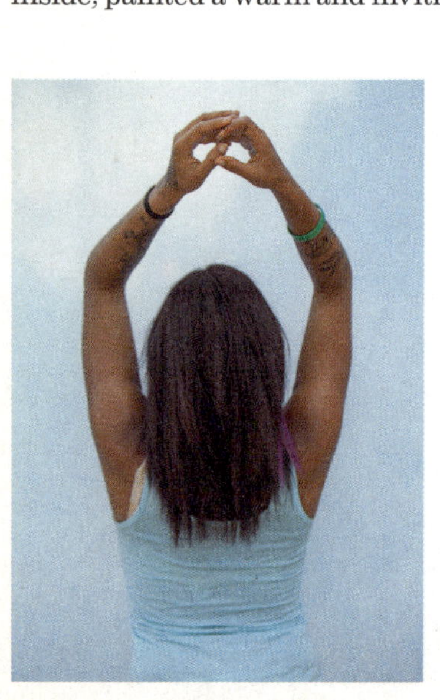

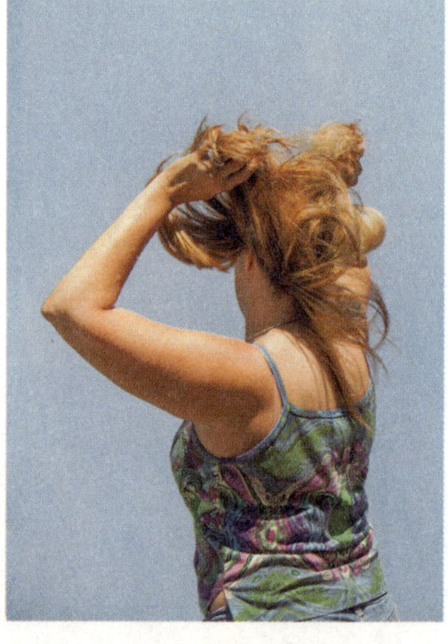

Previous spread: View of salon truck, *Beauty in Transition*, New York City, 2015.

Left: Portraits from *Beauty in Transition*, Philadelphia, 2015.

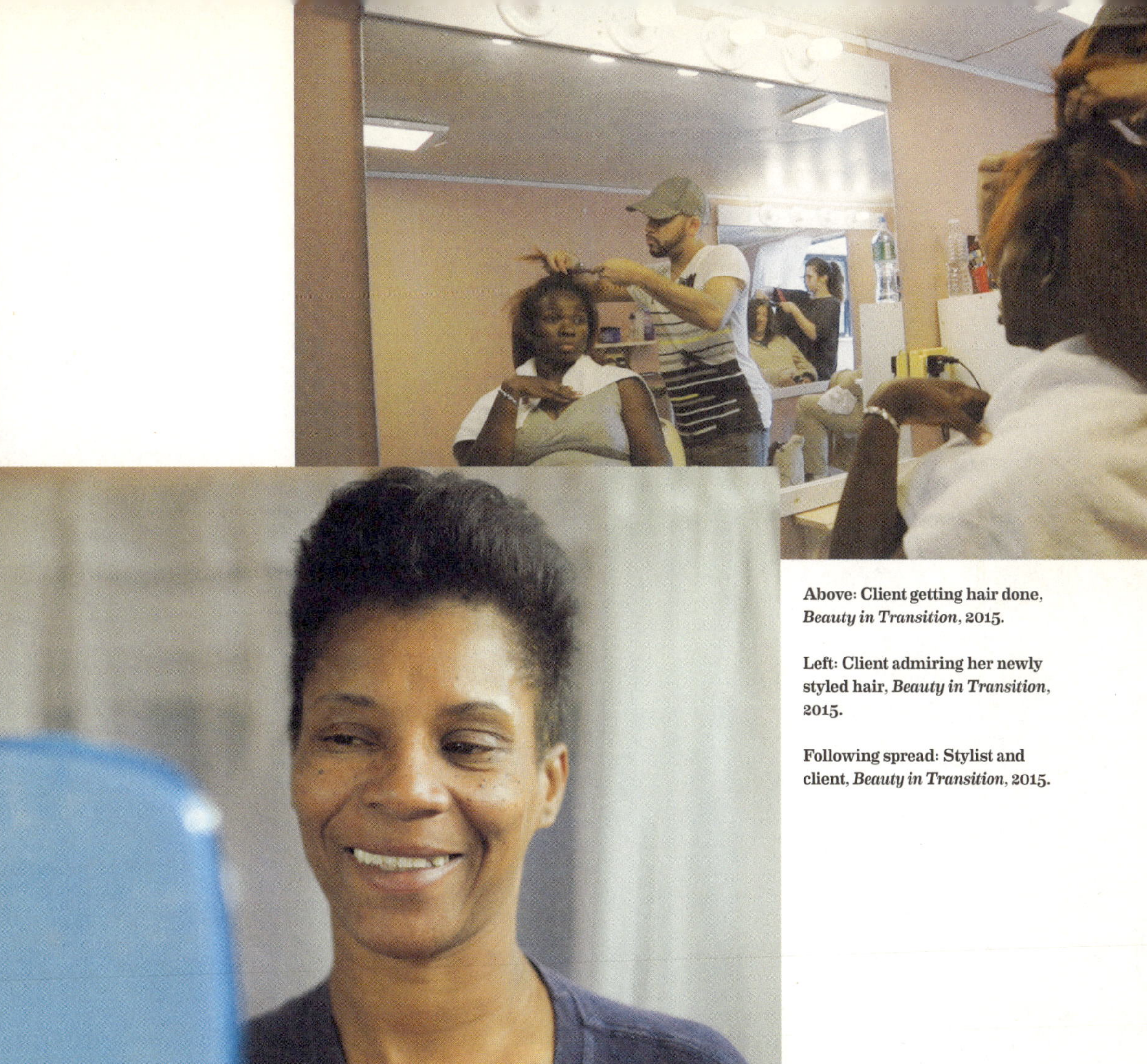

Above: Client getting hair done, *Beauty in Transition*, 2015.

Left: Client admiring her newly styled hair, *Beauty in Transition*, 2015.

Following spread: Stylist and client, *Beauty in Transition*, 2015.

Beauty in Transition with Nahomie Marcena

Elizabeth M. Grady in conversation with Nahomie Marcena
October 17, 2014

ABOG Fellow Jody Wood and a team of volunteer hair stylists traveled to homeless shelters throughout New York City in fall 2014, providing free beauty services to willing participants in a truck custom outfitted into a fully functional mobile beauty salon. Elizabeth Grady corresponded by email with Nahomie Marcena, one of the stylists working with Jody, about what it was like to take part in the project, and we've reprinted the conversation here.

Elizabeth M. Grady (ABOG)
What prompted you to get involved with Jody's project, *Beauty in Transition*?

Nahomie Marcena
What prompted me to get involved was to help women like me to enjoy the beauty within themselves. This is not only a project but an experience of a lifetime, to give love the way it was given to me. Jody's love for people prompted her to show beauty in every aspect of life, and show that despite your situation or circumstances you can always look and feel beautiful.

ABOG
What was it about the project that made you say "yes," in spite of the extra work it would mean for you?

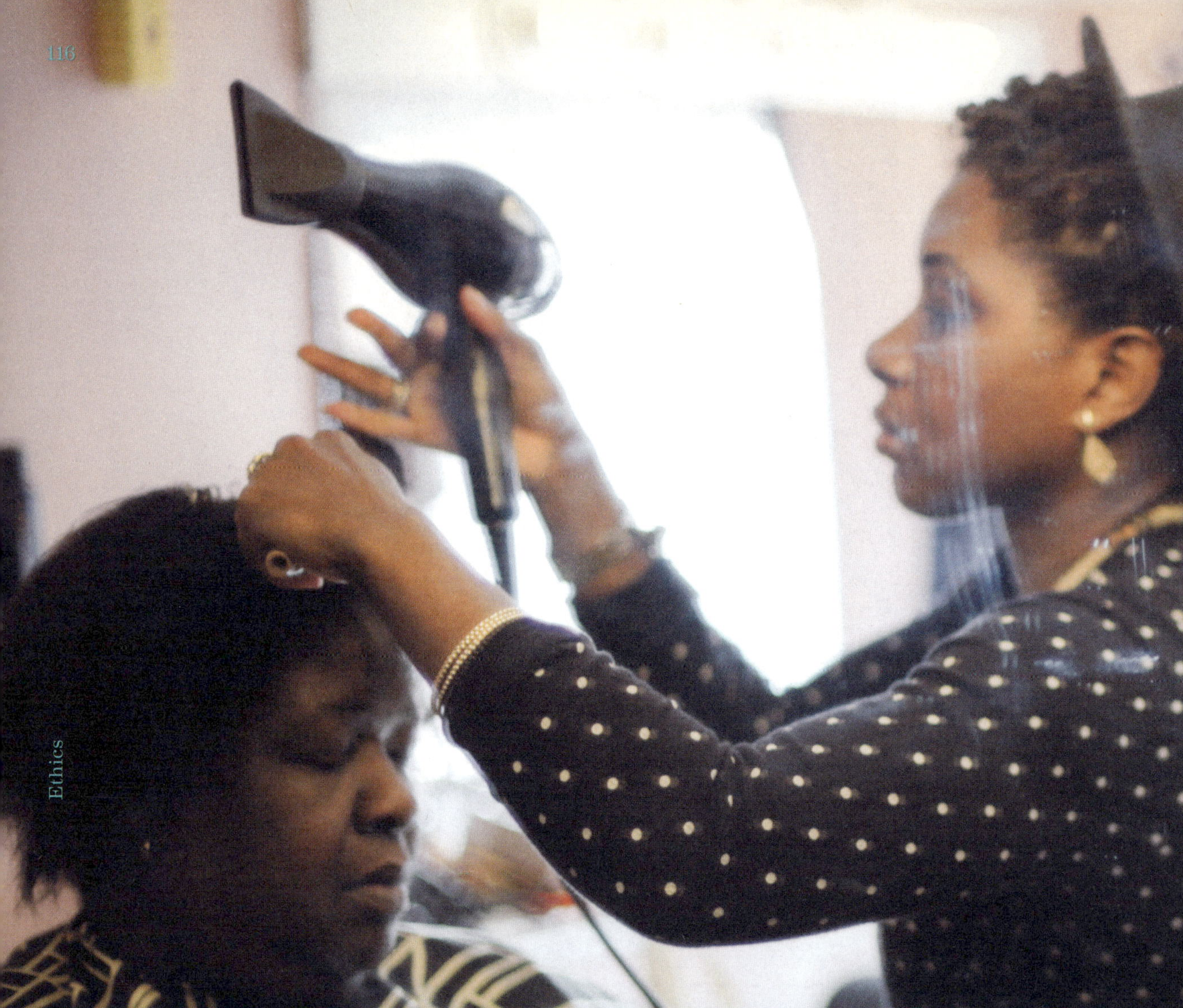

NM
I said yes to the project because of what it represented for the community, and the message that it's trying to convey across this beauty in transition; women being seen for who they are, despite what race, ethnicity or look we portray to the world. I think that's the message Jody was trying to get across when she established this particular project. Art is in you, it's just waiting for an opportunity to mold and present itself to you, to show you what you're made of.

ABOG
Do you feel that there was "beauty" in the project as art? If so, what was beautiful to you about it?

NM
I feel there was not only beauty in this art project, but passion. Before any art is made, written, molded or designed there must be an inspiration and love in something you believe in or do to make it become a reality. To make it become yours, you first have to have an inspiration for the art you believe in. Doing this in life you must have the faith that people, or someone, will see it and be touched and become encouraged or inspired in life by the message you are trying to convey.

ABOG
If you had to pick one moment that was the most meaningful for you, what would it be?

NM
The most meaningful part of this project for me was letting go of my past; having the courage to help someone along the way where I was 14 years ago. Even though my past hasn't stuck to me or labeled me, I identify with the young ladies there at the shelter. I too was in a shelter, and was looked down at and ridiculed. My faith kept me strong that it wouldn't always be like that. My dedication, and inspiration from strangers kept me going.

An experience is not a good one if you can't tell a story behind it to change someone's life, to encourage, to touch their heart and show love. You must first show them through a touch, a style, or words

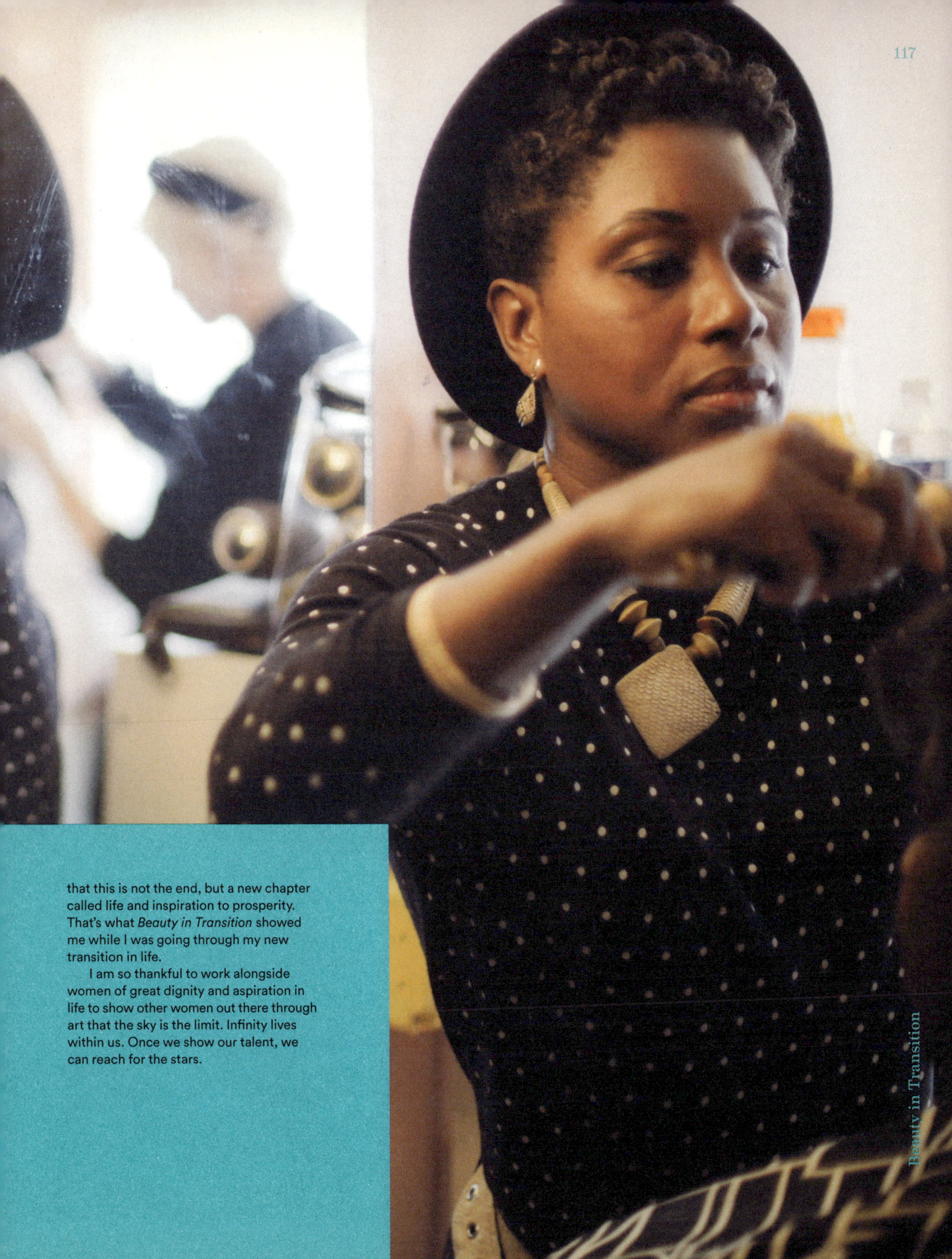

that this is not the end, but a new chapter called life and inspiration to prosperity. That's what *Beauty in Transition* showed me while I was going through my new transition in life.

I am so thankful to work alongside women of great dignity and aspiration in life to show other women out there through art that the sky is the limit. Infinity lives within us. Once we show our talent, we can reach for the stars.

scarcity in which resources, which appear meager in the face of the massive and growing problem of homelessness, are spread as far as possible. This often results in a minimal baseline of standardized service, offering just enough to keep people alive but not quite enough to really help them transform their lives. Wood offers something beyond mere necessity, which suggests an abundance to which most shelter residents have become unaccustomed.

Positioning *Beauty in Transition* as an artwork rather than simply a service has significant implications. Wood is not bound to meet benchmarks in terms of the number of people she is able to help, or to provide a general, baseline service that is offered to everyone on an equal basis. She does not work for a government agency where such standards would be required, nor is she subject to a performance review based on how she uses scarce resources. In her case, the removal of such limitations has offered the opportunity to approach those she engages with as people with unique talents and identities, and tailor her response to the way they perceive their own circumstances and needs. Not only do the beauty treatments offered have the effect of transforming her clients' outer selves so that they match their inner lives, but her careful attention and ability to calibrate her response to the needs of individuals validates them and reinforces their belief in their own humanity, potentially reinforcing the kind of inner strength that they may be able to draw on to pull themselves back out of the condition of homelessness. Because art is a space of creative imagination, her services work as a tool for clients to imagine an alternate situation to the one they are experiencing, to envision a new or unexpected path into the future.

A common indicator of a society's basic ethics is the way it treats its weakest members. To protect the vulnerable and ensure their just treatment is the marker of an evolved culture. Justice is something only afforded to people by people. If people are reduced to a category, they lose their humanity, and with it their claim on just treatment within human society. The interesting

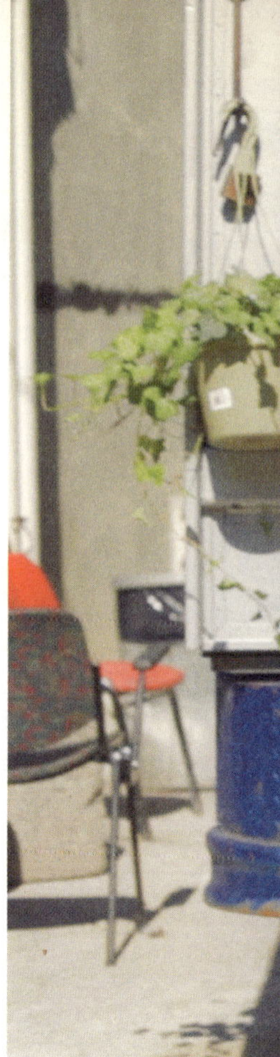

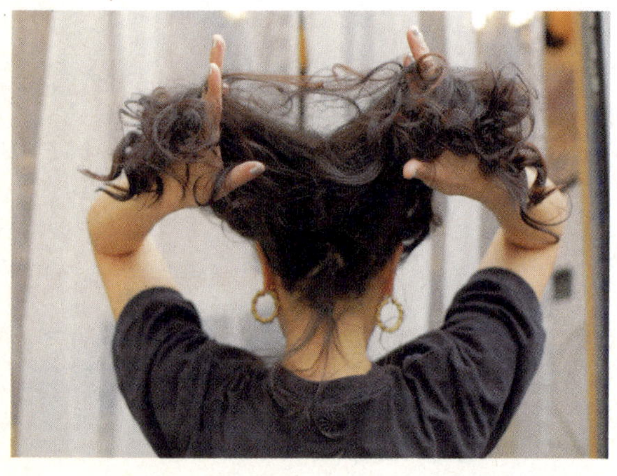

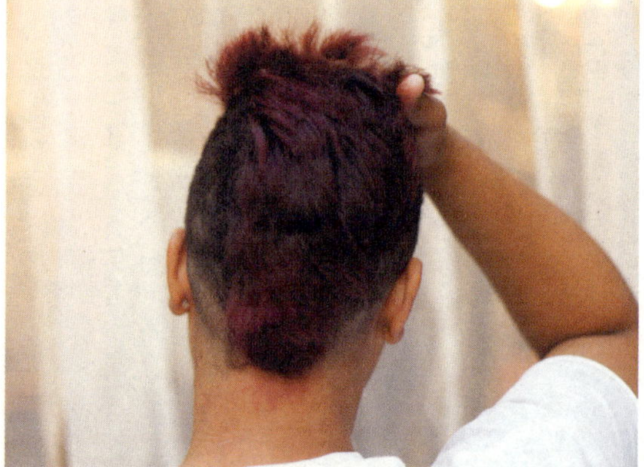

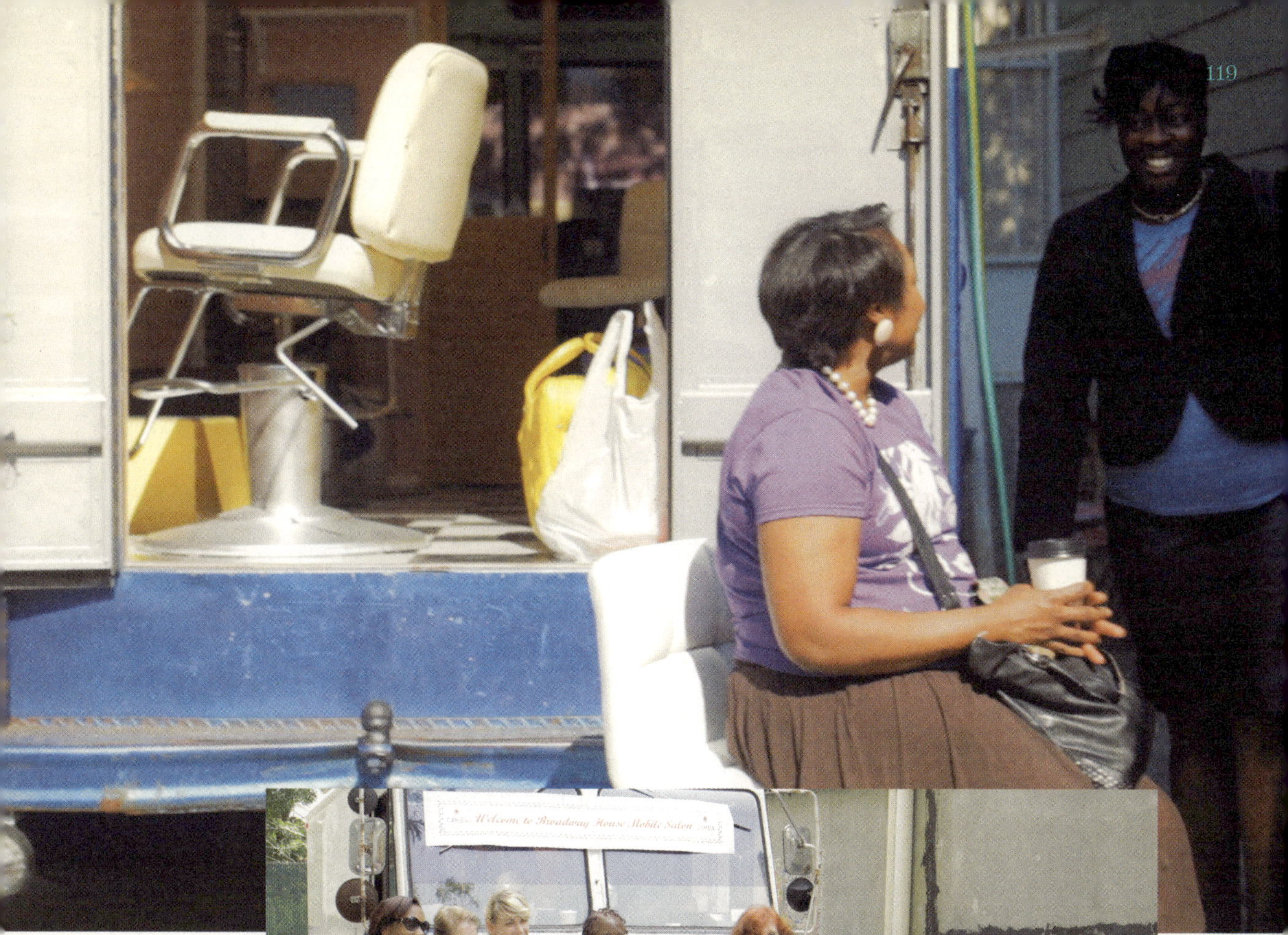

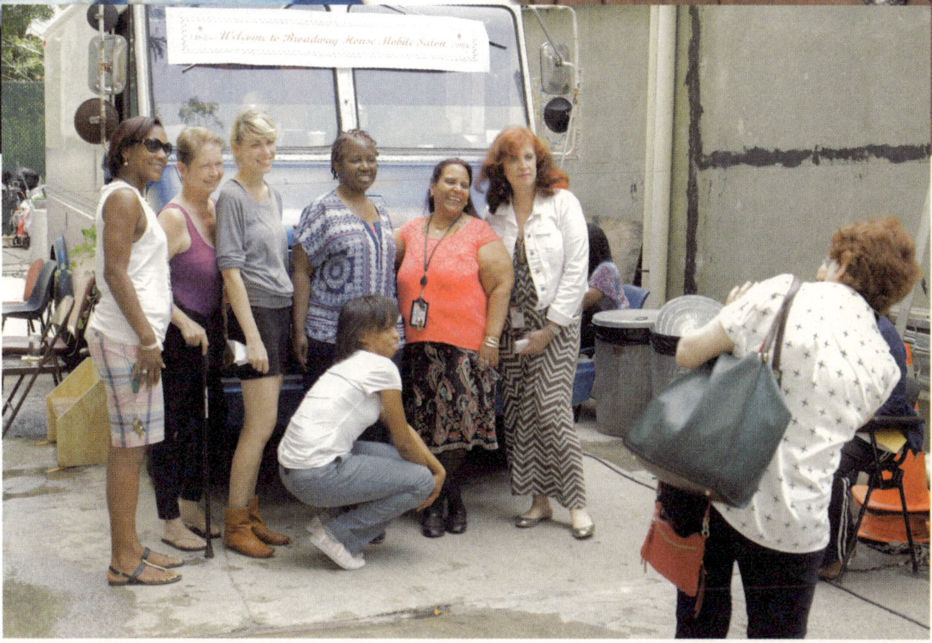

Left: Newly styled hair, ***Beauty in Transition***, 2015.

Top: Carol Thomas and Nahomie Marcena, volunteer stylists, ***Beauty in Transition***, 2015.

Bottom: Participants, Broadway House location, ***Beauty in Transition***, 2015. Jody Wood third from left.

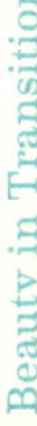

thing about society's view of humanity is that appearances matter a great deal. As Wood observes:

> Having the means to choose and control one's self-presentation is something most of us take for granted. Hair in particular has a deep connection to cultural identity expression. Without the ability to control how we appear to society, we lose our ability to control our cultural signifiers and risk being ostracized and isolated from larger and more sustaining social participation.

Further, those who have lost this ability become, in essence, untouchable. Avoided because of social stigma, or perhaps simply because we fear that some of their misfortune may rub off on us, we avoid even a brush with them. This social isolation is a little like a brand of psychological solitary confinement. Refusal to touch—or even see—them; walking by without any acknowledgement implies that they don't count as people, as citizens of our society who are subject to the same laws and protections as the rest of us. The prison-like controls that are in place in shelters reinforce this strange sense that they exist outside society's purview. By helping people reclaim their identities through controlling their appearances, Wood lays the foundation for a more just treatment of those experiencing homelessness. Choosing haircuts, which involve touching, works actively against stigmatization. And her services give her clients a fighting chance to claim the treatment and protections that most of us take for granted.

The aesthetic quality of Wood's project is not necessarily, as it might at first seem, in the "installation" of the salon in a box truck. Nor is it found in the results of the treatments her clients receive, as lovely as those results might be. Rather, it is found in the inner transformation of individuals who have restored to them a whisper of their former selves, and a bit more fortitude to fight for their basic human right to exist in the world.

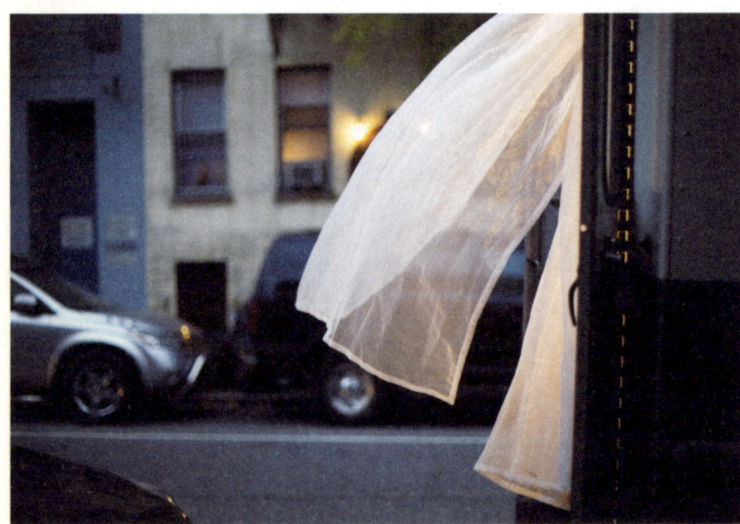

Curtained entrance, *Beauty in Transition*, 2015.

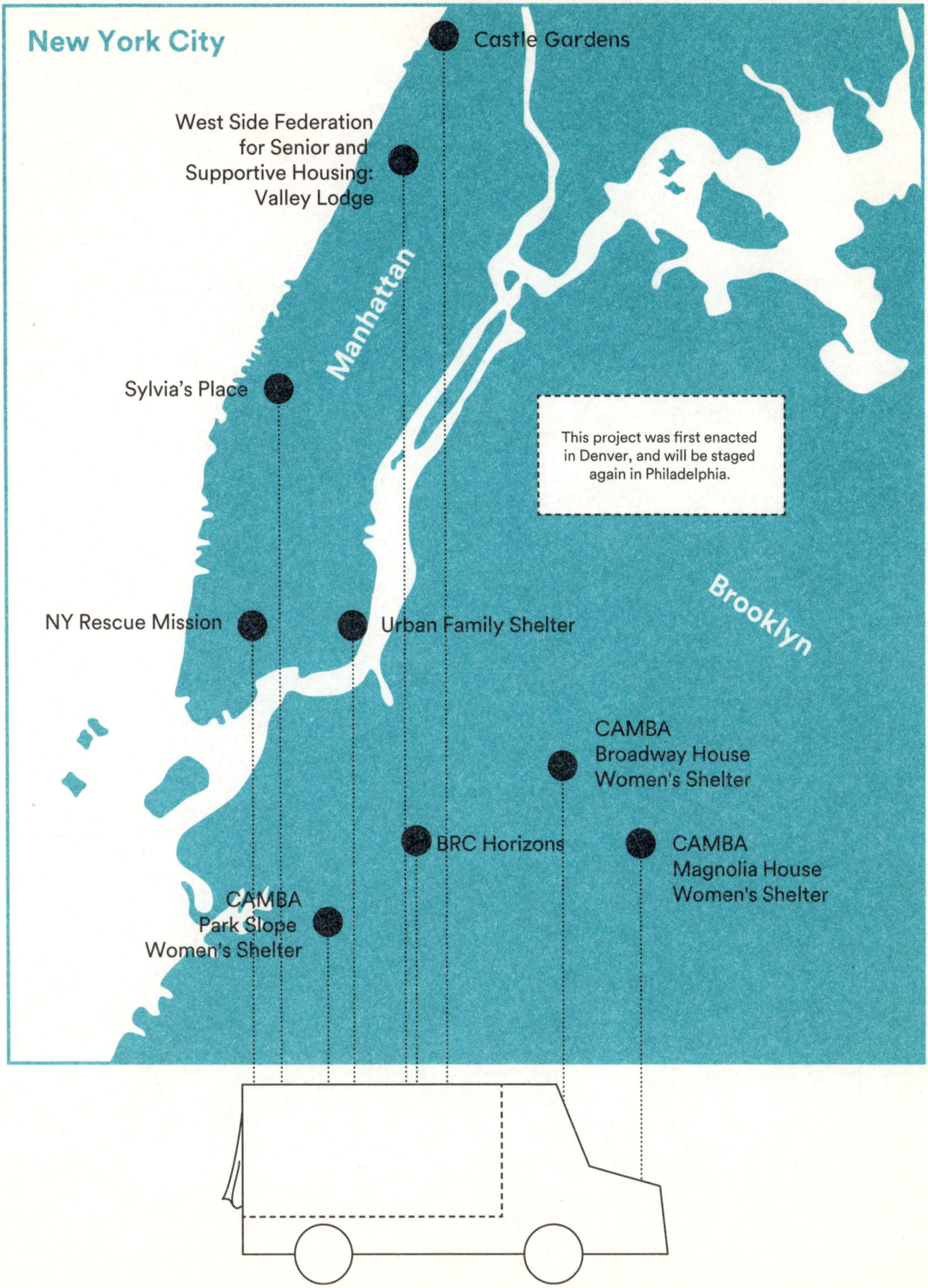

New York City

Castle Gardens

West Side Federation for Senior and Supportive Housing: Valley Lodge

Manhattan

Sylvia's Place

This project was first enacted in Denver, and will be staged again in Philadelphia.

NY Rescue Mission

Urban Family Shelter

Brooklyn

CAMBA Broadway House Women's Shelter

BRC Horizons

CAMBA Magnolia House Women's Shelter

CAMBA Park Slope Women's Shelter

PART THREE

EFFECTIVENESS

What is the Effectiveness of Socially Engaged Art?

Ben Davis' article, "A Critique of Social Practice Art: What does it mean to be a political artist?," which appeared in issue #90 of the *International Socialist Review*, sparked a lively conversation on socially engaged art that revolved productively around this question. This portion of the discussion includes contributions by Rick Lowe, Deborah Fisher, Tom Finkelpearl, Nato Thompson, Ben Davis, Elizabeth M. Grady and Ernesto Pujol.

Rick Lowe

In his article for the *International Socialist Review*, Ben Davis underestimates the role of the symbolic and poetic power of art. But its role has challenged many, as artists have tried to find new meaning for their work in the context of economic, political, and social crisis. For example, artists are seeking to move away from being the problem of gentrification to exploring ways to contribute to solving the problems of gentrification. Yet, I have learned to be careful about using the word "solving" and always try to temper it with words like "exploring" and "contributing" to lessen expectations that artists have the power or responsibility to "solve" problems.

Project Row Houses and our housing program have never been about "solving" the housing problem for Houston. We thought that by contextualizing housing as an artistic exploration, we could symbolically show the value of developing housing that embraced the existing people and history of the community. I agree with Ben Davis that *Project Row Houses* has not solved Houston's housing problem. But the symbolic quality of the project has generated dialogue about the value of existing community context when developing [property –Ed.].

"Placemaking" is a word being used to identify artists and arts organizations working in social/community contexts. A main indicator of the "placemaking" value of the work is "outcome," or the solution to some problem. This is troubling for me as an artist who works within the context of community development. *Project Row Houses* sought to contextualize the social in an aesthetic way. From an artistic standpoint, the economics of real estate is the least interesting part. However, now in the era of "placemaking," economics has made its way to the top of the list of concerns. I find this problematic for the continued growth of the field of creative social/community engaged work.

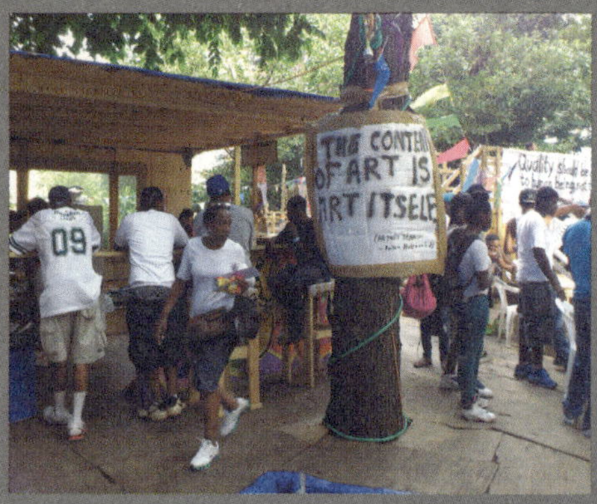

Thomas Hirschhorn, *Gramsci Monument*, 2013. Gramsci Bar, Forest Houses, Bronx, NY.

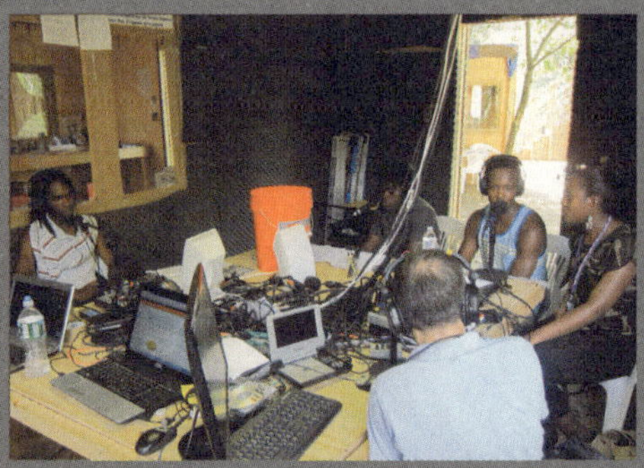

Thomas Hirschhorn, *Gramsci Monument*, 2013. Gramsci Radio, Forest Houses, Bronx, NY.

Deborah Fisher
The notion of measurable outcomes can be considered through art, can't it? I think that contextualizing the social aesthetically relies in some ways on sociology. Social art should be a branch of aesthetics that leans heavily on the existing knowledge and methods of sociology, which include assessment. To assess something is simply to evaluate its nature or qualities in a meaningful way. Is there no such thing as an aesthetic assessment?

Tom Finkelpearl
Yes, aesthetics is all about assessment—finding meaningful ways to talk about art. How can aesthetics be bent toward the social without simply becoming sociology or political science?

Nato Thompson
For me the better way to articulate the value of SEA is to place the questions of what artists do in a different light. How do places of intersubjective play and radical pedagogy produce different forms of collective behavior? How is the media used as a form that resists dominant conditions of power? What kinds of infrastructure can make social forms of play and politics? How can we produce spaces where autonomous action is actually possible? How can we produce spaces and situations that upend ideas of race and class in a way that is fun, strange and liberating?

Deborah Fisher
Your questions are helpful because they account for art's ability to expand the boundaries of what is real and possible. This is hard for us to talk about—it's easier to either essentialize this art and say it's inherently good, or instrumentalize it and make claims about its effectiveness that don't hold up to scrutiny.

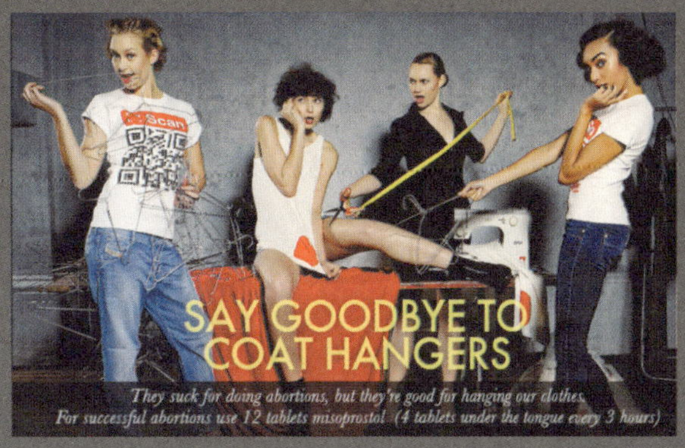

Women on Waves. *Say Goodbye to Coat Hangers*. dieselforwomen campaign. January 2012.

Ben Davis
My original article was written for a very specific audience: activists. I lay out my agenda, right at the beginning, to explain, "how activists should interact with a strand of art that often looks so much like activism." What are people advocating for abortion rights to think of Rebecca Gompertz's Women on Waves? How do housing advocates approach Thomas Hirschhorn's *Gramsci Monument*? What do my friends who have been organizing around immigrant rights in Jackson Heights for years think of Tania Bruguera's *Immigrant Movement International*? My own experience is that many are enthusiastic, or at least amused. But a substantial number of activists roll their eyes at the attention accorded to such things. In his introduction to *Living As Form*, Thompson himself quotes Josh McPhee: "I am tired of artists fetishizing activist culture and showing it to the world as if it were their invention."[1] The potential for a hostile relationship between movement activists and "social practice" artists exists—particularly as the latter become institutionalized and celebrated in a way that the former aren't.

My intention was to explain such art-making practices to people who might be liable to dismiss them outright, and to try to lay out the conditions for a possible productive relationship. To do that, one does have to give an honest account of possible pitfalls, it's true. But when I end the article by saying that for activists such artistic-political phenomena should be treated as an opportunity, I am not being flip. Activists should be looking for ways to engage with such gestures, not excuses to dismiss them. In general, I'm not trying to argue for (or against) this or that type of art but for an overall way of relating to the questions raised by "social practice."

Elizabeth M. Grady
SEA can at worst be unhelpful, masking real problems with deceptively warm and fuzzy interactions, if it fails to remain conscious of its political aims and real-world goals. This is not to say that the work should be instrumentalized, turned into a mere tool or engine for achieving specific aims, but that in order for its aesthetic and social goals to have impact and carry meaning, its practitioners need to remain mindful of their political and social position. This is doubly true when communities are engaged, and the work's "success" or "failure," however defined, has a marked and observable impact on the lives of those who work with the artist and activate their networks on his or her behalf. I'll leave aside definitions of success and failure for another debate, but the question you raise here is critical.

Tom Finkelpearl
So, is the response to Sandy by Occupy and others akin to what Rick Lowe has set in motion at *Project Row Houses* in Houston or what Tania Bruguera has done at *Immigrant Movement* in Corona, Queens? I believe it is. Both projects have psychological value in their communities, bring outside

attention, and offer creative alternatives to traditional activist approaches. While Lowe and Bruguera live in the communities of their projects, they started to some degree as outsiders, and this can have value—helping folks wake up, bringing new energy, stepping in more nimbly than the government is willing or able to do. They have focused attention on the local issues, brought media attention, and have brought new sorts of thinking to the table relative to local problems. Maria Canela, a frequent participant from Corona, once told me that *Immigrant Movement* is the "free space" in the community, both because all the workshops are free of charge and because anything can happen there—it is free of constraints.

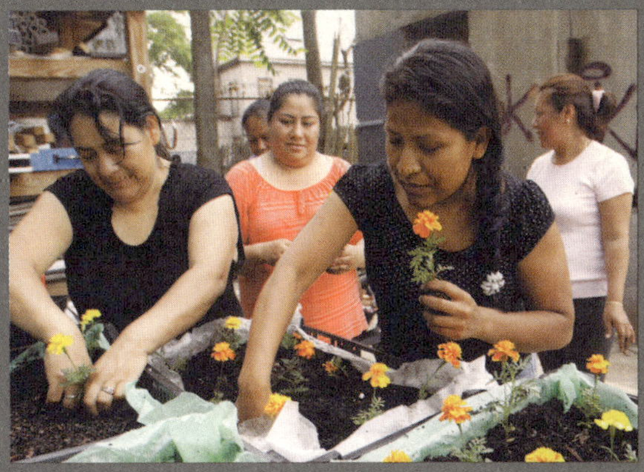

Tania Bruguera, *Immigrant Movement International*, Jason Gaspar's Plant Justice class, 2013.

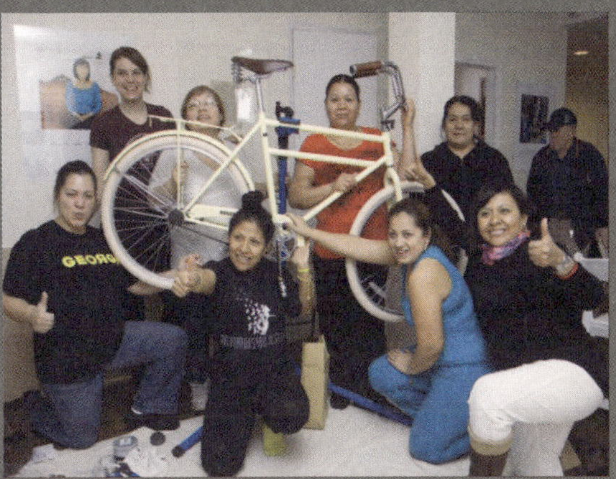

Tania Bruguera, *Immigrant Movement International*, women attending bike maintenance class led by Liz Jose of We Bike NYC, 2013.

I do not think that either *Project Row Houses* or *Immigrant Movement* claims "#WeGotThis," nor do I see danger (identified by Davis) in their substituting for non-artistic activism. In fact, from what I have seen, both projects are well integrated into the local activist communities. But as artists they have latitude for openness in their approach that can be not better, not a substitute for, but often more flexible than

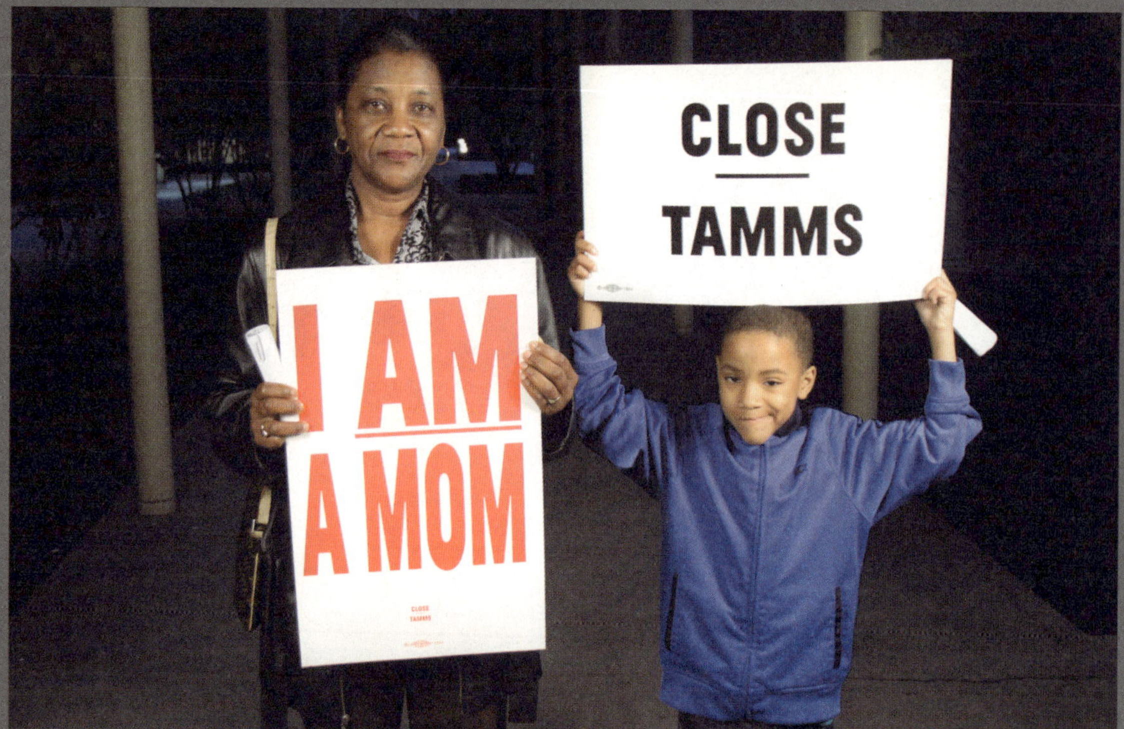

Laurie Jo Reynolds, Tamms Year Ten project. Annette and A.J., Jane Addams Hull House, Chicago, May 6, 2012. Photo: Community Based Art Practices Group, School of the Art Institute of Chicago, Instructor Lora Lode.

Annette's son Alonzo had been at Tamms supermax for ten years. In that time, Annette said he lost a lot of weight, became depressed, and nearly stopped writing: "He was once a very strong person, and now talks about giving up." Tamms was difficult for her whole family, who found it hard to visit him through glass walls, and see him handcuffed and shackled to a concrete stump. Alonzo was sent there for a ticket he received in 2002 which was supposed to be expunged. He was not given any other reason for his placement at Tamms.

immediate campaign-based actions. In general, then, I agree with most of what Ben Davis is saying, but feel his target is perhaps too broad. There is such a range of work under the heading of Social Practice, much of which is relatively uninteresting and ineffective (just like there is a lot of uninteresting and ineffective abstract painting). But there are social art projects that complement local activism while keeping a clear eye on their own limitations.

Ernesto Pujol

Art and social engagement, or socially engaged art must seek the consciousness (enlightenment) of individuals and groups as one of its primary goals. Otherwise, it runs the risk of being

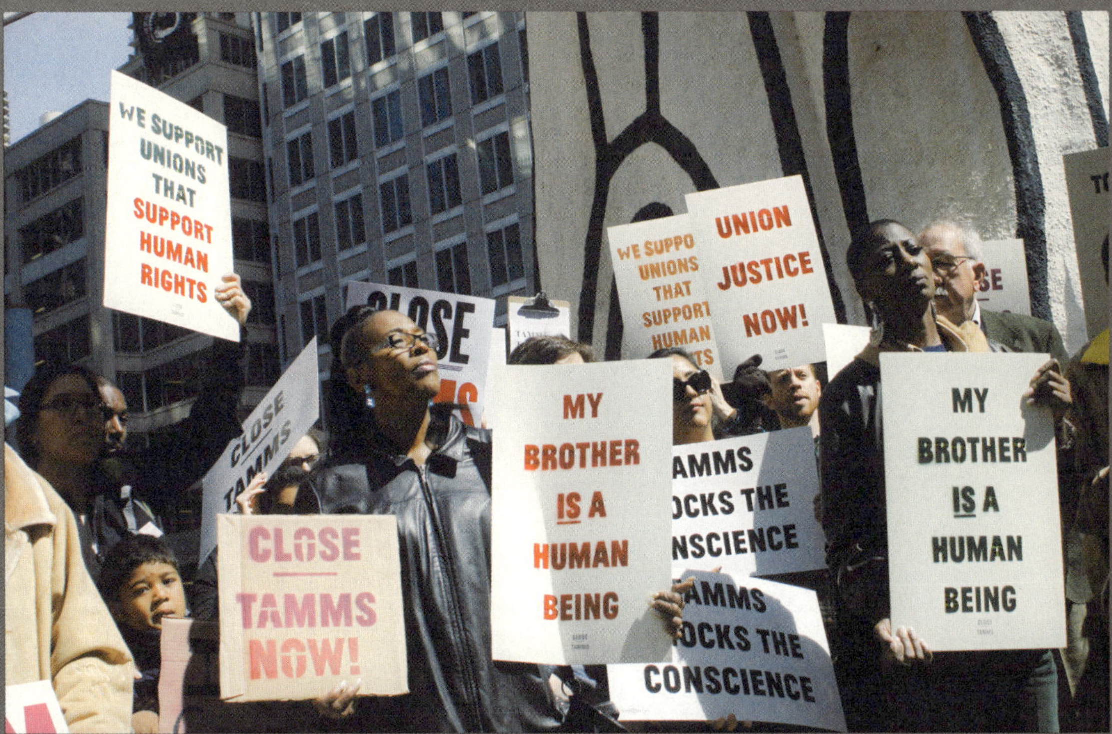

Laurie Jo Reynolds, Tamms Year Ten project, My Brother is A Human Being, 2012. Photo by Catherine McMillian, April 4, 2012.

Family members of men in isolation at Tamms supermax protest the guards union AFSCME for supporting a prison condemned by international human rights monitors. Their signs are based on the "I AM A MAN" placards first used by striking AFSCME sanitation workers, whom Martin Luther King, Jr. supported just before he was assassinated in Memphis in 1968. The mothers said that closing Tamms is about human dignity, not jobs, and reiterated King's message that workers' rights and human rights are inseparable. They marched to AFSCME headquarters on April 4, 2012, the 44th anniversary of King's death, and told the crowd, "Human suffering cannot be the basis of the southern Illinois economy."

a liberal intervention that seeks the redistribution of material wealth, promoting unsustainable notions of American Dream abundance, and ongoing materialism.

In addition, and long before any intervention, art as social engagement demands a group of fully conscious (enlightened) practitioners who are not going to turn groups (society) into their laboratory, becoming the site where a new generation of young white artists used to virtual social media but little human field contact learns about existence on the backs of working class people of color. Socially engaged art projects should not be about the education of artists at the expense of the poor.

Deborah Fisher

I appreciate your insistence on enlightenment as a goal. I think this serves the important purpose, particularly within this discussion, to get beyond separating language and dualisms that come out when we talk about political change. I wonder about how this goal of enlightenment, and the specific language of compassion that surrounds it, jibes with your own condemnation of a wide swath of artists practicing SEA as white privileged kids making careers on the backs of poor people of color. While I agree that this is a problem of SEA, I am curious about the best approach as a community to solving it. Do we want to create a dualism, build a wall between those artists who get it and those who don't? Or do we want to create a community of support that's both critical and generous—that helps artists grow and learn from mistakes?

I've made mistakes as an artist working in communities. I've made mistakes with race and class. When I messed up, I was treated dismissively by a handful of mostly white people with a stake in identity politics as currently practiced, and I received a generous, rigorous education and a clear path forward from the people I actually messed up with. This is important because you're talking about such huge concepts—materialism and class and consciousness itself. I agree that artists should take on these big ideas! But to do so you need to be able to fail. How do we infuse criticism of SEA with those qualities of both rigor and compassion? It's not generative to condemn everyone who gets it wrong.

Ben Davis

Since this exchange has certainly helped me clarify my own thoughts on the question of "social practice," I wanted to offer some general takeaways.

I think artists have a very important part to play in political struggle—but they don't have any particular special access to political wisdom. I respect art enough to grant it its own kind of logic, just as politics has its own particular needs. The demands of these two fields can and do converge, but it is an uneasy relationship, and the emphasis ought to be on that fact. For instance, *originality* is something artistic practice puts a lot of stress on. And of course a certain degree of imagination is important—vital even—for sustaining political momentum and inspiring new audiences. When, at the 2013 Creative Time Summit, Laurie Jo Reynolds presented art projects connected with Tamms Year Ten's years-long work building solidarity with prisoners in solitary confinement, I sent the link to my friends who do criminal justice activism. These are some great ideas!

At the same time, while originality *can* be a virtue in activism, it would be easy to overemphasize it as the missing piece of the political puzzle. There are tried and true tactics that work, but that simply aren't very fun. Sometimes you need to be repetitive, unrefined, inelegant, blunt, when you are trying to make an urgent point. In general, the dire state of left-wing politics can't be explained by a lack of creative ideas. It is better explained by a lack of sustained organization, coherence, clear goals, and commitment to stick it out through the unpleasant parts—all those tired old non-creative things that make social movements possible. The right isn't particularly creatively inspiring, but it is relentless and well organized, and its agenda has dominated official politics for decades.

When all you have is a hammer, every problem looks like a nail, and when you relate to politics through art, it is easy to look at every problem as an artistic one. But even creative activism, if it is to be effective, entails a lot of old-fashioned non-artistic organizing and outreach. "[R]eal political work involves continuous interpersonal negotiations, meetings that never end, and receiving and responding to hundreds of emails a day," the filmmaker Astra Taylor wrote recently, reflecting on how her work as part of the *Strike Debt/Rolling Jubilee* initiative sat uneasily with her more artsy side. "It's reactive, not contemplative, and I prefer life with more of the latter." But the trade-off, she thinks, is worth it in order, possibly, to inspire bigger and better things.

The actual debate about the hazards of these relationships, which is what my original article was about, is part of taking art's political role seriously. It is the cultivation process that transforms what Rick Lowe rightly identifies as the art world's "bullshit" into the "fertilizer" that Fisher hopes can grow something socially meaningful. I'll end with a real-life parable about the expanded field of cultural action, an episode that I come back to when I think about the question.

* * *

Back in 2008, I went to a demonstration against the Iraq and Afghanistan wars in Union Square in New York. It was led by the coalition United for Peace and Justice, and titled "River to River: Join Hands for Peace." The intent was to form a human chain across the island by linking hands. This gesture could be read as an effort to give protest an artistic twist, rather than doing the same old thing. More cynically, you could say that the symbolic action was a symptom of the diffusion of the antiwar movement in the lead-up to the 2008 presidential election, an attempt to avoid making too uncompromising an antiwar demand so as to get a Democrat into office.

"River to River: Join Hands for Peace" was a bust. The day was blustery, the crowd scattered. Not enough people came together to belt the island. Perhaps the movement was already on the decline, and the gesture would have been beautiful if more people had shown up. But in the event,

I wished that our numbers had been more concentrated instead of symbolically spread out.

As I left Union Square, somewhat dejected, I became aware of a new and different tide of people flooding in. They were carrying pillows. This was World Pillow Fight Day, a bit of viral fun apparently staged in jolly obliviousness to the anniversary of the carnage in Iraq. And the incoming throng of people thwacking each other with pillows completely dwarfed the United for Peace and Justice protest.

To escape the fracas, I ducked across the crosswalk. There, once again, I found myself in what appeared to be a rally. Demonstrators were brandishing professionally printed placards: "Elect Harvey Dent!" The signs featured the image of a beaming politician who looked uncannily like actor Aaron Eckhart. In fact, it *was* Aaron Eckhart, and this mystery "rally" was part of a countrywide viral marketing campaign for the upcoming Batman movie, shortly to become one of the largest blockbusters of all time.

You can take a lot of different lessons away from this particular conjunction of events, where demonstrators try to look to escape traditional forms of protest while Hollywood promoters clone them, and a goofy flash mob drowns them out. You might say that it points to the need of politics to be both more and less symbolic at once. In any case, I think that it is in navigating this triangle that the real stakes of the "social practice" question will become clear.

1 Josh McPhee, quoted in Nato Thompson, "Living as Form," *Living as Form: Socially Engaged Art From 1991–2011*. New York: Creative Time Books, 2010, 31.

Laura Raicovich

The Urgency of the Unseen

> Now it is a matter of seizing and admiring a new art, which ... opens up to the artist unsuspected possibilities ... in the very spectacle of things ignored and silenced.[1]

In her series of essays for *Tropiques* magazine, collectively titled *The Great Camouflage: Writings of Dissent* (1941–45), the Martiniquais poet, writer, and co-founder of the Negritude movement Suzanne Césaire confronts a wide swath of subjects: colonialism, aesthetics, resistance, identity, camouflage, poetry. Among these extraordinary writings, Césaire takes up art in its many guises, and argues forcefully for an art that is urgent, unexpected, and expresses elements of the unknowable. In doing so, she asserts, art might provide a path to the radical liberation and reinvented freedom for which she advocates in her work.

At the outset of my journey as the Queens Museum's director, I think of Césaire's exhortations for this art, and for the intersectionality it implies, and wonder how an institution might best serve this art, the artists who produce it, and its audiences. How the Queens Museum might contribute to urgent discourses of the everyday, of dreams, of liberation and equity. Césaire posits liberation via celebration of that which has been marginalized—the dark, the demanding, the surreal, the difficult to categorize, the ambiguous, the excluded, the camouflaged, the real, the painful, and the anti-colonial. How can I step forward to steward an institution, and simultaneously foreground the methodologies and ideas that will question conventional terms for culture and art, recreate language, decolonize rhetoric, and enable multiple, variedly focused lenses through which we might see the world again?[2]

Queens itself is a physical site of diaspora and hybridity, a longtime home to migrants and immigrants to New York City,

1 Suzanne Césaire. *The Great Camouflage: Writings of Dissent (1941–45)*. Middletown, CT: Wesleyan University Press, 2012, 17.

2 The term *intersectionality* was first used in Kimberlé Crenshaw, "Demarginalizing the Intersection of Race and Sex: A Black Feminist Critique of Antidiscrimination Doctrine, Feminist Theory and Antiracist Politics." *University of Chicago Legal Forum* 1989, 139–67.

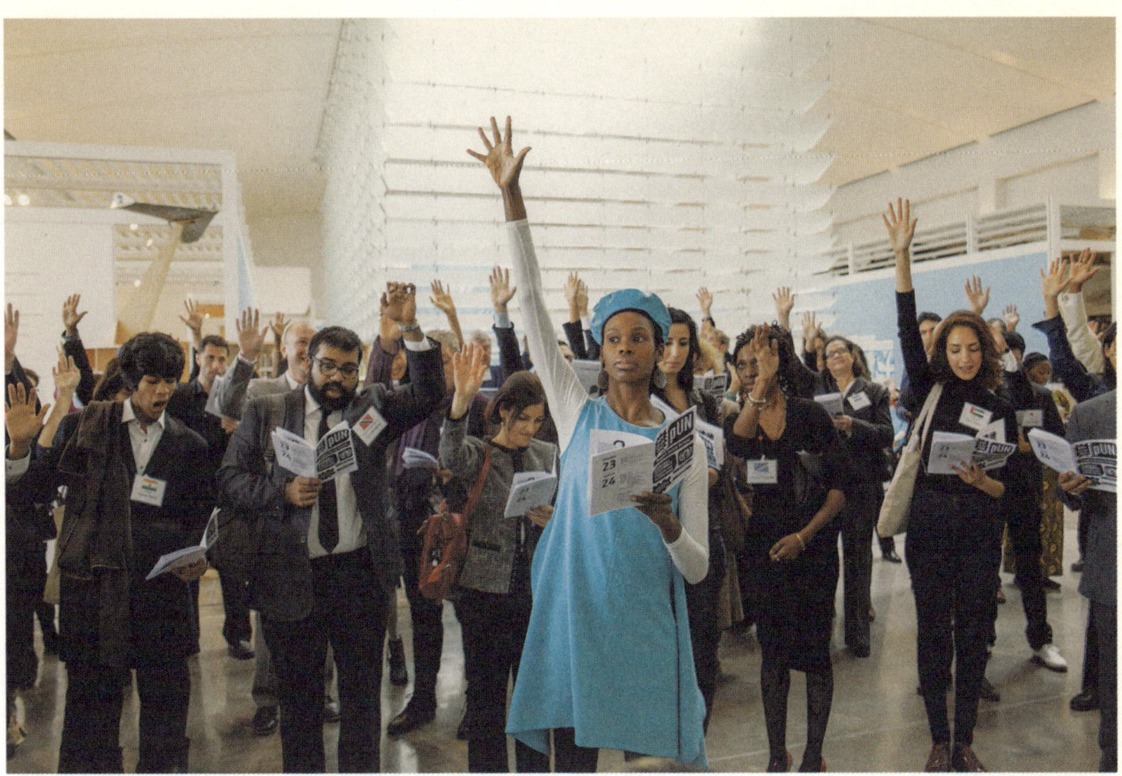

Participants in Pedro Reyes' exhibition "pUN" at the Queens Museum read "The Blessing of the Bees," a poem written by Jesús del Toro.

a geography that is rich in multi-rootedness and rhizomatic conditions. How might we envision the Queens Museum as a site of divergent, complex, specific experiences for both makers and visitors? I will try to map ways the Museum can offer more to artists and to audiences who might contend with these circumstances. How can the Queens Museum be a place that highlights and celebrates these practices, artworks, and conditions, celebrating them, and in so doing, perhaps achieves a space for Césaire's particular brand of liberation?

Carol Becker, writer, cultural commentator, and Dean of the School of the Arts at Columbia University, has written eloquently of her own childhood experiences at the Brooklyn Museum:

> What I do remember is the freedom the museum represented. It was our place, albeit a grown-up place, within which we could be transported to multiple other realities and moments of cultural history. It made Brooklyn seem huge. It made my life seem huge ... I could journey back in history aware of the possibility that I might actually travel forward into such realities in the future ... The most important thing for me, then, was that it was our museum to roam in freely, just as we did on our streets.[3]

3 Carol Becker. *Thinking in Place: Art, Action, and Cultural Production*. Boulder, CO: Paradigm Publishers, 2009, 30.

My desire is that the Queens Museum can function as a space for envisioning other worlds as Becker writes about it; as a site for wonder and co-creation and experimentation; and as a space that not only feels like it belongs to its audiences, but actually does so. While I am profoundly aware that Becker's or my childhood experiences of museums are inextricably connected to privileges of race, class, and education, can the structures that build these requirements be dismantled to allow for broader participation? What does it take to achieve such a space? For the Queens Museum, with deep histories of engagement and the textures of its physical location embedded in its DNA, the best means to locate possible answers to these questions is in the place itself.

There is a great deal to overcome. The word "museum" is loaded down, not least with its twinned history as a place of wonder for the curiosities held within, and for its exclusion of large portions of the population, financially, socially, racially, politically, and physically. The word "museum," and perhaps worse, "contemporary art museum," does not elicit thoughts of easily accessible space. Barriers to entry are very high in the public imaginary. Museums conjure notions of the display of art that are to be revered rather than interacted with, under circumstances that are often over-crowded, over-mediated, or unapproachable. Further, the financial structures that support museums often confer the values and priorities of the wealthiest classes in society to the perceived, and often the actual, exclusion of many visitors.[4]

The Queens Museum occupies a particular zone in the cultural landscape of New York City, and has spent the better part of its existence in the pursuit of reversing the popular perceptions mentioned above. It is the way the Queens Museum is physically embedded in its site that conveys clues as to how it might operate in some unmuseum-like ways. Particularly relevant are the history of the site of the Museum itself, the building's former uses, the ethos of the borough in which it resides, and its history as an institution profoundly connected with its surrounding audiences.

A very brief building and site history: the Queens Museum was founded in 1972, in a building originally constructed to house the New York City Pavilion for the 1939 World's Fair. After the Fair, it was converted to a public recreation space with a roller and ice skating rink. From 1946 to 1950, it served as the first meeting place of the General Assembly of the United Nations while the UN's Manhattan location was being constructed. Subsequently, the building served as the site of the New York City Pavilion for the 1964–65 World's Fair.

The Museum sits at the edge of Flushing Meadows Corona Park at the foot of the massive Unisphere, one of the most lasting

4 See Carol Becker, "Museums and the Neutralization of Culture: A Response to Adorno" in *Thinking in Place*.

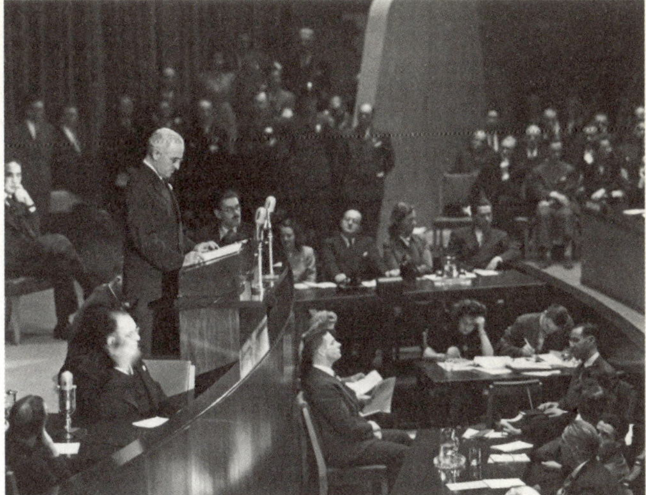

President Harry S. Truman addresses the General Assembly, 1946.

symbols of the 1964–65 Fair. The park, the second largest in New York City, is a well-used public space, home to innumerable casual soccer games, cricket matches and family picnics, as well as the US Open and National Tennis Center, the Mets' home stadium, and sundry cultural spaces. It has the possibility to embody publicness, and a possibility for play, as well as to take on the challenges and opportunities posed by the lingering texture of past manifestations of internationalism via the World's Fair and early days of the UN.

The Queens Museum is a public space within a public park. It has a robust history of deep local engagement, particularly via the innovation of including community organizers as permanent members of the staff. Within the next 24 months, it will add a Queens Public Library branch within its walls. As I contemplate the library's presence, John Cotton Dana's Progressive ideas and library reform provide some fodder for thinking about public spaces, the educational role of public institutions, and what they have to offer as platforms for ideas that fall outside of the mainstream, as settings for the incubation and exchange of thought and dissent. In Dana's words:

> The public library ... is not an institution in which the accepted canons alone are taught ... It is the extension to the humblest of the chance of learning the latest thing that is being taught and said.[5]

Dana advocates most forcefully for, "an open, laissez-faire environment of uncensored discourse, an environment in which the freedom to think and speak is guaranteed by law and safeguarded by institutional practices."[6] Indeed, libraries and museums should be at the forefront of institutions embodying such practices, both in administration and in programming. Both of these institutions must be locations for such exchange and experiment. The museum and the library can and should provide both resources (intellectual, financial, educational) and physical space to locate the freedoms that Suzanne Césaire wrote about so passionately. Furthermore, they should also, "have the wisdom to understand that new forms of discourse might not be immediately evident or even seem threatening to 'business as usual'."[7]

5 Carol Duncan. *A Matter of Class: John Cotton Dana, Progressive Reform and the Newark Museum*. Pittsburgh: Periscope, 2009, 29.

6 Ibid., 32.

7 Email conversation between Laura Raicovich and Lisi Raskin, January 2, 2015.

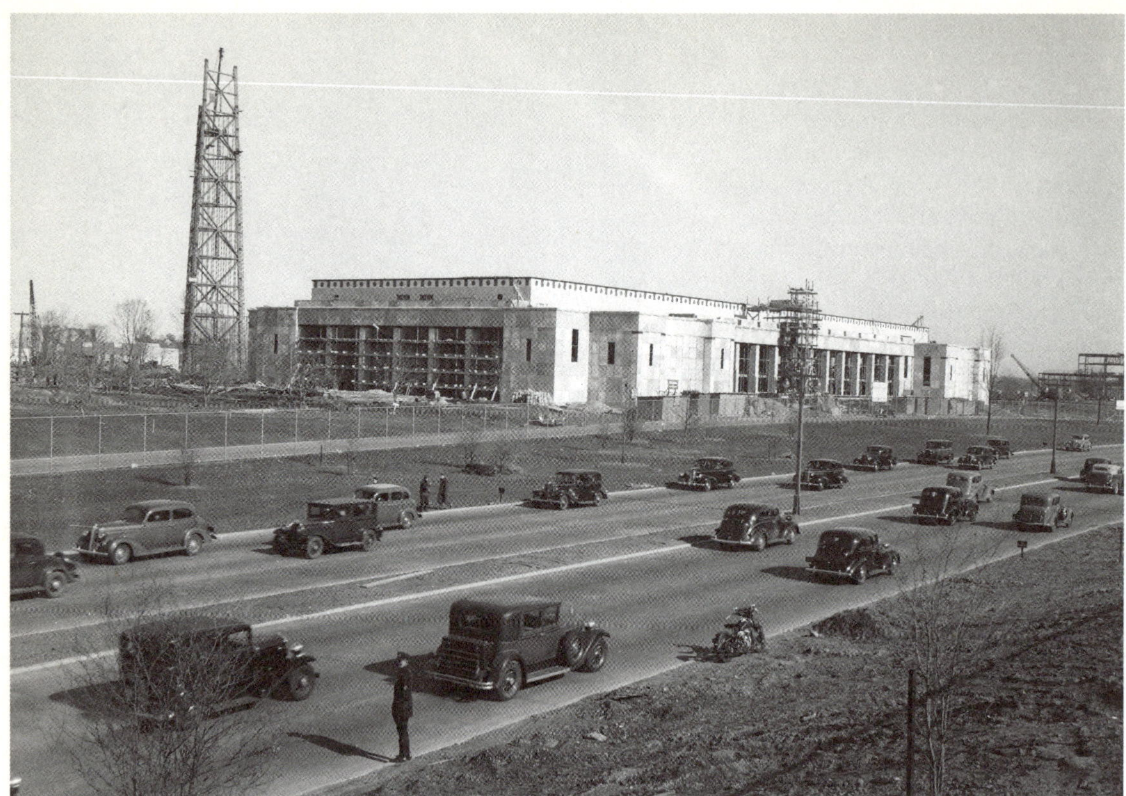

New York City Building and Trylon under construction, June 21, 1938.

The Queens Museum is a case study for such a space: a flexible institution that learns with and from its audiences, including, importantly, the artists with whom it works. Perhaps the Museum can be so flexible that it functions radically differently at different times, to support artists and communities in ways that they require, as well as supporting artists working with radical methodologies, and those whose work fosters alternative views on our past, present and future. Radical American pedagogue, activist, and writer bell hooks comes to mind here, with her "self-interview" on the impact that reading Paulo Freire (1921–1997), influential Brazilian educator, had on her thinking. In particular, her need to engage with "education as the practice of freedom," interests me. She writes of "how difficult the politics of everyday life was for black people in the racially segregated south when so many folks did not read and were so often dependent on racist people to explain, read, and write."[8] Not only is this practical need for interpretation one that remains particularly necessary in Queens as a location of multilingualism, it is also a requirement of cultural institutions that wish to enact their politics in their operations as well as in the art they display.

8 bell hooks. *Teaching to Transgress: Education as the Practice of Freedom*. New York: Routledge, 1994, 51.

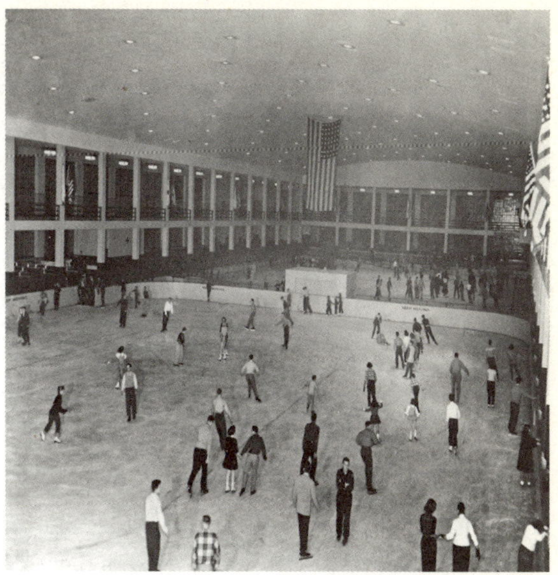

View of roller and ice skating rinks, New York City Building, 1941.

Artists continue to challenge us to see the world in a new light and require a multiplicity of creative, structural, financial, and intellectual resources to realize their ideas. Becker writes:

> There are now artists who exist within the structure of their multiple identities as sculptors of public space, functioning as community organizers, instigators, interventionists, environmentalists, archivists, curators, and writers. Perhaps more than any notion of interdisciplinarity, there is an expanded notion of art and artists finally large enough to include everything that artists choose to address and all the ways in which their projects are actualized.[9]

It is our great challenge to envision and realize scaffolding that can foster such work.

Further, our global interconnectedness and the conditions of late capitalism loom large in our activities. These realities are felt in Queens particularly keenly. As the most diverse county in the United States, where over 138 different languages are spoken, the realities of diaspora are a constant. "Crisis globalization," a term coined by TJ Demos in *The Migrant Image*, describes an international condition "divided between the neoliberal claims of free markets and democratic participation, and the politics of economic inequality, statelessness, and military conflicts."[10] These are global realities, and the ways they are made manifest in our daily lives are the material, in a Césairian sense, that might serve as our most inspiring cultural moments.

It is up to institutions like the Queens Museum to enact and reflect the shifting patterns that describe points on the arc of our cultural moment. And just as bell hooks insists that we "open our minds and hearts so that we can know beyond the boundaries of what is acceptable, so that we can think and rethink, so that we can create new visions ... enabl[ing] transgressions—a movement against and beyond boundaries,"[11] places like the Queens Museum must create spaces, exhibitions, and programs to question and explore that which has been excluded and disregarded, and for inspiration and beauty in all its manifestations. Within this web, we may find our liberation.

9 Becker, 78.

10 TJ Demos. *The Migrant Image: The Art and Politics of Documentary during Global Crisis*. Durham, NC: Duke University Press, 2013.

11 hooks, 12.

Jan Cohen-Cruz

The Imagination and Beyond: Toward a Method of Evaluating Socially Engaged Art

> Because you have imagined love, you have not loved; merely because you have imagined brotherhood, you have not made brotherhood. You may feel as though you had, but you have not.
> —Muriel Rukeyser[1]

This essay is about evaluating art that aspires to *affect,* rather than be about, the social issue it addresses. It is about artists who create a process, environment, or event that they put directly into the world, unconstrained by the parameters of galleries and performance spaces. I believe such art ought to be more valued than it typically is, and held to criteria that fit its purposes rather than to generic metrics like attendance numbers and ticket sales, which may or may not elucidate success. Engaged art is tricky to evaluate, and is often difficult even to recognize as art. It is less about an object than a relationship, and rather than intended as a complete manifestation of an artist's imagination, it is purposely incomplete, requiring social interaction to reach fullness.

The first part of this essay describes principles of evaluating socially engaged art and how I came to them, initially drawing on my experience making socially engaged performance. In the second part, I provide examples of these principles in practice, drawn from evaluating the socially engaged art projects funded in 2014–15 by A Blade of Grass.

Principles

My evaluation process is rooted in having been part of socially engaged performances, and eventually having written about them. The constant in socially engaged art is a palpable aesthetic experience—the joy, bursts of imagination, self-knowledge, insight beyond surfaces, and temporary experience of what anthropologist

1 Muriel Rukeyser. *The Life of Poetry*. Ashfield, MA: Paris Press, 1949, 1996.

Victor Turner called *communitas*, a connecting spirit that transcends hierarchy. But equally fundamental to socially engaged art are principles that I learned first through experience:

1. *An active relationship with those who would otherwise be strictly an audience contributes to social purpose.*
When I was 17, I toured with a theater company in New Hampshire's White Mountains. A federal grant covered half the cost of our shows. A group from a small community proposed hosting a potluck dinner before the performance whose proceeds, they assured us, would cover their half. We accepted. We were not only treated to a savory meal, but the proactive stance their preparation entailed, and our informal conversation over the meal, connected us more directly than just seeing a play allows. Theorist Richard Schechner's 1973 articulation of an entertainment/efficacy continuum, with "spectators" characteristic of the former and "participants" of the latter, further suggests why an active relationship is needed in socially engaged work.[2]

2. *A participatory art-making process is often more useful in social contexts than finished work.*
I co-facilitated a theater workshop in a maximum security prison, providing the participants with the means of self-representation, communication around issues of concern, and dialogue with people of multiple points of view. The workshop met weekly for a year, enough time to have a social impact, such as community building among participants—something that strictly seeing art, though valuable, could not provide.

3. *Partnering with people whose expertise is related to the social context brings in what the artists do not know.*
I was working with drama students on a play advocating for endangered community gardens in New York City. Wanting not only to express the value of the gardens but also to help protect them, we needed additional skills that are not taught in art schools. To build a case, we depended on organizers to strategize how our advocacy could be applied politically, and gardeners who knew from experience the individual and collective value of their activities. When the goals are not purely aesthetic, it's unlikely the means will be either.

4. *Identifying impact from the points of view of all the key partners is in keeping with socially engaged art's goals.*
A few years ago, I was the evaluator of smARTpower, a collaborative cultural diplomacy program designed by Sergio Bessa,

2 Richard Schechner. *Environmental Theatre*. New York: Applause Theatre & Cinema Book Publishers, 1973, 2000.

Director of Curatorial and Educational Programs at the Bronx Museum of the Arts, and funded by the US State Department. The program intended for US artists to meaningfully partner with people and organizations in each of 15 countries where the projects took place, and in so doing to positively impact perception of the US. Assessment thus required responses from multiple layers of participants. These included the State Department funding us from Washington, the Embassy in each participating country, the artists, the workshop participants, and the host cultural organizations—sometimes responding in contradictory ways, which was most instructive.

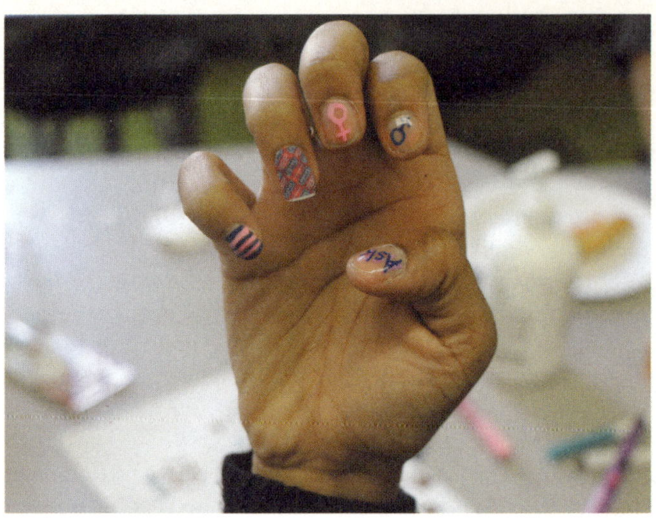

SexEd, *Wearing Consent*, 2015, custom manicure.

I would be remiss not to mention a criterion for the evaluator: writing in a way that is accessible to everyone who has been part of the project, whatever their profession or education. Theorists sometimes undervalue such writing but accessibility and depth of thought are not mutually exclusive.

My evaluation principles proved compatible with A Blade of Grass' values. ABOG foregrounds:

1 *Artistic excellence*. To me this means identifying what the ABOG artists create in addition to objects and how they apply aesthetic knowledge in social contexts.
2 *Artists in leadership roles to promote social change*. Here I focus on how the artist situates the work to have societal impact, including gathering partners and publics to partake in the vision-in-action.
3 *Relevance to the participating communities*. This is evidenced through observation, interviews, and conversations with people in the intended communities, be they geographic, circumstantial (e.g., people struggling with the same issue like homelessness), tradition-based (e.g., sharing a religious or cultural orientation), or aligned by spirit (e.g., a similar philosophical or political base).

The 2014–15 ABOG projects were centered in the following venues and activities (detailed elsewhere in this book):

— At homeless shelters, Jody Wood's refitted truck functioned as a mobile hair salon for residents;

— At meetings of political activists of all kinds, Fran Ilich provided full-bodied Zapatista-grown coffee to energize work in a kindred, collective spirit;
— In a Brooklyn College lab, Jan Mun experimented with a particular mushroom's soil remediation potential;
— At a public international high school, Liz Slagus and Norene Leddy taught students in two sex education classes through a process of making t-shirts about consent;
— In a pop-up Spanish-language used bookstore in Red Hook, Brooklyn, Pablo Helguera celebrated the Spanish language and intellectual life;
— In DeFremery Park in Oakland, California, alongside healing workshops at the Life Is Living festival, Brent Cook displayed portraits of local healers, and also brought the images to the Oakland Museum;
— In Illinois living rooms, Laurie Jo Reynolds gathered families of people formerly incarcerated in Tamms Correctional Center, the notorious supermax prison designed for sensory deprivation, which they helped close, and which now risks reopening, to plan the next art-informed campaign;
— In elementary schools, children at risk of lead poisoning drew "Fundreds," their interpretation of hundred dollar bills, which, Mel Chin writes, "represent the tangible voices of millions speaking to those with the power to end this national problem."

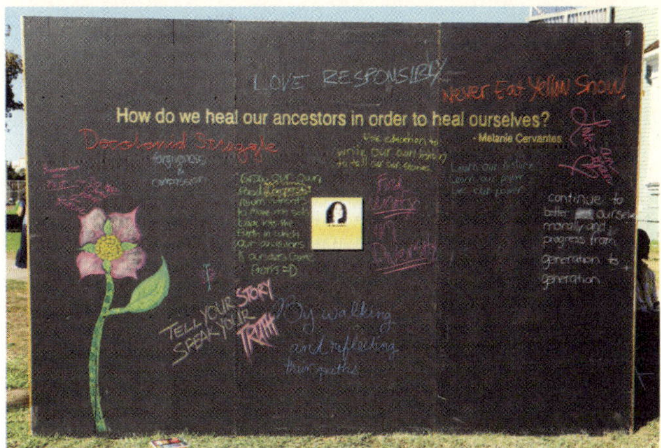

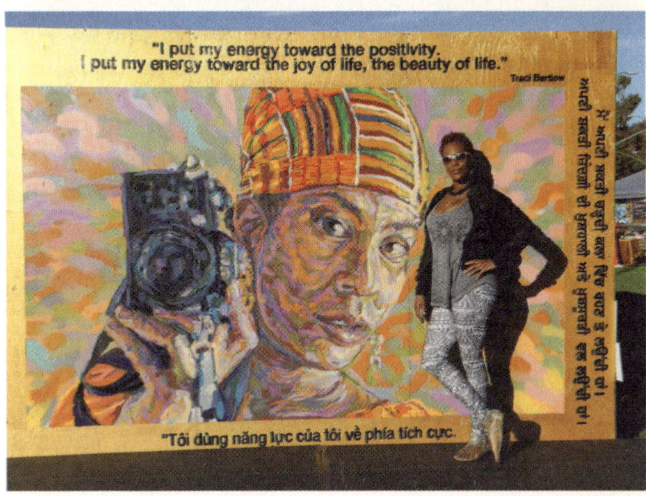

Brett Cook, ***Reflections of Healing***, **2014, top: community response wall; bottom: portrait of Traci Bartlow with workshop leader.**

I evaluated the New York City-based projects and was point person for the field researchers evaluating projects happening elsewhere. What do these projects tell us about socially engaged art's many forms, diverse participants, intended benefits, and array of locations? What social goals can they achieve? How do these artists' aesthetic orientation, training, and vision propel the social contribution? Responses to these questions, as perceived not by only the artist but also by the range of people intended to experience each project's impact, informed my evaluation and suggested metrics by which to assess the value of art whose purpose is as much social as aesthetic.

Evaluation in Practice

I try to position myself as a supportive witness who shares what I observe with the artist along the way. I do not wait until the project ends to let the artist know about a concern, or a desire to do more of something, that a participant voices to me. This stance aligns with ABOG's framing of evaluation as one of the ways they support artists, rather than, as artists have sometimes experienced, something punitive or secretive.

I began by reading the artists' proposals, and then discussing with them how their projects evolved in the months since submitting them or from their original conception. It was important to know, for example, that Helguera's pop-up, Spanish-language used bookstore had begun some years earlier as an art installation in a gallery, and now was an actual bookstore. While still a careful reproduction of his mother's library in his childhood home, with comfy armchairs, soft lighting, and a warm rug, where he had developed a love of reading, it was now also a shop where people could buy one book at a time, for a contribution of at least one dollar. The store format made it available to a broader constituency than frequents galleries.

Given the process orientation of socially engaged art, my approach to evaluating it is ethnographic, requiring that I (or the field researcher) go to the project sites multiple times and observe, and in some cases participate in, artist-generated activities. Our reports feature a lot of detailed description and interpretation of what we've seen. We request dates, times, and places where the project will happen. We sit in on meetings where activities are set up, to see how all the partners' goals are included in the unfolding design. For example, Slagus and Leddy met with the teacher in whose sex-ed class they would be designing t-shirts with the students on the topic of consent, and at her request included more handouts of the art terms they would be using so they could double as vocabulary words.

As the partners join in, I observe relationships being built. Indeed, the center of gravity for socially engaged art is less an object and more what Mel Chin calls a "sustained cultivation of relationships" to bring a project to fruition. In the Cincinnati iteration of Chin's *Operation Paydirt (OP)*, the desired outcome was to "prove the concept" of local engagement, action, and transfer of ownership of *OP* tools and tactics, so that responsibility for details of implementation is local and that local artists, educators, and healthcare professionals share efforts for awareness and action. Local stakeholders already involved in the effort separately are drawn together by the freshness of Chin's tactics, such as children, who are those most at risk of lead poisoning drawing "Fundred" dollar bills, representing, in Chin's words, "the value of informed public voice, to be exchanged for real resources to leverage 100% prevention."

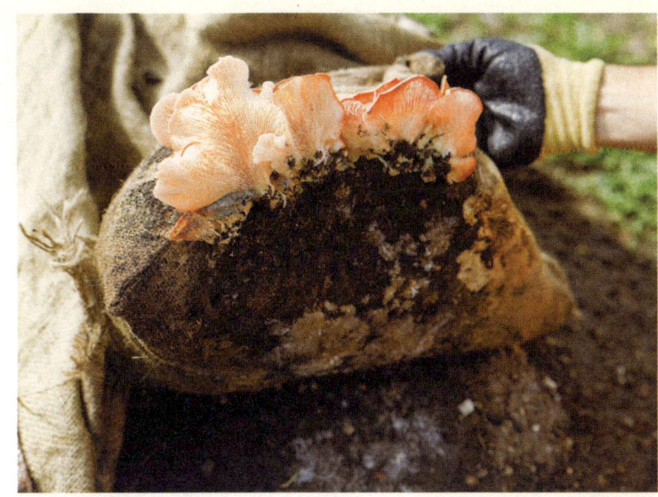

Jan Mun, *The Fairy Rings*, 2013, mushrooms used in soil remediation.

I look for how aesthetics is manifested in the projects. Sometimes the forms are recognizable as art, like Brett Cook's ABOG project portraits of people that in some way play a healing role in their communities. He exhibited the portraits, which also feature the subjects' words, as a form of acknowledgement in the Life Is Living festival in an Oakland park. His skill in portraiture is part of what must be evaluated because the beauty and energy of the portraits shows his respect for the subjects.

Sometimes art training shapes the project in more subtle ways. Jan Mun, for example, was trained in documentary photography but found it too small a world. She explains: "When I went sailing, I wanted to photograph the wind and not the effect of wind." She integrates an artist's curiosity, capacity for observation, and communication skills with her concrete efforts as an amateur scientist in order to make a social impact. Mun's colleagues said that her curiosity is infectious, piquing their interest in the world around them. Her capacity for observation is crucial in her roles of both artist and scientist. Her communication skills build public engagement into soil remediation efforts. She reaches both those people who come to neighborhood meetings out of concern about their local environment, and art audiences.

Some projects have both more and less recognizable aesthetic components. *Operation Paydirt* in Houston was timed to coincide with "Mel Chin: Rematch," a major retrospective of his work, jointly presented by Blaffer Art Museum, the Contemporary Arts Museum Houston, Asia Society Texas Center, and the Station Museum of Contemporary Art, from January through March 2015. As Sixto Wagan pointed out in his evaluation, Chin extended his art activities during that period to initiate community-based processes to further efforts for lead poisoning awareness and prevention, manifesting art as "not just the

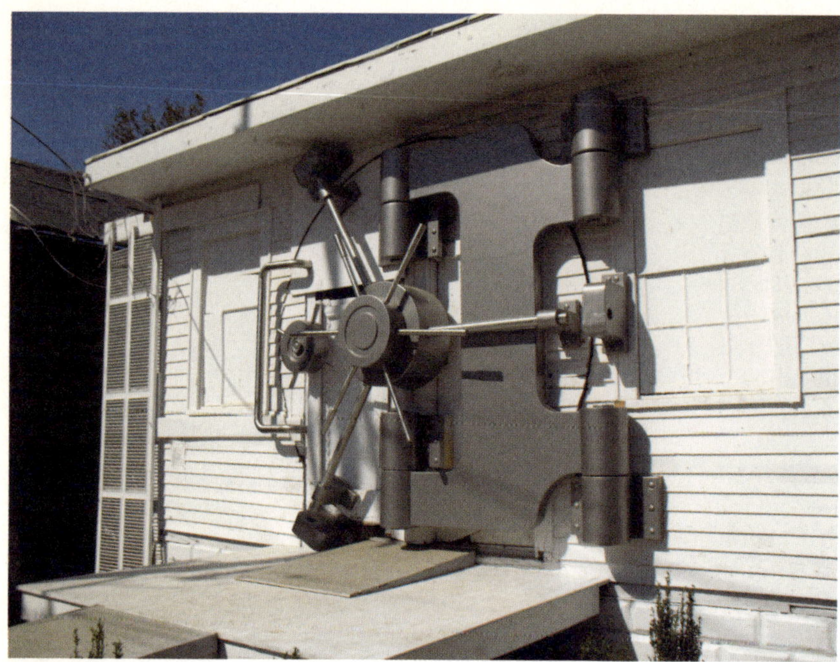

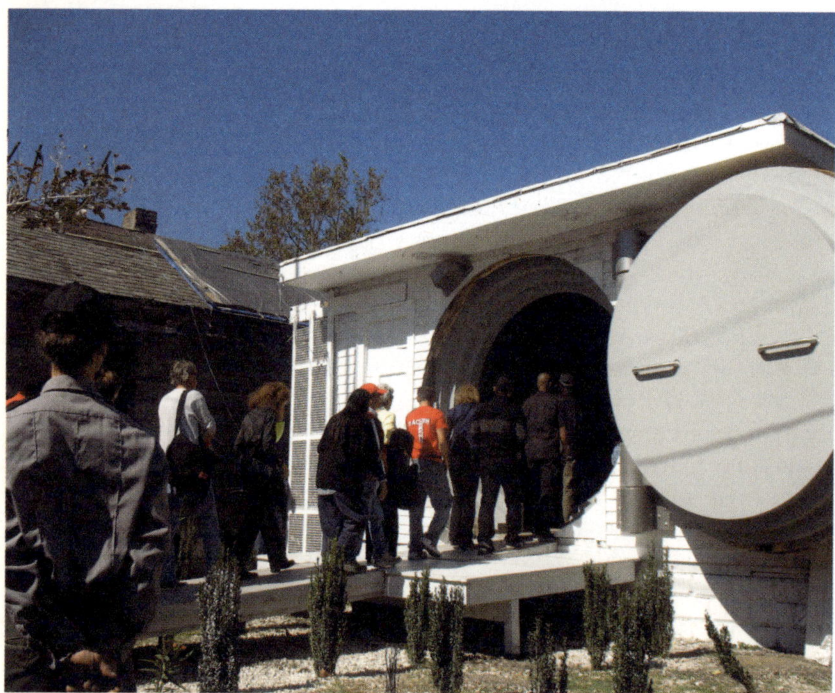

Mel Chin, *Safehouse*, 2008–2010 (both images).

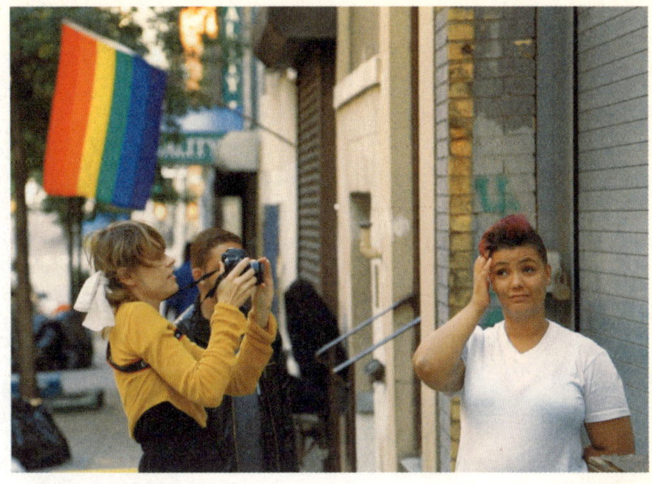

product, but a catalyzer of conversations and instrument for education and synthesis."

Art often manifests itself as the capacity to imagine something other than what exists. Community development specialist Doug Reeler writes that an obstacle to social action is "finding the will to actually change ... [and] working with resistance to change, most commonly rooted in fear of what might be lost, of doubt or self-doubt as to whether there is any real alternative that can be embraced".[3] As Brett Cook said to field researcher Brian Edgar, "I start thinking more about what I want in the world. If I want it to be more inclusive, let me make things that are inclusive. If I want the world to be peaceful, let me make things that are peaceful. If I want to see multi-gendered, multiethnic, multicultural, queer, whatever images in the world, let me make them and then they exist and then I am changing the world. I've realized that my experience, my choices define my world."

Jody Wood, *Beauty in Transition*, 2014, Jody Wood left; client right.

Artists working in social contexts play a range of roles, corresponding to their diverse goals. Slagus and Leddy are educators, integrating making things into learning, especially attractive in contrast to the many hours students spend sitting in classrooms. Laurie Jo Reynolds is a community builder, having brought together the families of incarcerated people through her art-infused, volunteer, grassroots legislative campaign that contributed to the closing of Tamms Correctional Center. Approaching Chin's *Operation Paydirt*, field researcher Pat Clifford drew on the Walker Art Center's "town square" framework for art and civic engagement that includes the artist in four roles: container, convener, connector, and catalyst (2015).[4] The *Operation Paydirt* production team sees itself as a "catalyst"—bringing attention to lead in the environment and the impact of lead poisoning in the lives of individuals and across society. It is also a "connector"—bringing together artists, educators and health workers. It is a temporary "container" for cross sector activities. However, Chin and his team are not long-term "conveners," a role they believe is more appropriately filled by local participants for the sake of sustainability.

While more qualitative than quantitative, our assessment includes numeric measures valuable to the artist; for example, Slagus and Leddy cared about the number of students who tested

3 Doug Reeler. "A Threefold Theory of Social Change," accessed at www.cdra.org.za/threefold-theory-of-social-change.html. 2007, 23.

Thanks to Pam Korza, Sylvia Gale, and the Assessing the Practices of Public Scholarship (APPS) collaboratory of Imagining America: Artists and Scholars in Public Life, for bringing Reeler and other assessment models to my attention. For more on APPS' excellent work around evaluating socially engaged art, in their case with higher education partners, see http://imaginingamerica.org/research/assessment/.

4 Walker Art Center. "Art and civic engagement: Mapping the connections," accessed at http://www.walkerart.org/education-community-programs/art-and-civic-engagement.

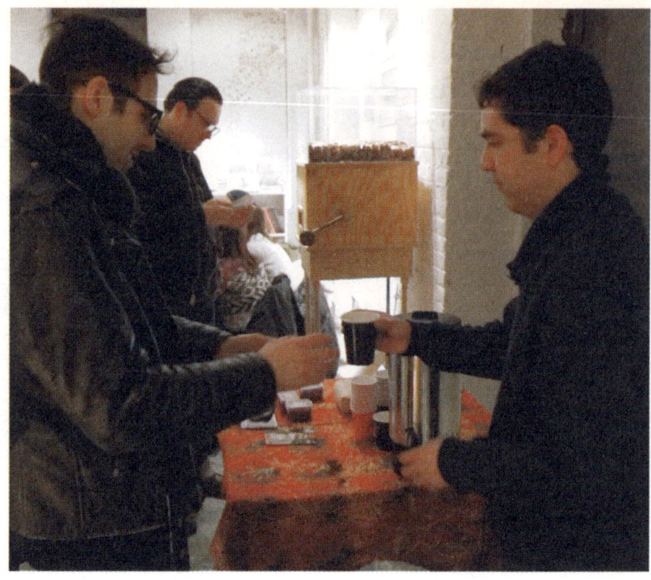

Fran Ilich, *Diego de la Vega Coffee Co-op*, 2014, the artist serving coffee.

their SexEd curriculum. We do not assume that the scale of the project is a metric for all ABOG Fellows. Some depend on the multiplier effect and need more than the fellowship year to reach their intended impact. Fran Ilich described his project "as ambitious and quixotic," more about influencing a handful of people who will in turn influence others than about reaching many people directly. Ilich serving Zapatista-grown coffee at political meetings in New York City is symbolically valuable, providing a glimpse of a world animated by collectivity, meeting everyone's basic needs, and connecting idealistic aspirations across national borders. Evidence of the power of his message was the standing-room-only crowd of mostly young artists at an ABOG presentation he gave.

A large part of my task is drawing out the experiences of people the project is meant to engage and benefit. In Jody Wood's *Beauty in Transition*, this included the homeless women who got their hair done, shelter staff, and volunteer stylists. A number of shelter residents indicated that their treatment by the mobile salon personnel was as important as the free hairdo. A client getting her hair washed said she went to a salon recently but because she is homeless the stylist just wet her hair down to limit physical contact—quite unlike the care she received from the mobile salon stylist.

Several shelter staffers noted that the mobile salon facilitated their work by raising the women's sense of worth, if temporarily. A recreation assistant at a Bushwick shelter said, "A lot of the residents have lost their way and to have this pick-you-up has been great for them. One who always has her head down got her hair done and it's the first time I saw her smile. And she put her head up."

Stylists participated for a range of reasons from "doing a good deed" to doing something in line with their already-established social commitments, to personal identification with the lot of the homeless. One stylist often interacts with homeless people through her church, giving old clothes and serving food at holidays. But she never before had an opportunity to do so through her profession, and was very pleased that she did now. She said, "When people are going through changes like these women are, hair helps that process. Being able to *see* themselves in good shape on the outside again helps them believe it can also happen on the inside."

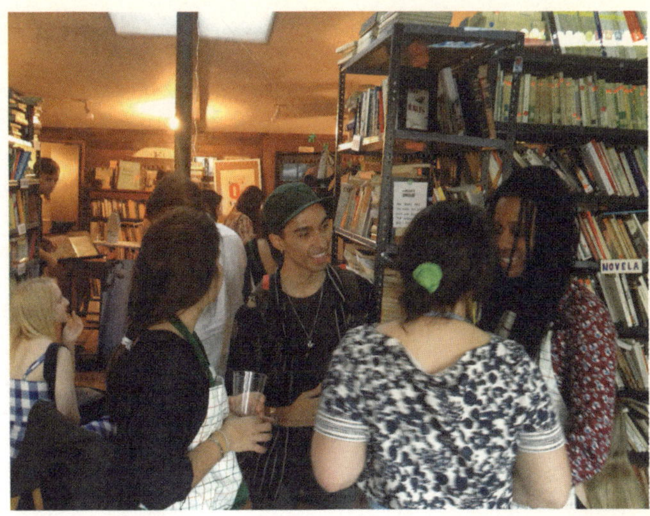

Pablo Helguera, ***Librería Donceles***, **2015.**

Persistent Questions

How do evaluators deal with the slow pace of social change? Community-based projects evaluator Chris Dwyer has noted indicators in cases when the full value of the work may not emerge for years:

- New relationships that are formed and existing ones that are strengthened, especially from boundary-crossing opportunities that the arts nurture so well;
- Overt recognition of stories and painful episodes previously unspoken;
- Public policy openings, even when not successful;
- New roles assumed by key players, whether formal or informal;
- Subtle shifts in power; and
- Involvement of the next circle of artists who can spark subsequent engagements with future issues.[5]

How does one evaluate a project whose manifestation changed radically from its original design? One fruitful approach is what's called Outcome Harvesting, beginning with what actually happened and working backwards to try to identify what led to those results.

How much must socially engaged artists know about the social context, issue, and basic organizing principles to be effective? So long as someone core to a project is knowledgeable about the social issue, the artist has some time to develop direct understanding. As field researcher Arnold Aprill pointed out, Reynolds' partners in her prison project include the incarcerated, formerly incarcerated, and their families; prison administrations and staff; legislators and their staffs; curators of exhibitions and conferences; and socially engaged and prison reform activists.

Where is a socially engaged project's spectatorial opportunity if it is fully inserted in everyday life? That is, how can the public experience a kind of art that they can't hang on their wall or see in an aesthetically marked venue? Some projects, like

5 Chris Dwyer. "Time Tested Tools for Evaluation," accessed at http://blog.artsusa.org/2012/05/02/time-tested-tools-for-evaluation/. 2012.

Helguera's bookstore and Cook's exhibits and clinics, issue public invitations. Sometimes a whole phase of a project is political activity, with no art produced. How can such work nonetheless be recognized as art? Appreciating the long time frame of much social practice is essential, but more experimentation needs to be done around this question.

While some artists, like Reynolds, work on the same social issue in the same place for many years, other artists change focus or location. How important is length of focus on one issue in one place vis-à-vis sustainability as regards social change? Wood noted that her satisfaction is seeing the relationships between clients and stylists. She cares most that it be an experience of physical care, not a "social service." Though successful in terms of numbers of people reached in its time frame and level of meaningfulness of the experience, Wood recognizes a tension in *Beauty in Transition* between the project as art and as client services. If the mobile salon becomes regularized to fit into schedules, it loses some of its power as art, which Wood described as a sense of "renewed energy in the unexpected."

Helguera's bookstore built a community of attendees in Red Hook who found meaning in a place celebrating the Spanish language and participatory events shaped by artists around the books. It closed, as planned, after six weeks. Perhaps someone else could revive it, though as one of Helguera's assistants said, the bookstore is much better when he's there because of his knowledge of and love for the books. Significantly, Helguera plans to open a bookstore in Chicago; other iterations of the bookstore took place in Phoenix, Miami, and San Francisco. He is manifesting the vision across the country, emphasizing range of places rather than duration.

Can initiatives like ABOG remove prejudice based on where art takes place? Too often, art outside aesthetic spaces and art districts of urban centers is categorically assumed to be of lesser worth. As Rosalba Rolon, artistic director of Pregones Theater, said about their 2014 extension from their home base in the south Bronx to a theater space in midtown Manhattan, many assumed the move was a step up. Yet to Rolon and her colleagues, it was a lateral move; they could expand their audiences but had no intention of forsaking their base community.[6] When the money that changes hands around art, the people it engages, and its location underpin assumptions of worth, we miss out on some of the most imaginative and useful expressivity around us.

Does it matter if participants know that the initiator is doing an art project? On the one hand, no. What matters are the social impact and the quality of the work, the experience for

6 Rosalba Rolon. Scholars Circle, Unpublished round table, New York: Puerto Rican Traveling Theatre, April 19, 2015.

participants, and the relationships that develop. On the other hand, knowing that such projects are art stretches understanding of its scope, for other artists, funders, policy makers, and the general public. That is where the contribution of appropriate evaluation may have the largest impact.

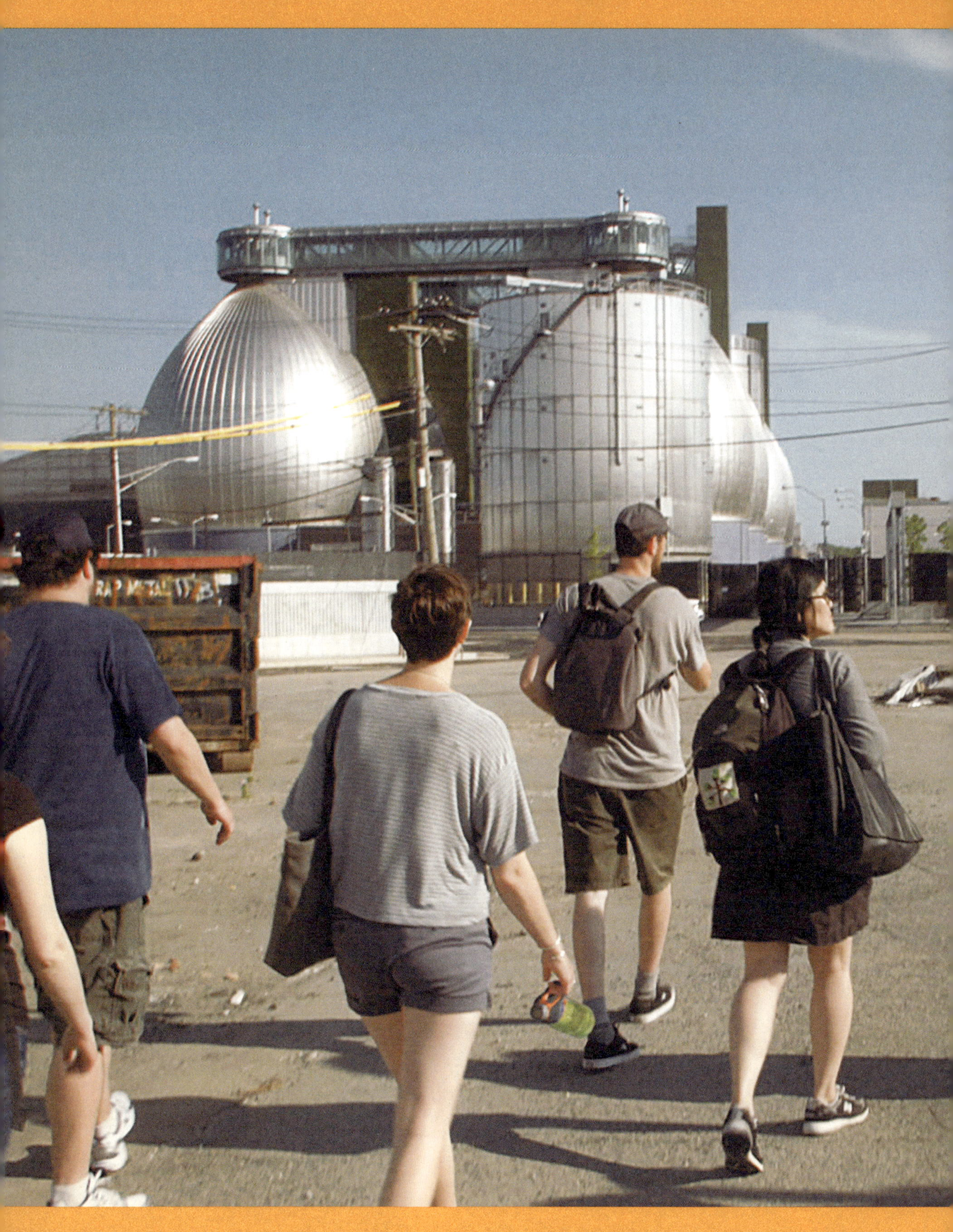

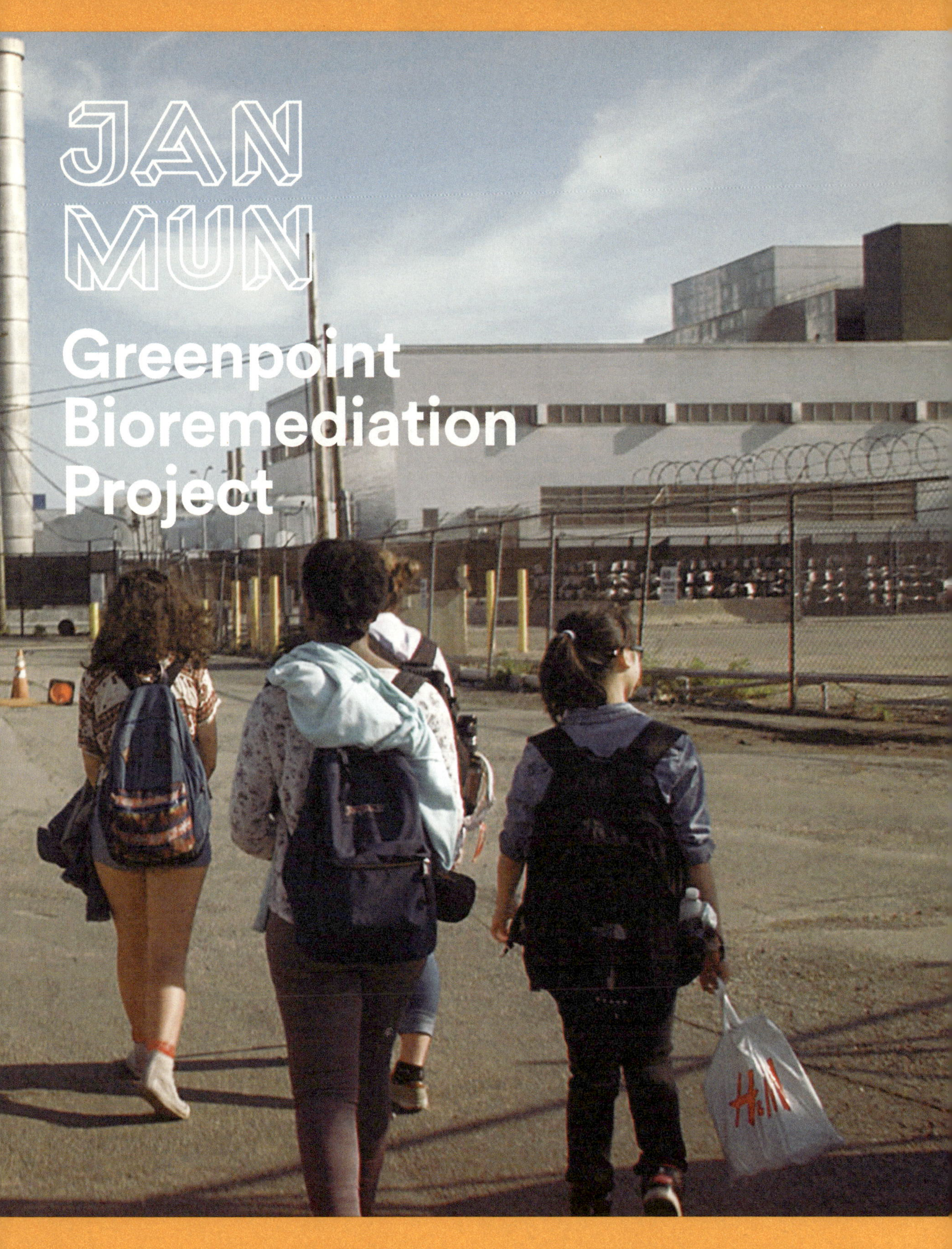
JAN
MUN
Greenpoint
Bioremediation
Project
H&M

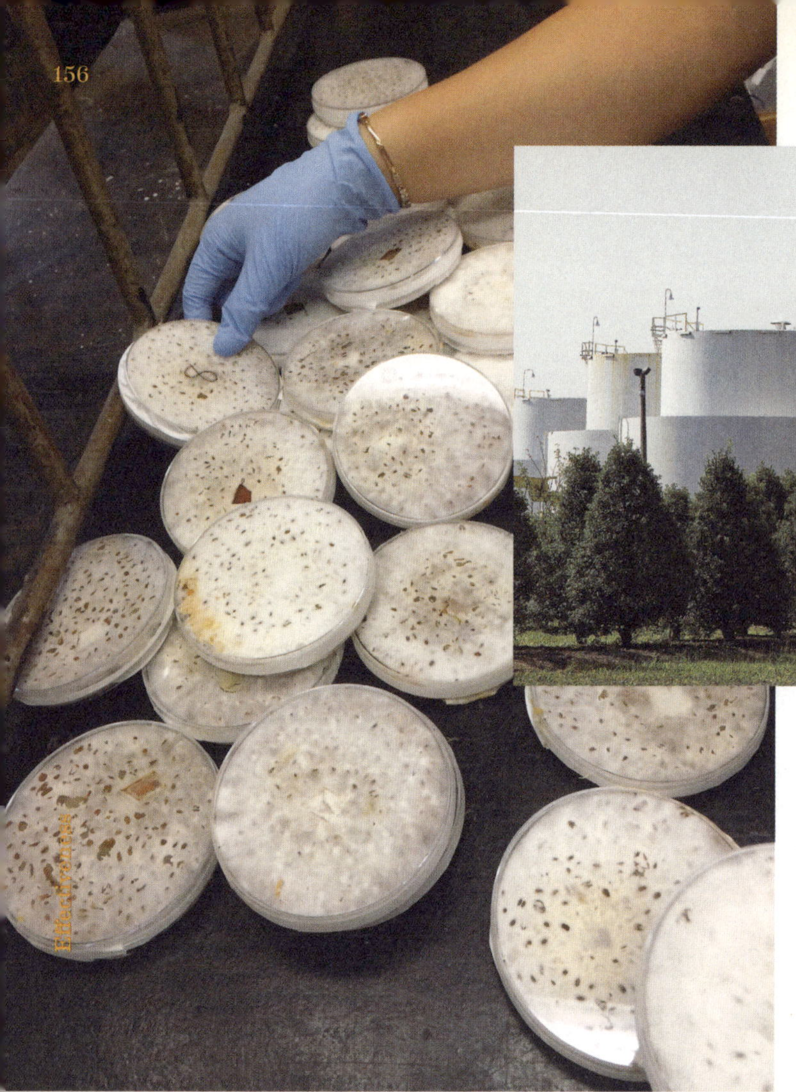

Previous spread: Jan Mun (with backpack, left of center) leading a tour of Greenpoint.

Left: Randomizing mycelium for research experiment, *Greenpoint Remediation Project*, 2014–15.

Right: View from the ExxonMobil Greenpoint Petroleum Remediation Project, Brooklyn.

Exploring Bioremediation in Brooklyn with Danielle Wagner

Joelle Te Paske in conversation with Danielle Wagner
April 30, 2015

In the past year, artist Jan Mun has developed her research of mushrooms' soil cleansing properties at the Environmental Science Analytical Center at Brooklyn College, which houses the only nonprofit soil lab in New York City. Danielle Wagner, who has a background in biochemistry, describes what it was like to collaborate with Jan and her core team of volunteer researchers.

Joelle Te Paske (ABOG)
How did you meet Jan and get involved in the project?

Danielle Wagner
I came to Brooklyn College to see if I could learn more about soil testing. As I was discussing available projects with Dr. Joshua Cheng, the head of the Environmental Services Analytical Center, he mentioned that an artist was working there with mushrooms to try to clean the soil. Whoa! I was instantly impressed, but didn't think I was qualified to work with such a rock star. By coincidence, the bioremediation group that Jan was coordinating was meeting that very day, so I thought it would be great to see what was happening with the mushrooms. As soon as I entered the classroom and showed interest, Jan said, "Let's see how handy you are," and recruited me to help make a filter for a mushroom mycelia demonstration bag.

The oil spill in Greenpoint, Brooklyn, discovered in 1978 and still little-known outside the borough, rivals that of the infamous Exxon Valdez disaster. Over several decades, sites owned by companies later acquired by ExxonMobil leaked an estimated 17–30 million gallons of oil and petroleum products into the soil. Controversy over the means, method and extent of cleanup led to rancor between the company and the community. In 2010, ExxonMobil agreed to pay $25 million through a legal settlement, and additionally has cleaned up 9 million gallons to date under the supervision of the New York State Department of Environmental Conservation. But there's still a long way to go. Jan Mun's *Greenpoint Bioremediation Project* was conceived in collaboration with community organizations to provide safe, immediate do-it-yourself (DIY) detoxification solutions that can be implemented on a backyard scale.

A couple of years ago, Mun began working as an artist-in-residence with the Newtown Creek Alliance (NCA). The Newtown Creek watershed that separates Queens and Brooklyn is located squarely in the affected area of the spill and its seepage, or "plume." With NCA, Mun developed a proposal for ExxonMobil that demonstrated mycoremediation—using mushroom mycelium (the vegetative, non-fruiting part of the fungus) to clean toxins from surface soil. Certain fungi and microbes absorb heavy metals like mercury, and break down petrochemicals into less harmful compounds. As an artist, Mun gained rare access to ExxonMobil's carefully secured petroleum remediation site. There, she created a living sculpture called *The Fairy Rings* in which mushrooms were planted in circles, mimicking the natural growth patterns of certain fungi. Program Manager of the Newtown Creek Alliance, Willis Elkins, in an interview with Jan Cohen-Cruz, said of the experience:

> Her work with mushrooms, described as art, doesn't need to meet the same standards and quality assurance as a science initiative, so [it] can be a demonstration

From there I talked with the group about the project and decided that it was an honor to be involved. I went every week, mostly as an observer. I was too new to the world of mycoremediation in Newtown Creek to participate in the discussion. Eventually, Jan asked me to help tie it all together by playing the scientific role as lead research designer in the project. Looking back, it makes a lot of sense that I ended up having this role.

ABOG
Had you worked with other artists before?

DW
In my sociology courses in college I worked with a few artists in group projects. The way the tides were rolling was similar to this project, in that I don't have a creative mindset, so they were able to bring something to the presentation that I would never have thought of. In other words, my thoughts tend to be very focused on completing a task at hand, and by working with such souls I learned that even though certain topics might not directly address the question at hand, they can help round out the project and establish the importance of it.

A few weeks ago, Jan gave each of us a Petri dish with drying mycelia and said, "Do something with it by next week." It had nothing to do with mycoremediation. Or did it? Since another project I am working on involves gypsum [a mineral composed of calcium sulfate], I decided to add some gypsum to the mycelia. Usually when you are working with fungi on Petri dishes, they have to satisfy two conditions: lack of contamination, or else they must compete with other microbes; and a food source. As I was preparing Petri dishes with gypsum and fluffy mycelia, I didn't add any food, and I was breathing all over my samples, adding contamination. Unexpectedly, the mycelia grew well and without visible contaminants. We can only speculate why, but it was very project and can lead to conversations about what is possible without going through the long process of getting all the permissions before you can do anything.

In this case, art opened up a space for investigation and communication between the NCA and ExxonMobil, who now enjoy a working relationship. Mun continues to be in dialogue with Exxon staff, who are similarly interested in minimally invasive, sustainable, inexpensive remediation methods. Artist, Newtown Creek historian, and community activist Mitch Waxman has written:

> ExxonMobil is very security conscious, with a big wall around [their remediation site], such that people who walk past it are very put off. So Jan getting in, and working with ExxonMobil, directly in touch with site managers, created a conversation and relationship that has continued. Now EM is less adversarial to community members ...

Armed with the knowledge that fungi could remediate soil polluted by industrial contamination, Mun set out to see if the mycelium could work in Greenpoint. Although the project has specific remediation goals, Mun has no illusions about being able to clean up the entirety of one of history's largest toxic spills on her own. Instead, using art as a vehicle for exploration and conversation, she has been able to forge new connections, and build surprising bridges of communication between ExxonMobil and advocacy groups in the affected area, making room for NCA and Exxon to work together on remediation strategies. Just as fungus permeates the soil in an ecosystem, helping roots to bind, use and exchange nutrients, Mun's project identifies common ground where historic opponents can find ways to work together.

In pursuing the project, Jan was sought out by Dr. Zhongqi "Joshua" Cheng, Chair of the Department of Earth and Environmental Sciences at Brooklyn College, who was interested in working with communities. He had the expertise to help her in her

interesting because it showed the importance of gypsum. It did lead us to research it more, and I am still thinking of future projects that I can do with it.

ABOG
How do you interpret the project as art? Do you? Is it helpful to think about it as art?

DW
The word "art" scares me, actually. I try not to interpret anything as art. As a nerd, I did look up the definition, and art includes "works to be appreciated primarily for their beauty or emotional power." The beautiful thing about this project is that it seeks to bring justice to an area that has been dirtied because of neglect. I think that one of the ways it differs from a science project is that Jan is consistent in working on an issue she wants to see solved, instead of following the path where there is money.

ABOG
Do you think research, design and art are interrelated? How so, in your experience?

DW
I think research, design and art can be related, but it takes a certain kind of culture to make them be that way. If design isn't involved in either research or art, the projects will go a completely different way. For example, one can have a goal to solve a certain problem, but there are many ways of investigating—guess and check, variable isolation, endless reading, and theoretical speculation. In the end, it's hard to fathom doing something without designing your next step, if even a millisecond before it's carried out. As long as we are thinking or moving we are designing, and as long as we are carrying out research or art we must be thinking or moving, right?

ABOG
If you had to pick one moment from working on *GBP* that has been especially

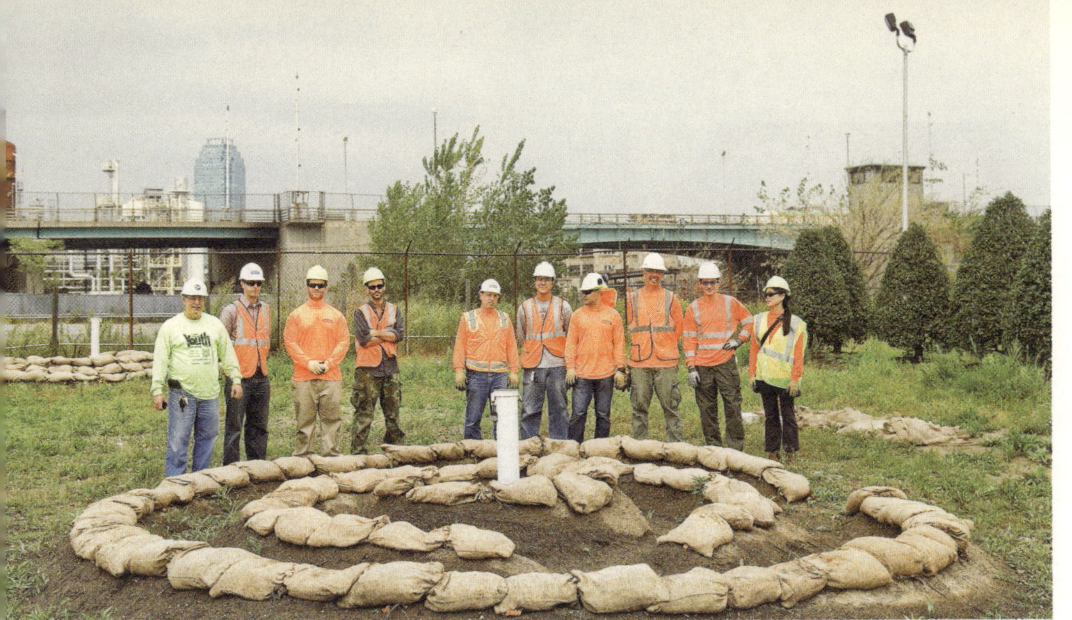

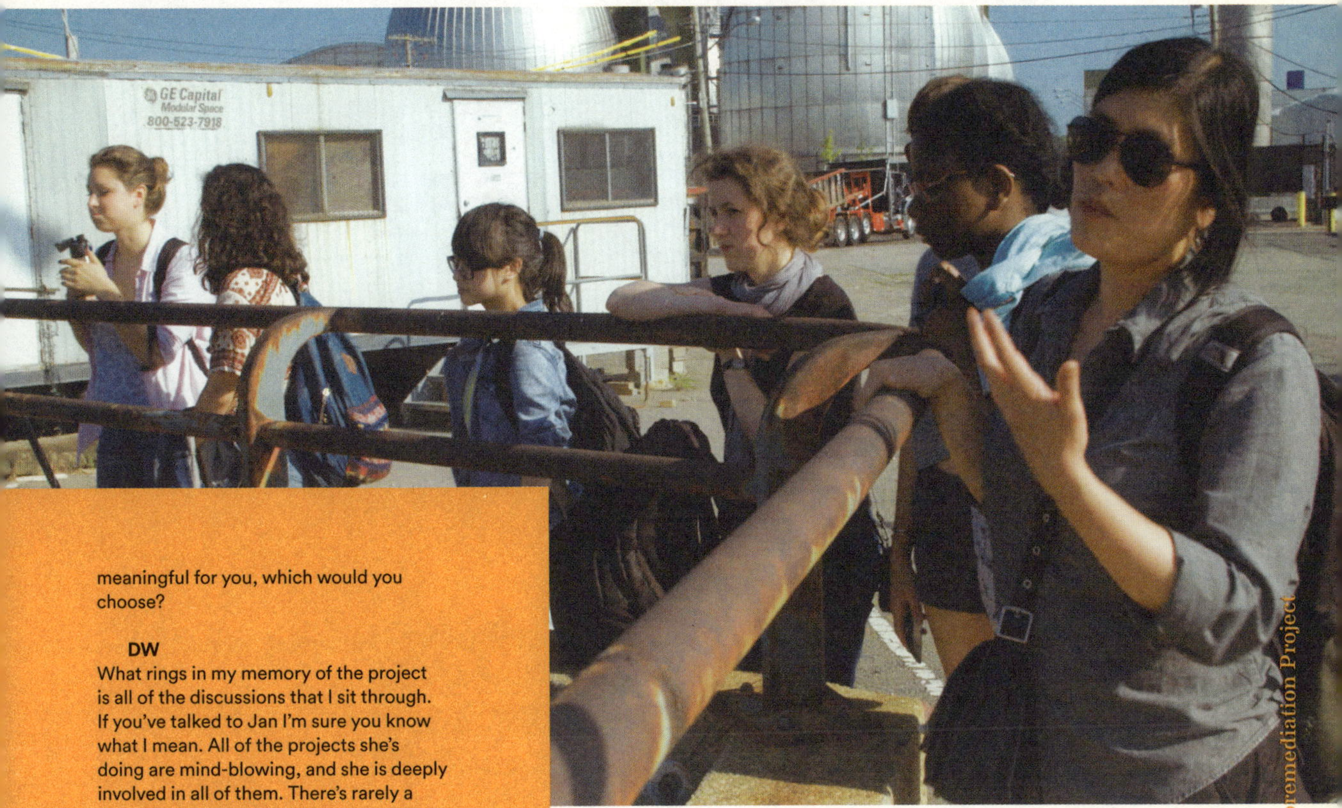

meaningful for you, which would you choose?

DW
What rings in my memory of the project is all of the discussions that I sit through. If you've talked to Jan I'm sure you know what I mean. All of the projects she's doing are mind-blowing, and she is deeply involved in all of them. There's rarely a discussion that ends in "I don't know," but usually an insight into something important or incredibly interesting.

Top: Tour for staff and engineers at *The Fairy Rings* at ExxonMobil Greenpoint Petroleum Remediation Project.

Bottom: Jan Mun leading a tour, *Greenpoint Bioremediation Project*, 2015.

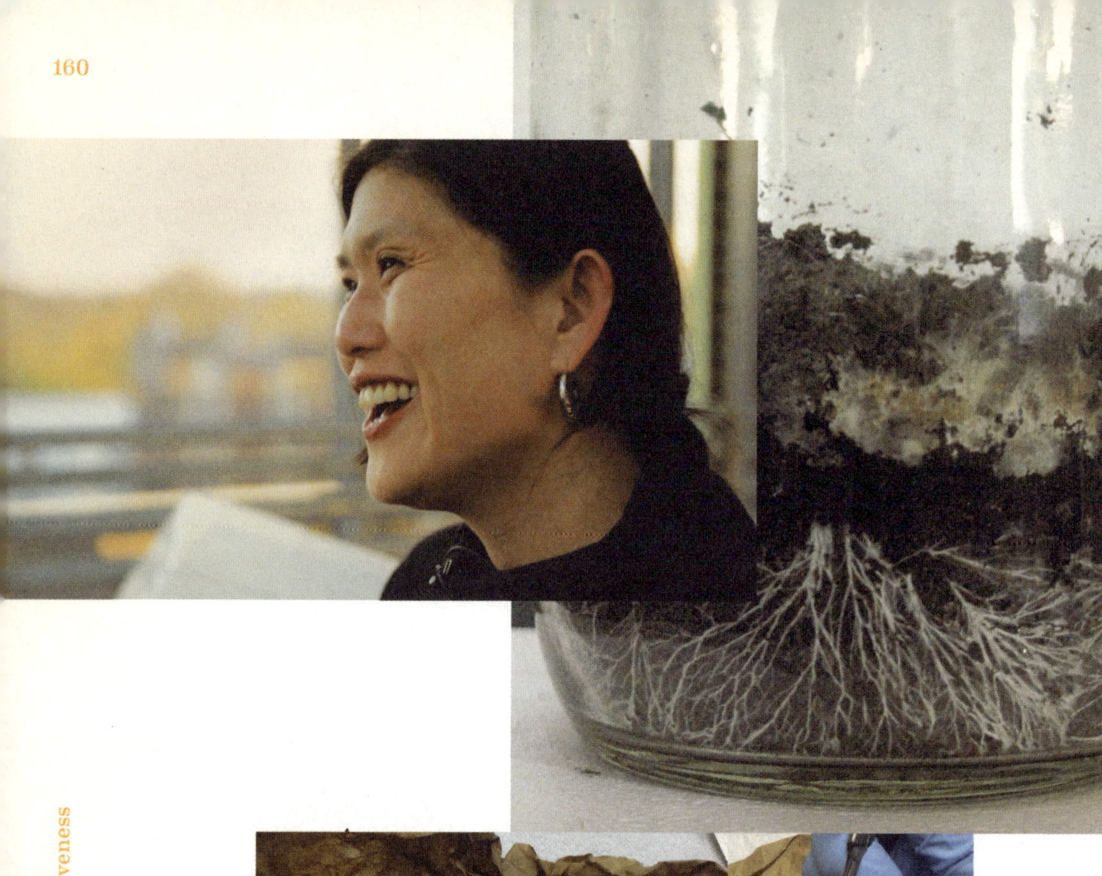

This page, clockwise from top left: Jan Mun.

Mycelium cultivation.

Mushroom tissue culture cloning.

Opposite page: Research Assistant Danielle Wagner, *Greenpoint Bioremediation Project*.

quest to find testing and DIY remediation methods local residents could use in their yards. Working with Dr. Cheng and his students, Mun developed a research project to identify beneficial microorganisms, contaminants in the soil, and test the effectiveness of mycoremediation in a lab experiment that could later be implemented in the field. In working with the scientists, Mun initially found that the data yielded by the experiments was presented in a way that was illegible to lay people, so she is working with lab staff to make the results useful to community members who send samples in to be tested for a small fee. The initiative benefitted Brooklyn College by contributing to their soil sample database, part of a broader mapping project of the soil makeup of Brooklyn. Thus the artist's input is becoming a conduit between hard science and community members.

Mun, with the help of high school students and volunteers at Brooklyn College, had access to a well-equipped lab and instruction in scientific methods of experimentation. This ad hoc workforce has since been testing the properties and effectiveness of various mushroom strains to see what will work best on the contaminants in local soil. Students have gone on to use their work with Mun to support applications to top college programs, with considerable success.

Part of *Greenpoint Bioremediation Project*'s strategy has also been to facilitate contact between activists, scientists, and community organizations, in order to share resources. Since beginning work with the Newtown Creek Alliance, Mun has become intimately familiar with local needs. She regularly attends meetings, and has managed to build a great deal of trust, even as her focus continues to be on the environmental concerns of the area's residents. As an art project, its ability to continue to forge and mediate previously unthinkable conversations is remarkable, just as its potential to make a real impact in the lives of Greenpoint residents remains promising. In the end, the foundation of trust she has woven into an ecosystem of communication and resources will ensure the long-term sustainability of the important work she has only just begun.

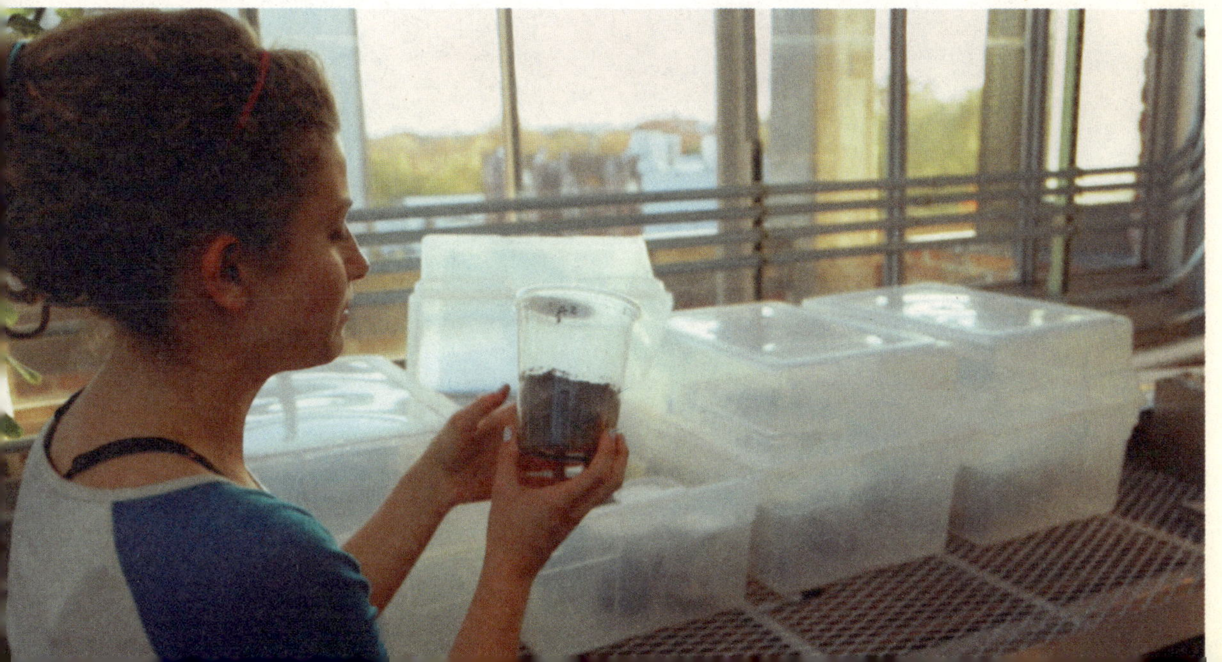

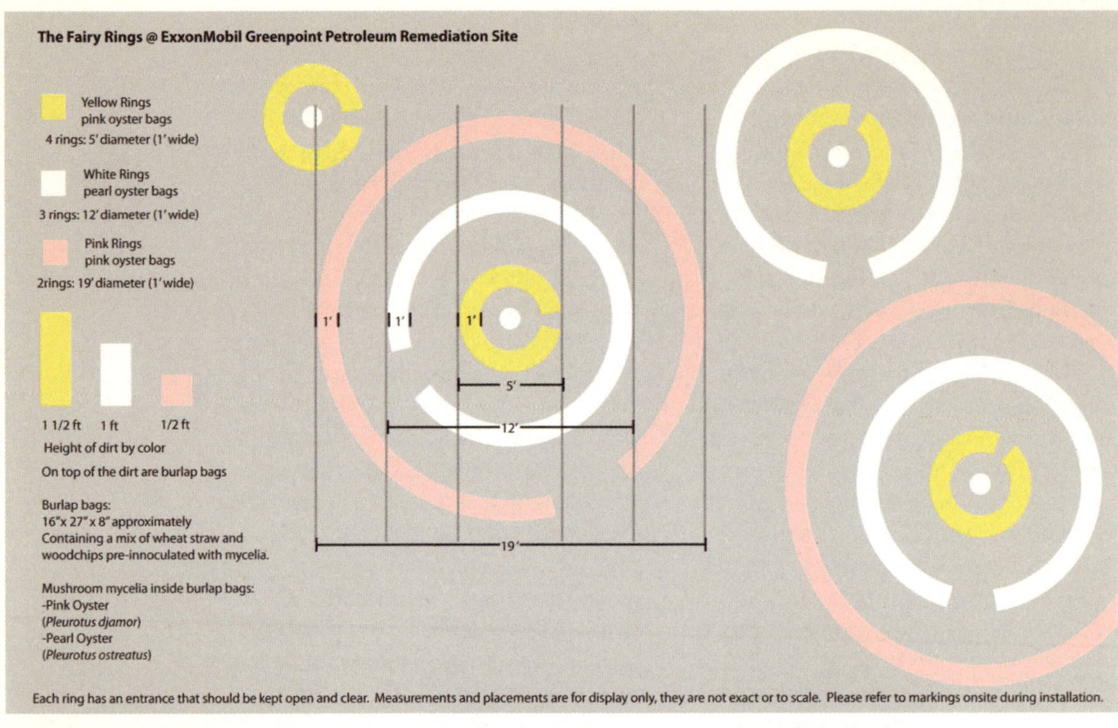

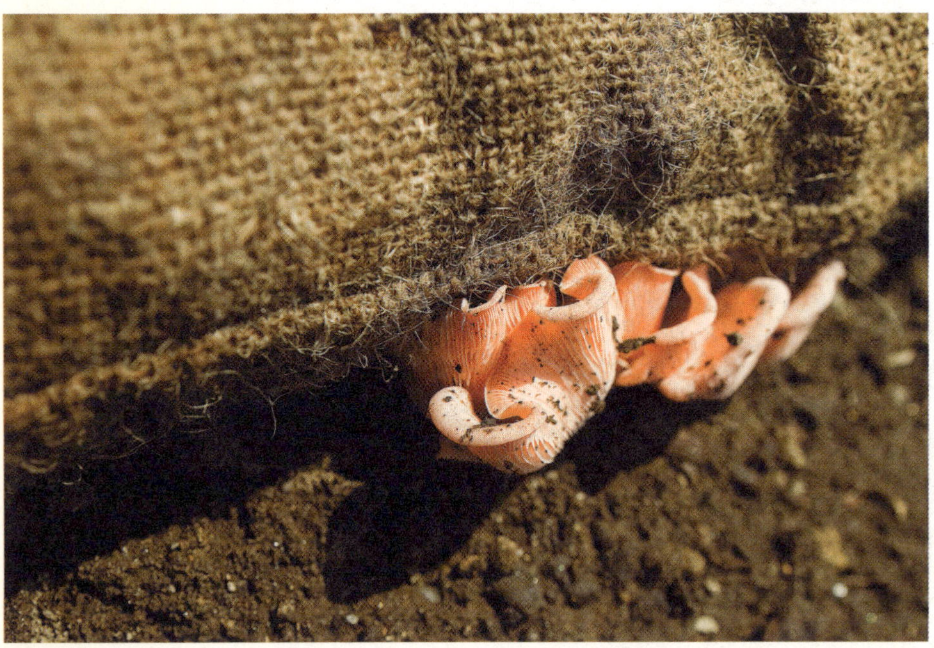

Top: Chart illustrating *The Fairy Rings* project.

Bottom: Mushroom growth.

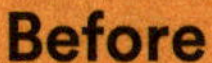

Before

Prior to Jan Mun's project, the Exxon site in Greenpoint Brooklyn was shut off from the community—literally surrounded by a giant wall.

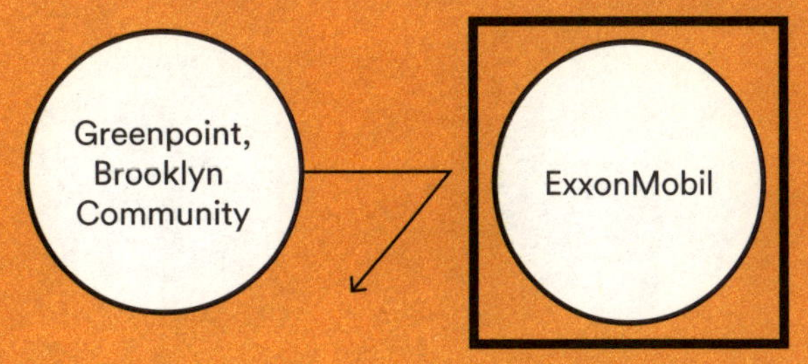

After

Greenpoint now has a healthy relationship with the oil company in its neighborhood.

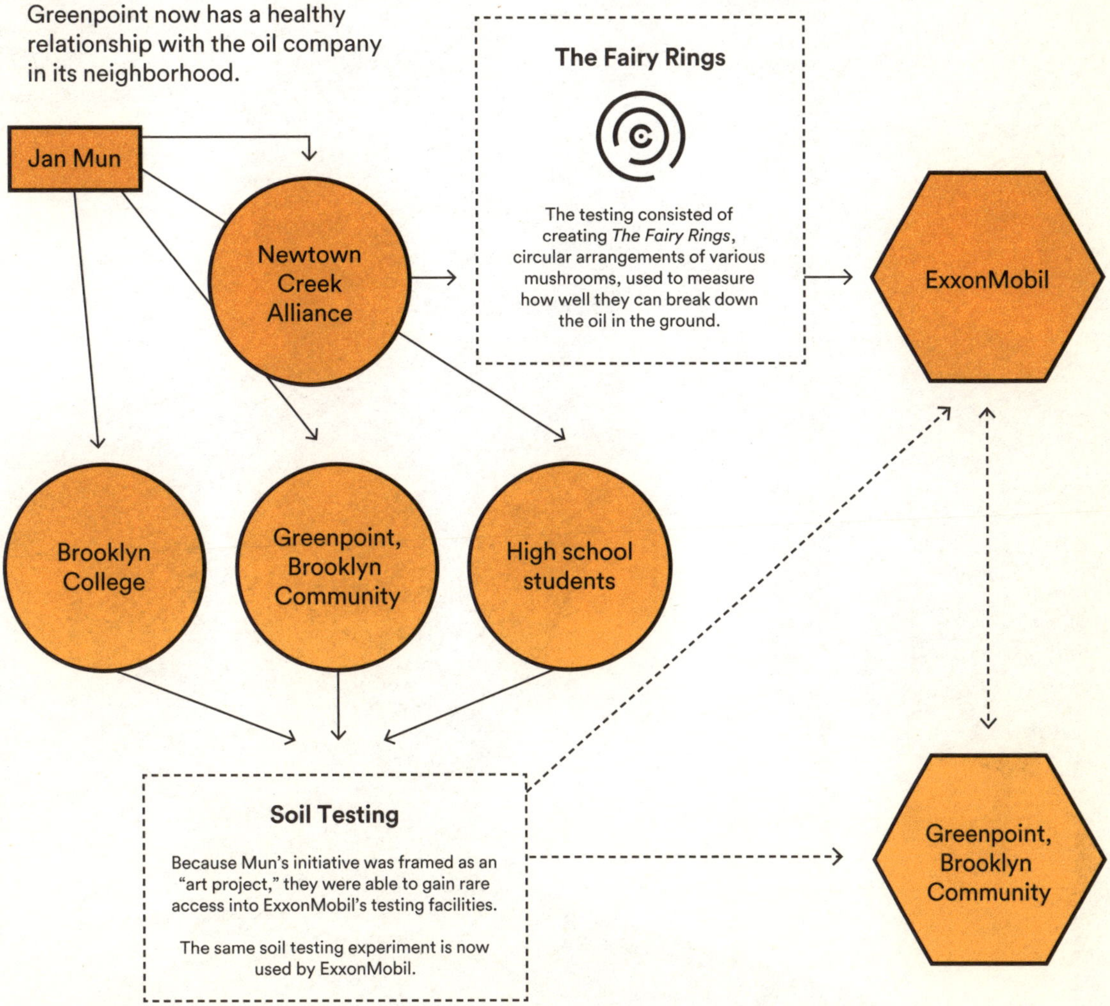

Jan Mun

Newtown Creek Alliance

The Fairy Rings

The testing consisted of creating *The Fairy Rings*, circular arrangements of various mushrooms, used to measure how well they can break down the oil in the ground.

ExxonMobil

Brooklyn College

Greenpoint, Brooklyn Community

High school students

Soil Testing

Because Mun's initiative was framed as an "art project," they were able to gain rare access into ExxonMobil's testing facilities.

The same soil testing experiment is now used by ExxonMobil.

Greenpoint, Brooklyn Community

Key: Artist | Stakeholder | Action | Antagonist/ transformed stakeholder

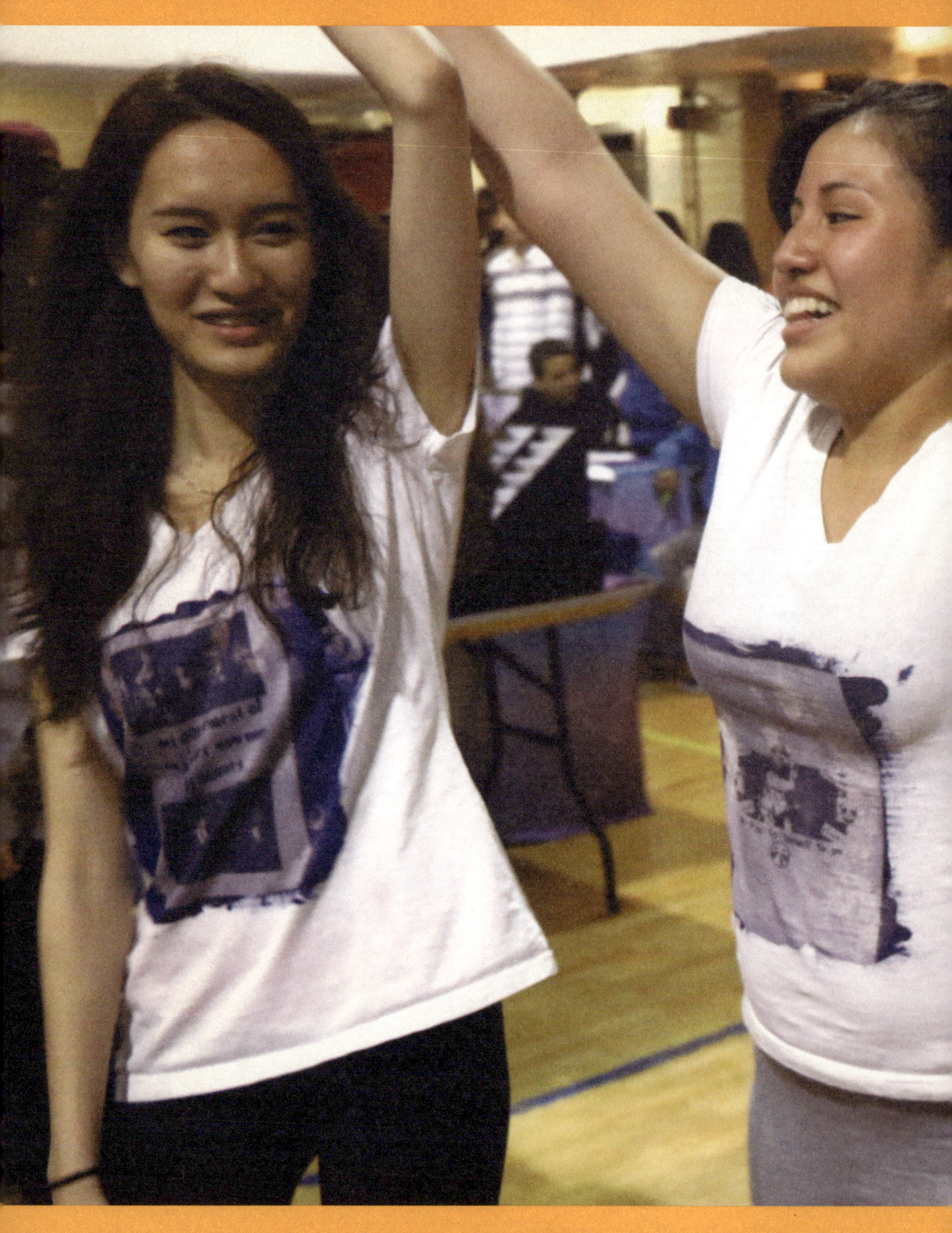

NORENE LEDDY & LIZ SLAGUS

SexEd: Wearing Consent

Remember squirming in health class as your wincingly awkward gym teacher tried to talk to you about where babies come from? As though you didn't already know? Most of us have high school sex education experiences that range from embarrassing to downright useless. Luckily for the students of Washington Irving High School Campus [WIHSC] in New York, there's another option. Liz Slagus and Norene Leddy, better known as the art collective SexEd, have found a way to use art instruction to make sex education fun and engaging, as they work with teens to consider issues beyond the usual "dos", "don'ts", potential infections and mechanics that so inadequately address the roiling hormones and drama-laced emotions of a teenager.

Norene Leddy and Liz Slagus met while Leddy was in residence at Eyebeam Art + Technology Center in New York. There, they discovered a common interest in women's empowerment around sexuality when working together on Leddy's *Project Walkway*, which taught high school girls how to hack their shoes with technology to create portable alarms and other useful wearable devices. They got to talking about the less than stellar sex education that most people receive, and wondered if similar art workshops could supplement the standard curriculum and raise questions about issues like pleasure and consent. Thus was born the SexEd collective.

Drawing on their experience working with high school girls, they sought out schools with staff that might be amenable to working with them, and were pointed toward Washington Irving. WIHSC is a complex of six schools near Union Square, where students have the benefit of access to a nonprofit in-house health center that is administered independently from the NYC Department of Education system. The health center offers free care, which includes but is not limited to reproductive health. Though heavily burdened with a large workload, the center's director, Caitlin Hanson, was open to SexEd's ideas, and predisposed toward any programming that could accrue additional resources toward the wellness of WIHSC students. She

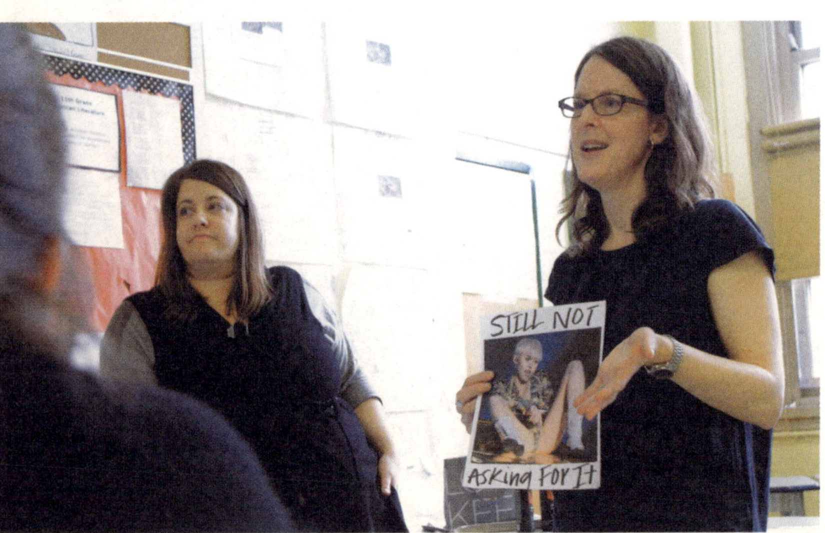

Previous spread: Student participants modeling their work at the SexEd Salon at Washington Irving High School.

Left: Liz Slagus and Norene Leddy.

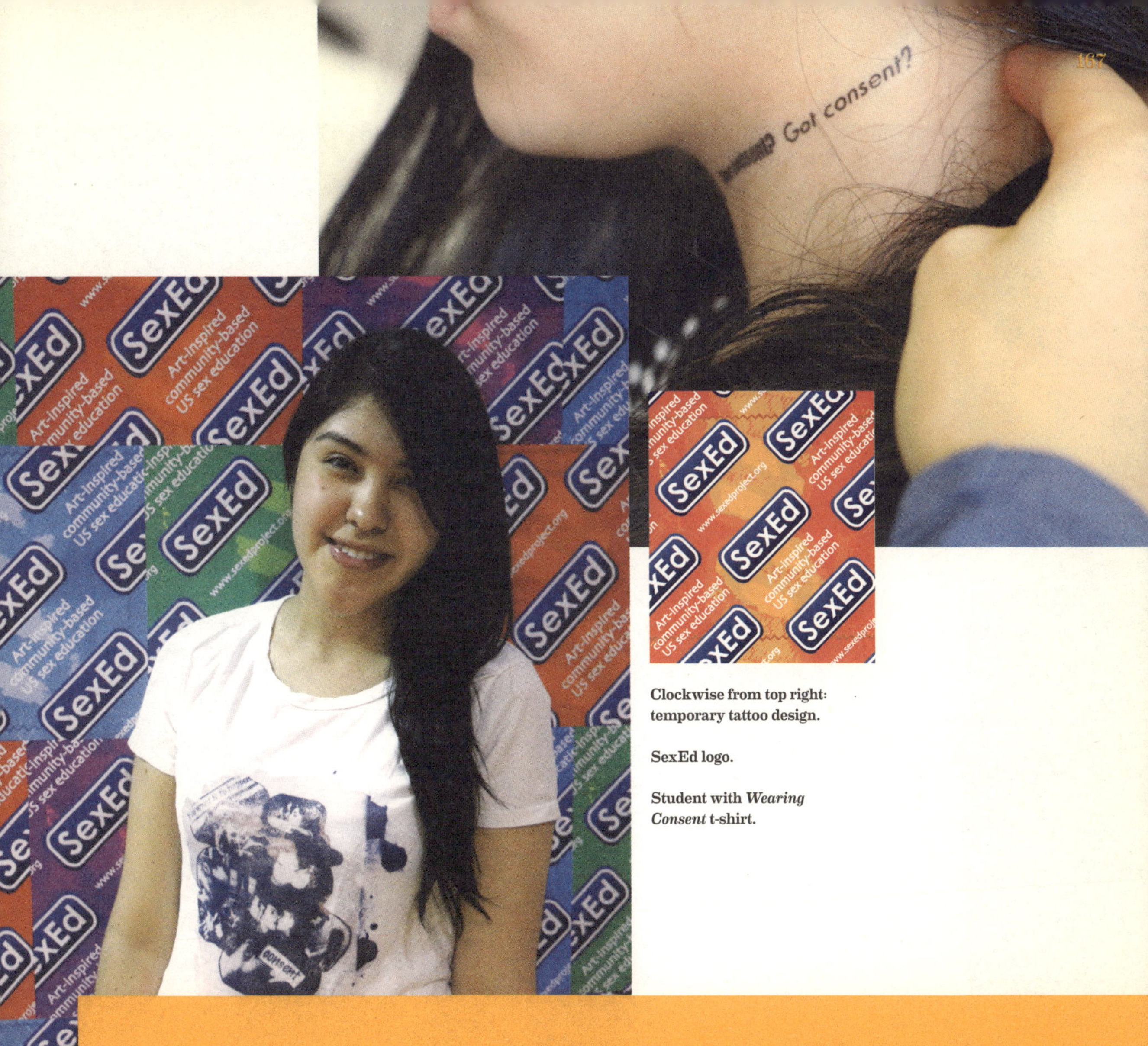

Clockwise from top right: temporary tattoo design.

SexEd logo.

Student with *Wearing Consent* t-shirt.

Wearing Consent: Educators on SexEd

Elizabeth M. Grady in conversation with Caitlin Hanson, Cory Silverberg and Bryana Williams
May 12, 2015

2014 ABOG Fellows Norene Leddy and Liz Slagus, also known as SexEd, have been collaborating on developing radical pedagogies that combine art, reproductive health, and participatory tools since 2008. On May 12, 2015, they shared their experiences of initiating an arts-based sexual health curriculum at Washington Irving High School Campus in New York City in a live panel discussion hosted by ABOG, along with project collaborators Caitlin Hanson, Cory Silverberg, and Bryana Williams. Excerpts from the discussion highlighting this collaboration are reprinted below.

Elizabeth M. Grady (ABOG)
How did you come to work with Norene and Liz on this project? What inspired you to be a part of SexEd?

Cory Silverberg
One of the things I'm very interested in is the question of who becomes a sex educator. Sex education is a weird career—it's not clear how one gets into it. There are two advanced degree programs in the US, but other than that, how one becomes a sex educator is a weird road. For years I certified sex educators, and I was getting emails from hundreds of people who wanted to be sex educators and wanted to know how to do it. There isn't one way

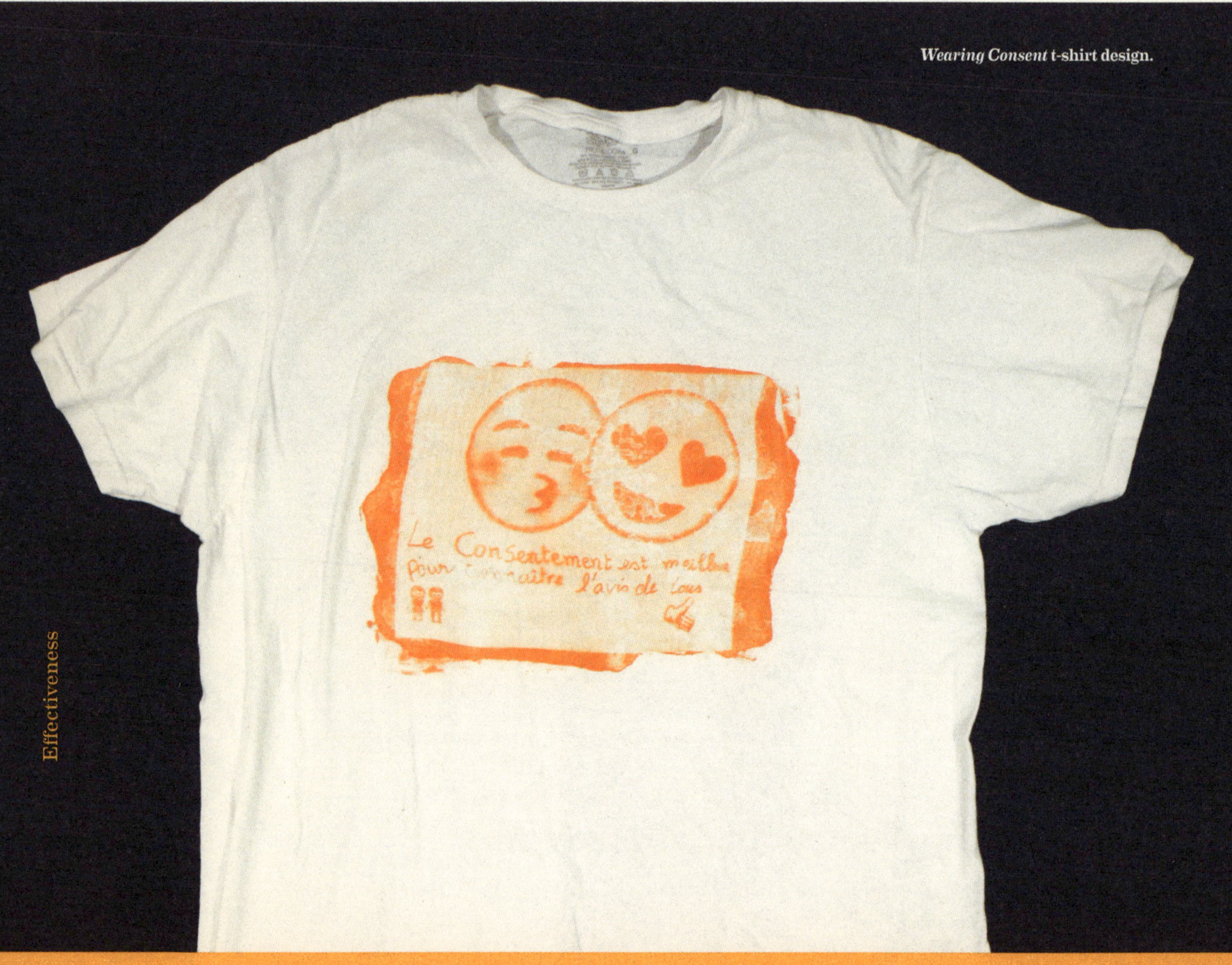

Wearing Consent t-shirt design.

to do it. I had worked in sex stores since I was 16 years old. When feminist sex stores began in the early 1970s, a lot of people who worked there felt like they were doing more than just selling vibrators and dildos. They felt like they were educating.

It was really interesting for me when Liz and Norene described what they were doing, in that they're artists and educators but they're not sex educators. That was one of my main interests in the project: who gets to go in and start conversations and what do those conversations look like? I'm concerned about how sex education is incredibly white, and it's incredibly medical, so all the conversations that flow out of that are white and medical. And when you're going into a school where the majority of the students are not white—and probably not doctors!—what comes out of it? I think that the idea of starting with something that's framed as art as opposed to some kind of educational curriculum is more interesting.

Caitlin Hanson

As a small school-based health center with limited funding, we're always looking for community expertise to bring in to enrich the programs we provide. A big part of this project has been about starting conversations, and that's absolutely what it does just to be around these inspiring people.

The school-based health center is a full-service primary care office located inside the school building, so we have a unique opportunity to get to know the students as students rather than just as our patients. We see them in the classroom, we see them interacting with their friends and with their teachers. We're not part of the Department of Education; we're an independent, federally-qualified, nonprofit community health center, so technically our zone is not a Department of Education space, and we can do a lot more.

Teens in New York City have decent rights when it comes to reproductive health care. They can make any type of worked with Leddy and Slagus to build trust with principals to allow SexEd to develop and run workshops during lunchtime and after school.

Leddy and Slagus developed a curriculum that was designed to build on issues of interest to students; a bottom-up approach that reverses the usual process of the New York City Department of Education. Working with students and facilitator Bryana Williams, they identified topics that were not generally covered in standard classes, and offered a number of suggestions. The students chose to address the question of what consent is and means. SexEd organized workshops that explored the question, asking teens to define the word for themselves. One challenge they faced was the multilingual context of the International High School at WIHSC; there were seven languages spoken by their group, and several people spoke little or no English. In an interesting twist, this led to heightened communication between the students, as they translated for one another and came up with definitions of consent in each of the seven languages. The potential of the process is clear: by translating the work of this core group, Leddy and Slagus suddenly acquired the potential to reach out into multiple immigrant communities, as workshop participants brought the fruits of their labor home.

Once a definition of consent was arrived at, SexEd worked with students on a number of wearable products that the young people could make to express their ideas. Using digital imagery sourced online, workshop participants created collages that were made into t-shirt designs. Their words were transformed into temporary tattoos, fingernail decals and stickers for the project, titled *Wearing Consent*. The students' work was displayed at the annual WIHSC Health Fair, which this year took on the guise of a beauty salon. Classes throughout the school were invited to attend, resulting in an audience of hundreds for the work. Not only did workshop participants have the benefit of working with SexEd, but the school as a whole had the opportunity to learn about consent and have fun with the idea. Indeed, the event was

reproductive health decision that they want to (without parental consent) and it's completely legal. That's what we're there to help them do, as a part of their general healthcare. We're also there to make sure the students in the building are healthy enough to engage in their education. Think about sitting in the class, not being able to see the board, or with a toothache, or terrified that you're pregnant. There's no way you're going to learn in those types of situations.

Bryana Williams
I began working with Norene and Liz through the school-based health center and also as the in-class health educator. I get to do a lot of going into the classes, developing curriculum, helping out at the after-school programs, and meeting with the students in the cafeteria. There is so much awesomeness embodied in these beautiful people, who are each unique and blooming flowers [*laughs*]. I get questions every day walking through the halls. Someone will come up to me and say:

"Miss, I think I did something ... I had sex yesterday."

"Okay, how was it? Did you enjoy it? Was it good?"

"Oh, um ... yeah."

That's an interaction right there. I get to spend a lot of time with the students engaging with them in whatever environment is best for them. Sometimes it's in an elevator, sometimes it's in their PE classes, but it's always fun—even more so with Liz and Norene, now especially that the students get to make stuff instead of having people talk at them all day.

CS
For people who have some kind of formal sex education in their school, it is usually someone just talking to you. That's one of the exciting things about the idea of doing something and making art. Sex education is often designed to be boring because it's not appropriate to have fun when you're talking about sex with young people—which in some ways is true, because there

clearly popular and enjoyable for the students.

Critical to the success of the work of Leddy and Slagus was the process of co-creating the art with students. Teens are notoriously suspicious of the motivations of adults, so it was a significant challenge to find a way to communicate so that they would not only listen, but have fun with a topic as prickly as sex education. Using the participants' own words and ideas as the basis for the work was not only a way to give them a sense of ownership, but ensured that the language and approach was accessible to other students, and "cool" enough that they would pay attention. This kind of shared authorship is outside the norm of many artists' practice, but here the success of the process illustrates the way that it made the art itself more compelling and effective.

Ultimately, Leddy and Slagus would like to see their process adopted as part of a district-wide health curriculum. They passionately believe that intervention during the sensitive but pivotal teen years can lead to emotional and physical health benefits that last a lifetime. It is striking that it requires the guise of art to move beyond a clinical approach and teach basic emotional intelligence. They have already reached out to other schools, and participated in conferences and other, more informal forums of the national sex education community. They hope that, in the end, the work will transcend art and pass into school systems nationwide, becoming part of a broader dialogue where art is only one approach in the toolbox of sex education teachers.

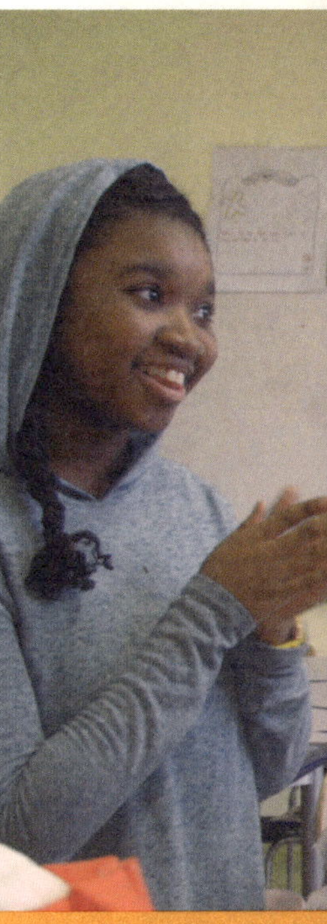

are boundaries—but getting to make art can be fun and appropriate.

ABOG
What's been the most meaningful moment to you so far in the process of working through this long-term art project?

BW
There are so many moments, with so many different students. One of my favorites happened during class. We work at an international high school, which is challenging because there are seven different languages in one room. When you're speaking English and the person in front of you only understands Spanish, and the person sitting next to them only understands French, you say something and just hope and pray that they'll get it, which is hard.

But the students took on the role of translator without me even having to ask them, for people who they might or might not have been friends with. And not just once, as in, "Oh, the definition ...", but consistently. Translating the directions, and translating back if someone at their table said something, without my asking them.

The students were so proactive in helping each other and getting the message across that it made me think, "If this is what they're doing in front of me right here in class, what else are they going to be doing with this information at home with their families, with their siblings?" Which brings into play that this is not just a single conversation that they're having with us, but that they're having it among themselves.

CH
I think that's what we concentrated on from the beginning. There is value in starting these conversations with no intention of doing any kind of follow-up research to find out where those conversations went, how many kids went to class and how many times. We put the value on the importance of starting these

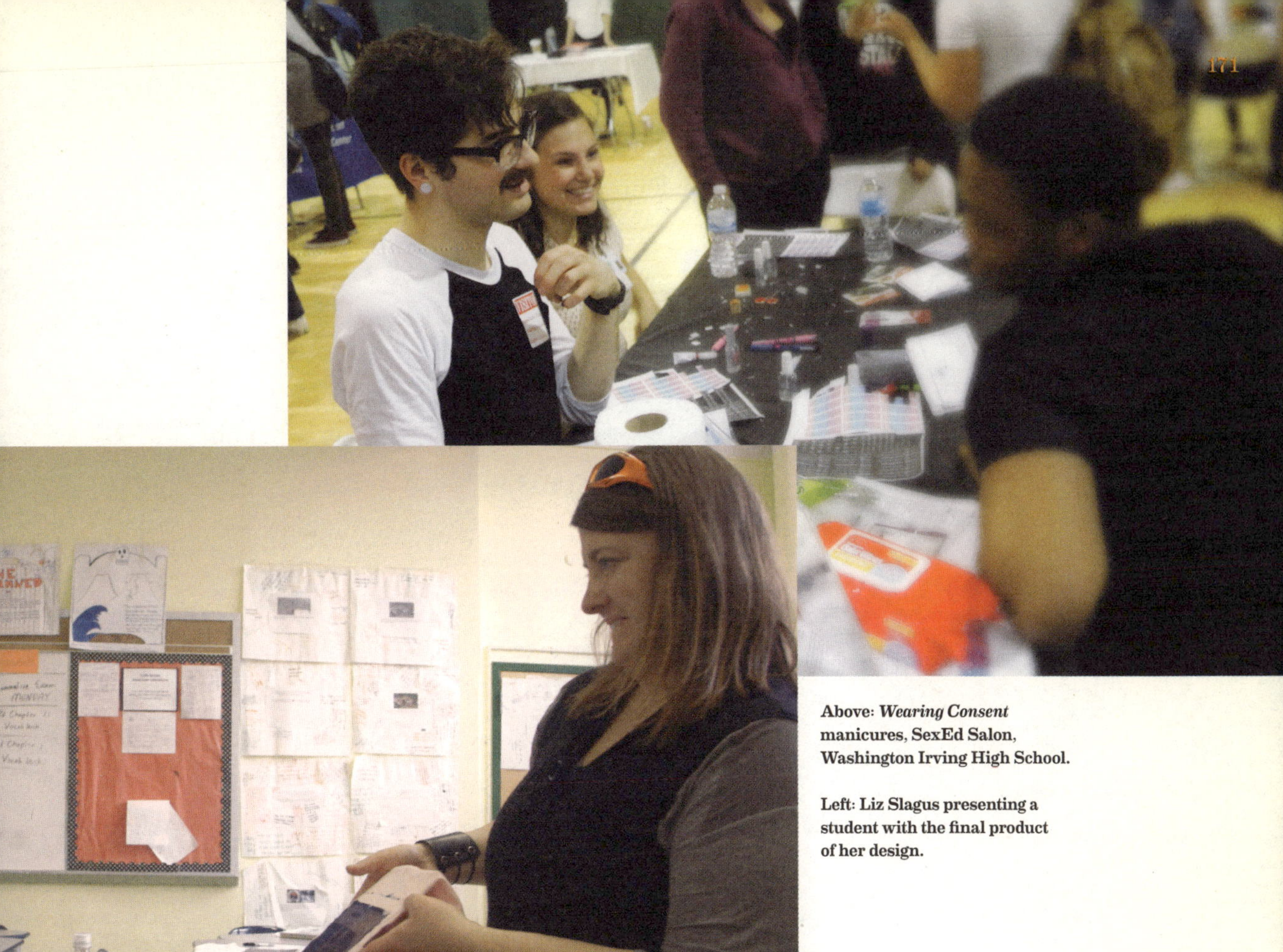

Above: ***Wearing Consent*** **manicures, SexEd Salon, Washington Irving High School.**

Left: Liz Slagus presenting a student with the final product of her design.

conversations, to see where they go, to let them go wherever the kids want them to go and to see all these light bulbs turning on over the course of the project.

CS
For me, the thing that was most exciting was they just did it. [*Laughter*] No, really, sex education is not very glamorous and really it's hard to go into a room and talk to a bunch of people about sex. And if they're different in any way it's even harder, so I was just happy that Norene and Liz did it. I often volunteer to help consult with projects and then people don't do it—because it's too scary, or because they can't get in or they can't get through the red tape.

But I'll say, one of my best moments was also just hearing Caitlin and Bryana talking, because one of the problems I have with so much sex education is that it is about the goal. It's that, "We're going to prove that 22% of students are going to use condoms 6 months longer than they would have, etc. ... " And it is all these nonprofits that are really just about keeping themselves funded and doing curriculum that is not helping students. Whereas we got to do something where actually we *weren't* saying, "This is the goal." The goal of the project was to have the conversation and to just let it go out there, which I think is one of the radical things about it—unfortunately, because that's what it should always be about.

Wearing Consent t-shirt design.

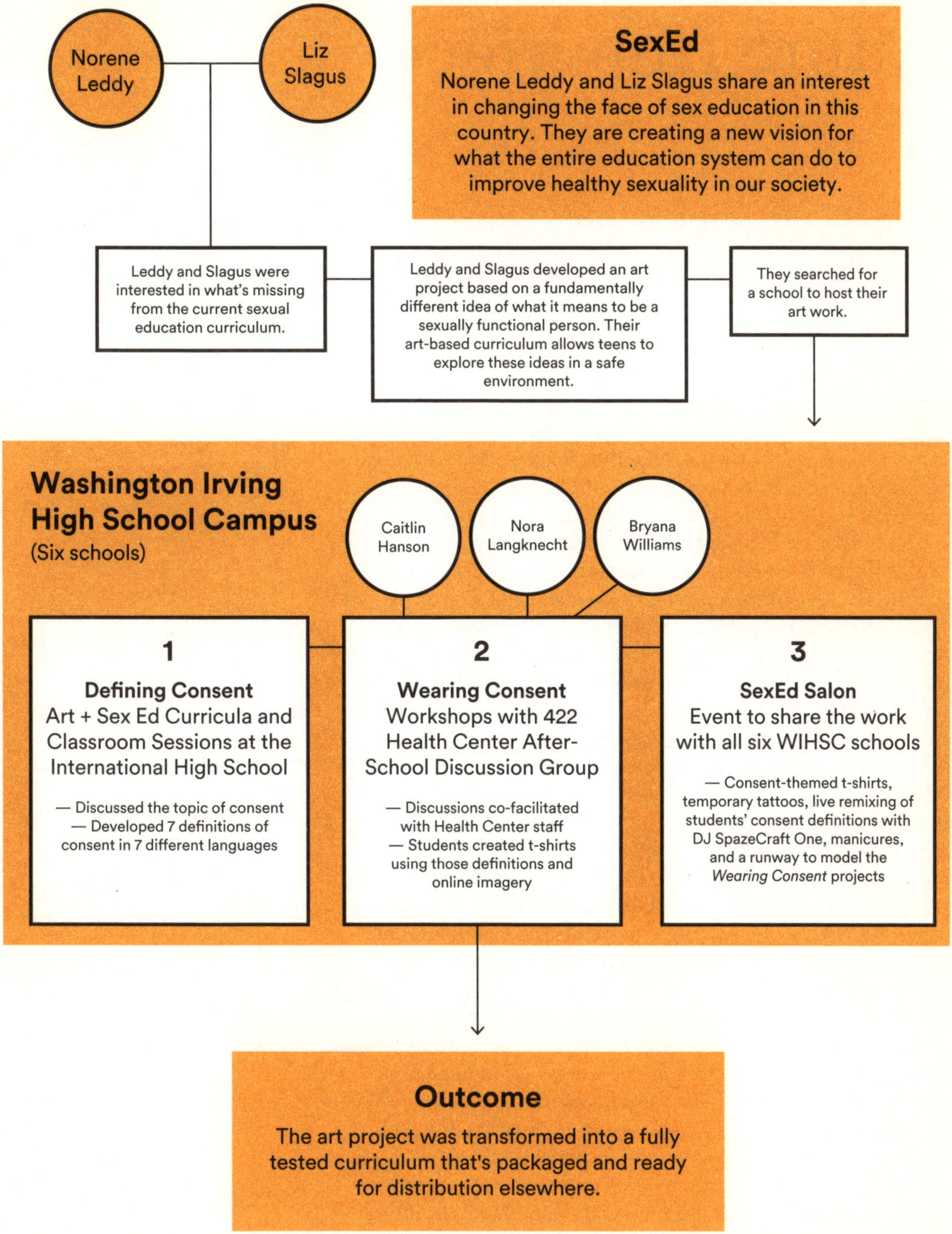

Norene Leddy

Liz Slagus

SexEd

Norene Leddy and Liz Slagus share an interest in changing the face of sex education in this country. They are creating a new vision for what the entire education system can do to improve healthy sexuality in our society.

Leddy and Slagus were interested in what's missing from the current sexual education curriculum.

Leddy and Slagus developed an art project based on a fundamentally different idea of what it means to be a sexually functional person. Their art-based curriculum allows teens to explore these ideas in a safe environment.

They searched for a school to host their art work.

Washington Irving High School Campus

(Six schools)

Caitlin Hanson

Nora Langknecht

Bryana Williams

1

Defining Consent

Art + Sex Ed Curricula and Classroom Sessions at the International High School

— Discussed the topic of consent
— Developed 7 definitions of consent in 7 different languages

2

Wearing Consent

Workshops with 422 Health Center After-School Discussion Group

— Discussions co-facilitated with Health Center staff
— Students created t-shirts using those definitions and online imagery

3

SexEd Salon

Event to share the work with all six WIHSC schools

— Consent-themed t-shirts, temporary tattoos, live remixing of students' consent definitions with DJ SpazeCraft One, manicures, and a runway to model the *Wearing Consent* projects

Outcome

The art project was transformed into a fully tested curriculum that's packaged and ready for distribution elsewhere.

Elizabeth M. Grady

Future Imperfect

Though initiated by an artist, socially engaged art[1] is a creative process that happens between people acting in the real world. It does not easily fit into traditional art institutions like museums and galleries. It evades efforts to codify and characterize it, manifesting in ways often surprising and unexpected even to those involved. It can be hard for those outside of a given project (the non-participant, secondary audience) to understand what happened and why it was significant. In a museum, live educators and written wall text often provide conceptual frameworks for viewers to use in their efforts to appreciate the work. Embedded in the fabric of society, socially engaged art frequently prefers a real-world context to an institutional one, and the usual interpretive help can be lacking or intentionally sidestepped to allow for open-ended outcomes.

A Blade of Grass documents and assesses such projects, working to expand the audience for the art and serving as a resource for those who want to learn more about it. In addition, we provide a full slate of public programming and moderated online content to supplement the concrete examples of our Fellows' work with broader ruminations on issues pertinent to them. It is not ABOG's aim to produce or, worse, reproduce existing institutional art world ideologies and their attendant pedagogical strategies. Nor do we mean to suggest that museums cannot play strong and beneficial roles in community-based projects. Rather, ABOG believes that artists and co-creative stakeholders are often the best windows onto their own work, and that each artist's project often provides its own interpretive framework. This is a starting point for our own work of audience building. So when we settle on an annual theme like that of 2014–15, "Future Imperfect," we offer it only as a lens—one of an infinite number

1 This term, defined by Pablo Helguera in *Education for Socially Engaged Art* (New York: Jorge Pinto Books, 2011) is not universally accepted. For example, among others Suzanne Lacy calls it *new genre art* in *Mapping the Terrain: New Genre Public Art* (Seattle: Bay Press, 1994), and borrowing from social theory, it is also called *social practice*. I use it here because it is the term of preference for A Blade of Grass, as it emphasizes active communication with a social entity or community.

of possible lenses—through which we hope to begin to bring into focus many diverse projects and outcomes. This work is curatorial, in that it offers interpretation, but is not prescriptive. The choice of a different theme each year reflects a desire to critically examine socially engaged art from a multiplicity of angles and approaches as we evolve as an organization.[2]

In this essay, I explore how the theme "Future Imperfect," with its grammatical and utopian implications, can contribute to our understanding of some of the ways that socially engaged art projects operate, and help us see their potential meaning and impact over time. As I wrote for the ABOG website:

> Future Imperfect
>
> Social change often challenges "the system." Sometimes the system is visible—the prison system, the health care system, the education system. Sometimes the system is a habit of thought or internal "cop in the head" that polices our behavior and governs the way we see ourselves in the world.[3]
>
> Perhaps the failures of our governmental, economic and social systems can be seen as a failure of the imagination. If so, what happens when art, an act of imagination, is used to creatively address these failures? What happens when instead of "fighting the man," artists become involved in reimagining the way things work? A Blade of Grass' 2014 Fellows for Socially Engaged Art and Organizational Grantees address this notion in different ways. By creating and expanding on ad hoc solutions to seemingly unsolvable problems, the artists' projects we are working with this year visualize ways of addressing, changing, getting around and otherwise confounding "the system" to foster greater freedom and equity in our society.

In spite of how it may sound, the invented term "Future Imperfect" is not a grammatical form. Nonetheless, it can be instructive to look at the two verb tenses it combines; the "future perfect" and the "imperfect." The "future perfect" refers to a time when something "will have happened." It's an odd notion, implying the belief that something will happen without fail. If it's something like the rising of the sun, that may be a fair assumption, but with anything less fixed it seems a little suspect. We cannot with certainty know what will happen—the future cannot be determined. Any unshakeable faith in the future—a faith that something "will have happened"—is illogical. On the

2 This is not to say that socially engaged art is exempt from working within or producing/reproducing ideology. Lane Relyea has observed that museums produce a kind of embodied ideology by instilling belief in audiences, through their cultural authority, in the viewpoints they present in their exhibitions and other programs. "By the same token, how does the art world ... continue to address those formerly dominant, more enduring institutional contexts such as the studio and museum, with their entrenched, repeatable practices, those rituals that instill belief within subjects and thus produce embodied ideology?" Lane Relyea. *Your Everyday Art World.* Cambridge, MA: MIT Press, 2013, 7.

By operating outside of such institutions socially engaged art may escape a specific ideology, but may also be doing the work of ideological paradigm formation. It is outside the cope of this essay to explore this question in depth, but it is necessary to consider it in writing an analysis of the impact of social practice art.

3 Augusto Boal famously coined the term, "cop in the head," referring to internalized oppression.

other hand, the "imperfect" tense refers to a continuing past state exemplified by phrases like "I was walking," or "I used to walk." In this case we become stuck in a feedback loop from which there is no temporal escape. As long as the circumstance is ongoing, as long as the grammar has us caught in its system, we remain in a condition of stasis. But what happens when we violate the rules of the system? What happens when we combine the two, and think of the "future imperfect" as a grammatical tense? We find the powerful possibility of an *ongoing state in the future,* something that not only "will happen" but "will be happening." Imagining it this way, for a moment, it is more robust than the future indicative tense (e.g., "it will happen") simply because it has the added punch of being a state or condition that is continually evolving.

Also implicit in the theme is a utopian reimagining of society, its problems solved and its structure transformed in the service of "freedom and equity." The only problem with utopia is that it is an ideal, and it may not be possible to agree on its essential features. Like the future in our grammatical exegesis, the form of an ideal society cannot be predicted with certainty. Assuming that the actions and work of socially engaged artists pursue the idea of a better world, the next question is what makes their work different and possibly more effective than other work motivated by dissatisfaction with the status quo. "Socially engaged art" is not simply a new name for the practice of community arts, an approach that has gained recognition in the US since the 1960s. This important, decades-old tradition often involves cooperation and collaboration with communities, as the name suggests. Perhaps because its aims are community focused, its practitioners have not often explicitly discussed their work in terms of *artistic* innovation. They have not necessarily intended to create new art forms or otherwise challenge the boundaries of existing artistic mediums (though some have done so). The new designation is a recent invention, which points to a shift in emphasis and perhaps a more critical approach to the work as an art practice, whereby the unique features of the medium like shared authorship and a frequent lack or transience of material presence can be brought into focus.[4]

I opened this study with an abbreviated definition of socially engaged art as a creative practice initiated by an artist that happens between people, acting in the real world. Such work does not rely on material objects, elaborate staging, identifiable events, performances or other art touchstones to be valid as art; thus it is often invisible to non-participants. It is avant-garde in its immateriality of form, since it is as likely to be composed only of relationship building, as it is to take on a material or

4 Pablo Helguera, *Education for Socially Engaged Art*. New York: Jorge Pinto Books, 2011.

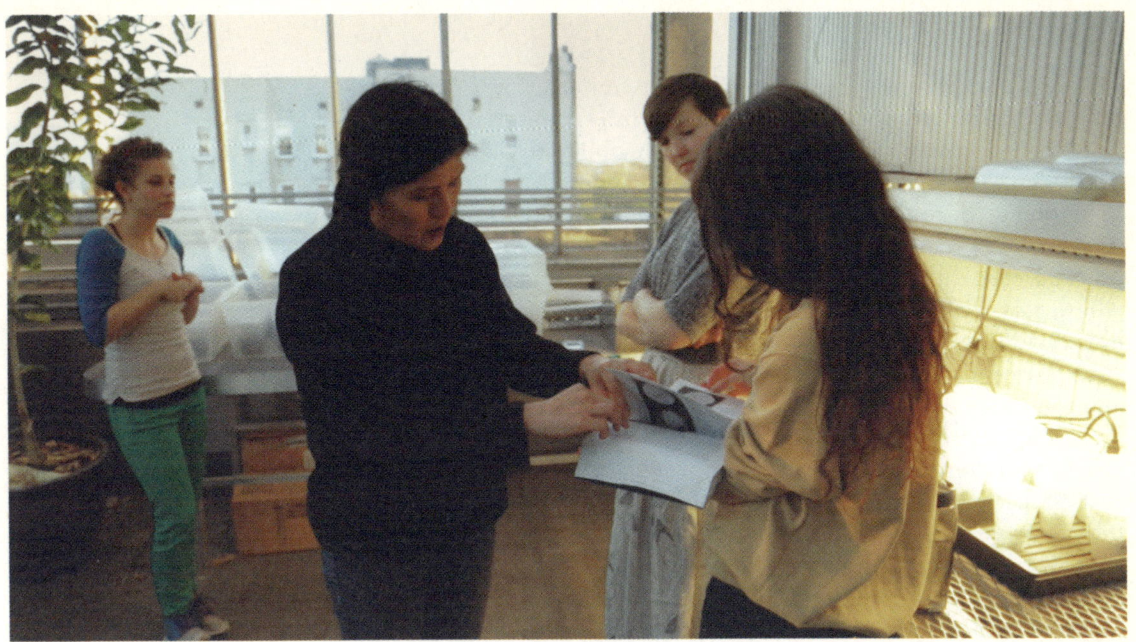

Jan Mun at Brooklyn College.

obviously performative manifestation. It is similarly groundbreaking in its radical sharing of authorship, which is the result of a co-creative process. Because it lacks two of the key features of the art of the modern age—clear and singular authorship and a material presence—people often ask what makes it art. The basic point is that aesthetic experience is located inside the individual, rather than within objects. Socially engaged art either removes the material distractions and spectacle, or strategically implements them in new ways through engineering opportunities for interaction and generating open-ended meaning. These tactics ask participants and witnesses alike to directly examine the aesthetics and meaning of everyday experience. In other words, it could ultimately fulfill one of the earliest goals of the modernist avant-garde by removing the separation between art and life. The process of co-creation is one means of achieving this goal.[5]

Co-creation is a central feature of socially engaged art, I would argue, because this aspect of the art form creates the condition for its success in promoting social change in two crucial ways: it allows for long-term impact beyond the scheduled life of the project, and it can lead to the disruption of power structures that hinder fundamental social change.

Co-creation ideally happens when an artist or art collective acting as a single artistic entity works in a dialogic and egalitarian way with members of a community to identify a common problem or area of interest. I use the term community rather loosely here, as artists working in social practice may engage a

5 I'm referring to historians' common characterization since the 1930s of the post-Medieval period as the Modern Era.

variety of communities, and define the very word community differently. Similarly, not all engagement is fully egalitarian. Nonetheless a co-creative process has the flexibility to be broadly useful. Together, the artists and community members agree upon a solution to the problem or means of exploring their common interest. They share authorship of the project in some way. In practice, co-creation moves along a continuum, falling somewhere between full collaboration and independent actions taken by individuals toward a common goal. Sometimes the co-creative process oscillates, as Kester observes, between conflict and consensus, which may occur either within or outside active phases of the project. He writes, "It's impossible to achieve the provisional consensus necessary to engage in action in the world without passing through moments of disruption or dissensus."[6] Indeed, it is often these moments of disagreement that generate new ideas and solutions, especially in projects of longer duration.[7] Actually, it is only through participation, interaction and dialogue that a co-created project can progress. Given this ideal condition of co-equal co-creation and the possibility of interactions between participants without the presence or input of the artist, real creation often happens at a remove from the artist. The artist becomes a builder of a system, a machine for generating aesthetic experience. The artist no longer controls the vessel for the experience as s/he did when making objects or performances; participants do. Artists thus become system architects, breathing new life into ideas like the death of the author (Barthes) and that everyone is an artist (Beuys).

The long duration of socially engaged art projects is not unique to the medium, but because of it the co-creation central to the way that such projects generate aesthetic experiences and outcomes can happen in a number of ways. They can be collaborative, with everyone working together at the same time. They can be concurrent, in which case participants act independently of one another but within the same timeframe. Or there can be subsequent moments of collaborative or independent creativity unfolding over time. The creative process has the flexibility to function both synchronically and diachronically. Because creativity does not reside within a specific individual, the co-creative process is a mechanism that allows for a project's longevity and sustainability. This is why *effects* (the achievement of specific social change goals) are hard to demonstrate: the creative players continue to evolve their thinking and actions over time in response to the original stimulus of the project.

But that doesn't mean those effects are not real and significant. This evolution may proceed from continued contact with or

6 Grant Kester, A Blade of Grass Post, May 18, 2015.

7 For further discussion of these points, see Ellen Feiss, "Response to Grant Kester's, 'The Device Laid Bare'", eflux Journal 54, April 2014.

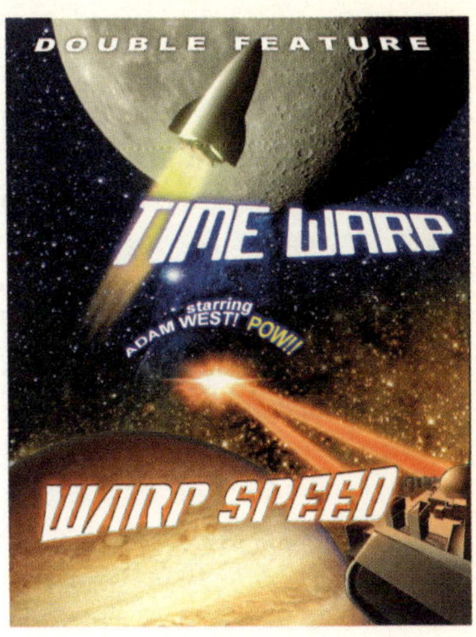

Poster for the film *Time Warp*. Sandler Institutional Films, 1981.

between one or more participants but may also happen independently. Once the creative seed is germinated by stakeholders and other participants, it may continue to grow along different trajectories followed by each individual. In this way a socially engaged art project may be rhizomatic, with productive shoots developing in unpredictable shapes and directions. Although there may be areas of agreement, each person's experience of the project—its success, the changes made, the outcomes achieved—will be different. To examine at any moment an individual's experience is to experience disjunctive simultaneity—the outcome will be perceived differently by each. This flexibility is the strength of socially engaged art.

ABOG pursues an ethnographic approach to assessment, where multiple stakeholders are interviewed, in order to capture the multiplicity of motivations and truths that come together in a project. An evaluator must be willing to listen to, account for, and report different and even divergent viewpoints about what exactly happened during the project, and why it was or was not important. In this way, s/he may arrive at an understanding of how each stakeholder perceives their actions, whether as art, community service, entertainment, or something else. "Even when they agree, as they may, they do so from different perspectives and different senses of the world."[8]

The Russian literary theorist Mikhail Bakhtin characterized this kind of simultaneity in literature as "polyphonic truth." He believed that multiple, even contradictory truths were possible, and that a broader notion of truth required multiple simultaneous voices. In their analysis of Bakhtin's work, Morson and Emerson write:

> It is clear that dialogue so conceived involves the constant redefinition of its participants, develops and creates numerous potentials "in" each of them "separately" and between them "interactively" and "dialogically." It is also clear that no single interaction could exhaust the potential value of future exchanges. Both dialogue and the potentials of dialogue are endless. No word can be taken back, but the final word has not yet been spoken and will never be spoken.[9]

Following Bakhtin's logic, not only are multiple truths possible, but through ongoing dialogue new truths are likely to be discovered. This dialogue may happen in real time among active participants, or even over a lengthy period of time through a distanced engagement with the ideas of others, including and perhaps especially the artist. Finding new positive and

8 Gary Saul Morson and Caryl Emerson, *Mikhail Bakhtin: Creation of a Prosaics*. Stanford: Stanford University Press, 1990, 236.

9 Ibid. 52.

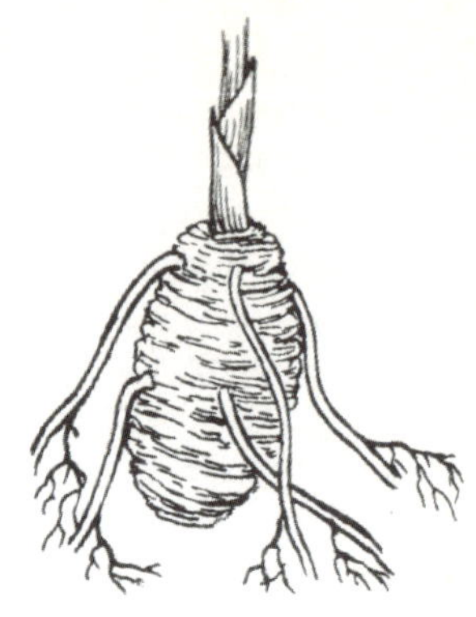

Diagram of a rhizome.

liberatory outcomes through dialogue lies at the foundation of Augusto Boal's Theatre of the Oppressed—the techniques of which socially engaged artists often deploy. In his Forum Theatre method, Boal invited spectators to take the place of actors on stage to change the direction of a narrative or come up with an alternate solution to a problem the actor has been presented with. This problem is often a real-world issue in the community. Socially engaged artists proceed analogously, initiating a conversation about an issue and inviting the community to offer new ideas about addressing it. The participants may naturally continue to discuss the issue when the artist is not present.

Similarly, walking the experience of participating in a socially engaged art project backward in time, each actor is likely to arrive at different ideas of the starting point. This is not only because memory is changed and reinterpreted by subsequent experience, but also because the original situation was approached differently by each participant at the outset. Further, because causality cannot be determined, you never really know if the later "achievement" of a goal was indeed caused by involvement in the art project in the first place!

If the dialogue born of co-creation creates multiple, sometimes contradictory truths that develop along independent trajectories, it can also slip out from under the project's power structures, as well as broader social structures. The creative agency of all stakeholders that is revealed through dialogic and co-creative practice means that the project's ideas proceed at least in part from the so-called non-experts. The implication is that they can take any proposition, idea, collaboration, project, stratagem, etc., and repurpose it for their own (liberatory) ends. This can allow stratagems and ideas to be repurposed in the service of different visions of the future—that is, to generate a counter-narrative or alternate ideology that could ultimately generate real social change. Boal's techniques are intended to foster precisely this, which is why his ideas have been so influential to socially engaged artists.

Since hallmark features of socially engaged art like co-creation, dialogic engagement, and a multi-voiced idea of truth rely on the duration of a project, it makes sense to return to the way that we talk about time in understanding the work. If we can be clear about that, at least, maybe we can begin to have a richer and fuller idea of how socially engaged art projects are sustained and continue to have an effect over time. This is especially significant because it is exactly the impact of such work that can be hard to measure. Often, the work doesn't necessarily impress in terms of sheer participant numbers and statistics. Yet socially engaged artists and the people who co-create with them still firmly believe in the efficacy of what they do. If a subtle, sustained impact is their real legacy, we need to find a way to talk about that—at least if we want the work to be recognized and ultimately funded.

To recap, in grammatical terms, the imperfect refers to a continuing state, usually in the past: "I was walking" or "I used to walk." The neologism I used for our 2014 theme, "Future Imperfect," suggests a continuing evolution. Just as causality cannot be determined, it is not possible to predict all outcomes. By suggesting a future state of ongoing or continuing effects as this grammatical construction would suggest (a specific action that will be continuing indefinitely in the future), a new definition of sustainability is arrived at, summarized by the new grammatical construction "I will be continuing to walk." Or, for an art project, "I will be continuing to work toward a specific goal or set of goals that I became interested in when I worked toward co-creating a socially engaged art project." The ongoing state described here is contingent upon the dialogue that comes from co-creation; it's the fuel that keeps the engine of the project's ideas running. The initial co-creative engagement thus gives rise to a wide range of impactful outcomes that mimic a rhizome rather than an arrow of focused trajectory. Shoots sprout periodically and unpredictably from the main tuber to generate new life. So, it's not really about the sustainability of a specific project, but the sustained endeavor over time to concern oneself with a set of ideas and actions. What we're talking about is really a social movement, rather than a narrowly defined field of artistic endeavor.

Parallel Fields: Coming Home
September 17, 2014
The 8th Floor
A conversation about the complex process of homecoming in military and civilian communities, with artist Brookie Maxwell and Allen Grane, First Lieutenant, New York Army National Guard; moderated by ABOG Programs Director Elizabeth M. Grady.

Fellowship Workshop with SexEd
October 1, 2014
The 8th Floor
Fellowship Workshops are designed for applicants to our Fellowship program and include hands-on, interactive approaches to helping artists with their proposals. This workshop began with a short presentation by 2014 ABOG Fellows Norene Leddy and Liz Slagus (SexEd), and was followed by small group discussions about what ABOG's selection criteria are and how artists can best apply them.

Republic of New York: Perfect City Discussions with Aaron Landsman
October 6, 2014
Abrons Art Center
Presented in partnership with the French Institute Alliance Française (FIAF) and Abrons Arts Center, as part of FIAF's 2014 Crossing the Line festival.
New York-based theater artist Aaron Landsman invited the audience to reimagine urban life outside of commerce in a performed public meeting, along with guest panelists Deland Chan, Urban Studies, Stanford University; Todd Lester, artist and founder of freeDimensional & Lanchonete.org; and Demaris Reyes, Executive Director, Good Old Lower East Side (GOLES).

Fellowship Workshop with Pablo Helguera
November 4, 2014
The 8th Floor
Fellowship Workshops are designed for applicants to our Fellowship program and include hands-on, interactive approaches to helping artists with their proposals. This workshop began with a short presentation by 2104 ABOG Fellow Pablo Helguera, and was followed by small group discussions about what ABOG's selection criteria are and how artists can best apply them.

Parallel Fields: Alternative Economies
January 14, 2015
The 8th Floor
A conversation about the use of art as a means of supporting an alternative economy, with 2014 ABOG Fellow Fran Ilich and financial journalist Felix Salmon, moderated by ABOG Executive Director Deborah Fisher.

Reports from the Field: Beauty in Transition
February 18, 2015
The 8th Floor
A conversation exploring the work of 2014 ABOG Fellow Jody Wood, whose mobile

beauty salon traveled to homeless shelters throughout New York City in the fall of 2014, along with project collaborators Jerry Anderson, JoAnn Copeland, Nahomie Marcena, and Carol Thomas; moderated by ABOG Programs Director Elizabeth M. Grady.

Open Engagement
April 17–19, 2015
Carnegie Mellon University, Pittsburgh, PA
Founded & directed by Jen Delos Reyes, co-presented by A Blade of Grass. 2015 Co-presenters: Carnegie Mellon University and the Carnegie Museum of Art
Open Engagement is an international conference and platform for supporting socially engaged art. The 2015 conference featured keynote presenters Rick Lowe and Emily Jacir and focused on the theme of "Place and Revolution."

Reports from the Field: SexEd
May 12, 2015
The 8th Floor
A conversation exploring the work of 2014 ABOG Fellows Norene Leddy and Liz Slagus, aka SexEd, who developed an arts-based sexual health curriculum at Washington Irving High School Campus in New York City, along with project collaborators Caitlin Hanson, Cory Silverberg, and Bryana Williams, moderated by ABOG Programs Director Elizabeth M. Grady.

Closing Party at *Librería Donceles* by Pablo Helguera
May 14, 2015
360 Van Brunt St., Brooklyn
A closing celebration for the Brooklyn iteration of 2014 ABOG Fellow Pablo Helguera's traveling used Spanish-language bookstore.

Aesthetics of Doing: Sleeping with the Enemy
June 3, 2015
The 8th Floor
A conversation featuring artists who work in cooperation or collaboration with companies or institutions whose values don't necessarily match their own, with artist Steve Kurtz, 2014 ABOG Fellow Jan Mun, and Not An Alternative's Beka Economopoulos and Jason Jones, moderated by ABOG Executive Director Deborah Fisher.

Aesthetics of Doing: Community Organizing
June 17, 2015
The 8th Floor
A conversation about community organizing in socially engaged art, with 2015 ABOG Fellow Sol Aramendi, Betty's Daughter Arts Collaborative CEO and Founder Ebony Noelle Golden, and artist Elizabeth Hamby, moderated by Prerana Reddy, Director of Public Events at the Queens Museum.

Parallel Fields is a discussion series that pairs an artist and a non-artist, both of whose work is socially engaged, to discuss with an audience how different professions are connected.

Reports from the Field presents the voices of community participants and collaborators in ABOG Fellows' socially engaged art projects, both in-person and online.

Aesthetics of Doing is a series of panel discussions that bring together artists, scholars, administrators and other members of the art community for discussions that critically address socially engaged art as it is practiced and defined.

Mel Chin

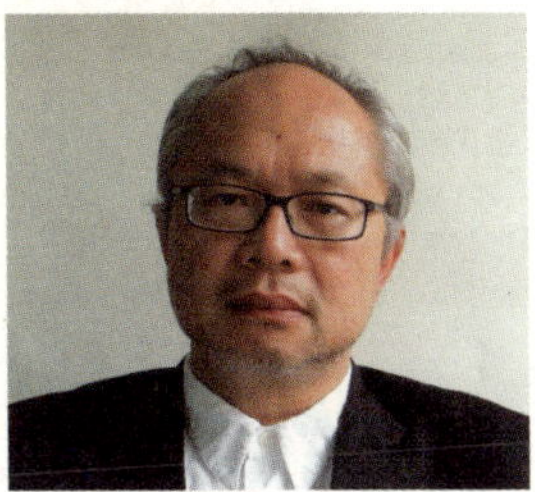

Artist **Mel Chin** insinuates art into unlikely places, including destroyed homes, toxic landfills, and even popular television, investigating how art can provoke greater social awareness and responsibility. Chin uses a broad range of approaches in his work, often emphasizing multi-disciplinary, collaborative teamwork and works that conjoin cross-cultural aesthetics with complex ideas.

In 1989, Chin developed *Revival Field*, a pioneering project in the field of bioremediation, to encourage the use of plants to remove toxic heavy metals from the soil. From 1995–1998, he formed the collective the GALA Committee and produced *In the Name of the Place,* a collaborative conceptual public art project that inserted 200 artist-made props into American primetime television. In 2000, Chin worked with software engineers to create *KNOWMAD*, a video game based on rug patterns of nomadic peoples facing cultural disappearance. In 2007, his film, *9-11/9-11,* a hand-drawn, 24-minute, joint Chile-US production, won the prestigious Pedro Sienna Award for Best Animation from Chile's National Council of Culture and the Arts. In these and other works, Chin seeks to produce collaborative artworks that question social and cultural boundaries, often by employing a technological or scientific approach alongside traditional artistic methods.

Chin has had one-person exhibitions at the Hirshhorn Museum and Sculpture Garden (1989), the Walker Art Center (1990), The Menil Collection (1991) and the Station Museum of Contemporary Art, Houston (2006), and has been featured on the PBS program *Art in the 21st Century.* He has received numerous awards and grants from organizations such as the National Endowment for the Arts, New York State Council for the Arts, Art Matters, Creative Capital, and the Penny McCall, Pollock/Krasner, Joan Mitchell, Rockefeller and Louis Comfort Tiffany Foundations, among others. In 2014–2015, a retrospective of his work traveled to the Contemporary Art Museum, St. Louis; and the Blaffer Art Museum, the Contemporary Arts Museum Houston, Asia Society Texas Center and the Station Museum of Contemporary Art, Houston.

Brett Cook

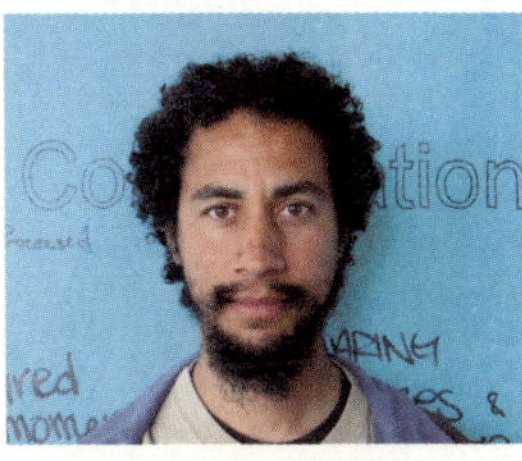

Brett Cook is an artist and educator who uses his creative practice of portraiture as a vehicle to explore and transform outer and inner worlds of being. For over two decades, Cook has produced installations, exhibitions, curricula and events across the United States and internationally. His work features drawing, painting, photography and elaborate installations that aim to make intimately personal experiences universally accessible. His public projects incorporate these artistic practices with community workshops that offer arts-integrated pedagogy along with performance, music and food, to create a fluid boundary between art making, daily life and healing.

Teaching and public speaking are extensions of Cook's social practice that bring communities into dialogue for shared reflection and insight. He has taught a variety of subjects to students of all ages and academic levels, and has been published in academic journals at the Maryland Institute College of Art, Columbia University and Harvard University. In 2009 he published *Who Am I In This Picture: Amherst College Portraits* with Wendy Ewald and Amherst College Press.

Recognized for a history of socially relevant, community engaged projects, Cook was selected as a cultural ambassador to Nigeria as part of the US Department of State's 2012 smARTpower initiative. He has received numerous honors and awards, including the Lehman Brady Visiting Joint Chair Professorship at Duke University and the University of North Carolina at Chapel Hill in 2008, and the Richard C. Diebenkorn Teaching Fellowship at the San Francisco Art Institute in 2005. His work is in private and public collections including the National Portrait Gallery, the Walker Art Center and Harvard University.

Pablo Helguera

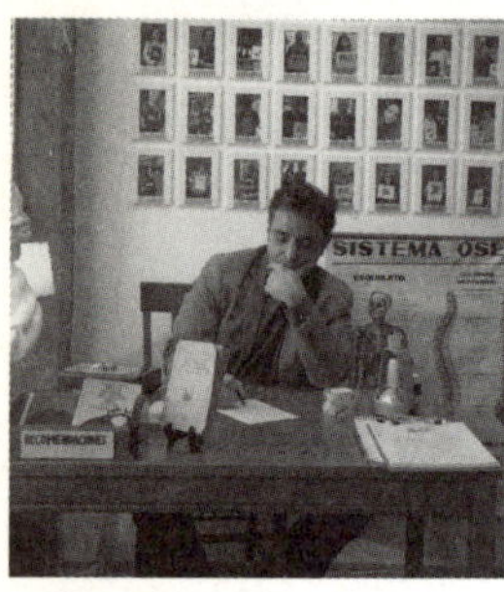

Pablo Helguera is an interdisciplinary artist working with installation, sculpture, photography, drawing, socially engaged art and performance. His work focuses on a variety of topics ranging from history, pedagogy, sociolinguistics, ethnography and memory to the absurd, in formats that are widely varied including lectures, museum display strategies, musical performances and written fiction.

Helguera's work as an educator has often intersected with his interests as an artist, and his work often takes a pedagogical approach to exploring the relationship between art and language, as well as the social dynamics of contemporary art in daily life. This intersection is exemplified in his project, *School of Panamerican Unrest* (2005), a nomadic think tank that traveled from Anchorage, Alaska to Tierra del Fuego in South America, making 40 stops over nearly 20,000 miles and facilitating discussions, screenings, performances and partnerships with organizations encountered along the way.

Helguera has performed and exhibited internationally at venues such as the Museo de Arte Reina Sofia, Madrid; ICA Boston; RCA London; 8th Havana Biennal, PERFORMA 05, Havana; MoMA PS1, New York; Brooklyn Museum; Tokyo Metropolitan Art Museum; and the MALBA museum in Buenos Aires, amongst many others. He is the author of several books, including *Education for Socially Engaged* Art (2011). In addition to his artistic practice, Helguera is the Director of Adult and Academic Programs at the Museum of Modern Art.

Fran Ilich

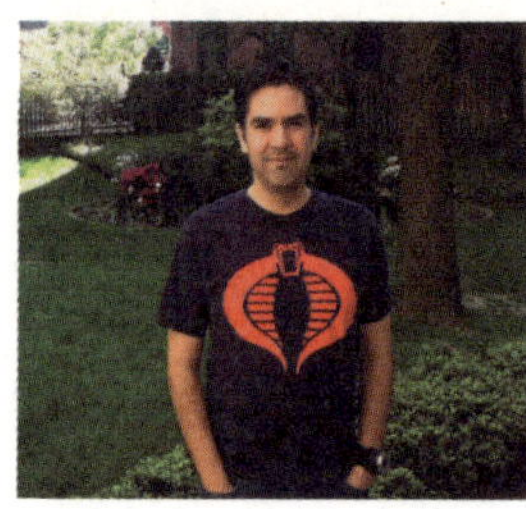

Fran Ilich is a writer and media artist influenced by cyberpunk culture, internet activism, and alternative economies. Born in Tijuana, Mexico, he began organizing with fellow artists in the early 1990s as part of the independent media scene in the city, co-founding the Contra-Cultura (menor) [(minor) Counter Culture] collective, and producing literature, photography, comics, videos, and electronic music.

Ilich has extensive experience in teaching languages, writing, and editing, and has held positions as a screenwriter for Discovery Channel Latin America, as an editor at the National Center for the Arts in Mexico City, and as editor-at-large for the magazine *Sputnik Cultura Digital*. Working with collective Laboratorios Cinemátik, he helped produce Cinemátik 1.0 in 1998, often considered the first cyberculture festival in Latin America, and Borderhack in 2000, which took place on the Tijuana-San Diego border and featured net art, films, workshops, and participation of the global hacktivist community. In 2005, after attending meetings in Chiapas with Subcomandante Marcos and the Zapatista Army, Ilich launched the autonomous server Possibleworlds.org and its economic body Spacebank.org to respond to the need of the Zapatista Army and other social movements to have access to web hosting services.

Ilich has presented his work at cultural institutions and art and media festivals throughout Europe and the Americas, in forums such as the Berlinale Talent Campus, Documenta 12, transmediale, MIT's Media In Transition, the Walker Art Center, The Economist 2011 Conference in Mexico City, and the Zapatista Army's Festival Mundial de la Digna Rabia. He is the author of novels *Metro-Pop* (1997), *Tekno Guerrilla* (2007), and *Circa 94* (2010), which won the 2010 binational Frontera de Palabras award from The National Council for Culture and the Arts in Mexico.

Norene Leddy & Liz Slagus

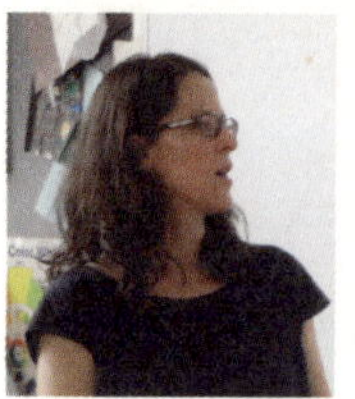

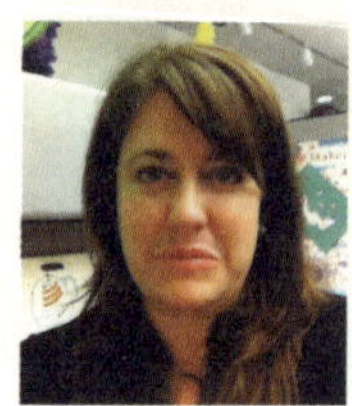

Since 2008 **Norene Leddy** and **Liz Slagus** have been collaborating as SexEd, focusing on developing radical pedagogies that combine art, reproductive health, and participatory tools in an ongoing quest to expose the current state of sexual education in the US, encourage a public discourse around the topics of sexual health and education, and develop a sex education curriculum that is artist-inspired and community-based.

Artist Norene Leddy came to SexEd with a long history of creating platforms to talk about technology, history, sex, art, and social justice. In her previous projects she has worked with LGBTQI youth, sex workers, young women, and others to create shoes, garments, alarm systems, maps, DIY electronics kits, and other ways to explore high and low technology for protection and self-expression. Her work has been shown internationally, at venues such as Eyebeam, New York; Henie Onstad Kunstsenter, Norway; and Sarai Media Lab, India. She has been the recipient of numerous grants, awards and residencies including a Fulbright Fellowship, two Eyebeam residencies, and funding from NYSCA, Bronx Council on the Arts, and the Experimental Television Center.

Liz Slagus joined SexEd with a background in consulting on art and technology education, public programming and community engagement. In 2009, the State Library of Queensland awarded her the Creative Fellowship for Art & Technology to develop the programming and outreach strategy for Brisbane's new digital culture center, The Edge. During 2008, she produced the youth component for the 01SJ Biennial in San Jose, CA, and co-curated "1800 Frames" for City Without Walls in Newark, NJ. Between 1998–2008, Slagus developed and managed Eyebeam's education programs, exploring new teaching and learning techniques and models for engagement.

Jan Mun

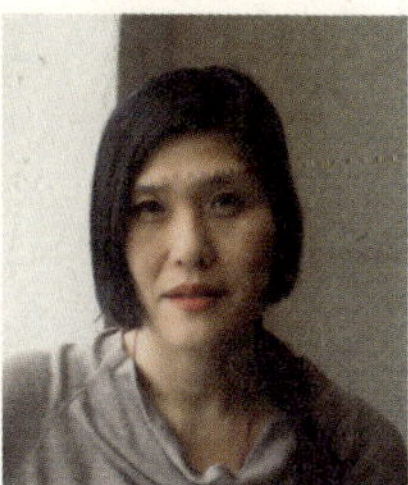

Jan Mun is an artist who explores the generative principles of how complex systems such as botany and fungi, economies, and social networks function and the effects of interactions between different entities, whether cultures, plants, or people. Working simultaneously as artist and amateur mycologist, microbiologist, and beekeeper, Mun works in collaboration with anthropologists, choreographers, composers, activists, gardeners, scientists and students to develop ways to communicate effectively with each other and the larger public.

As the artist-in-residence at the Newtown Creek Alliance Mun has previously partnered with ExxonMobil, one of the stakeholders conducting the cleanup of the Greenpoint oil spill, to create *The Fairy Rings*, a mycoremediation-inspired art installation. Another long-term project by Mun, *ProfileUS: Invasive Species*, examines the biopolitics of the migrations of non-native plants and people in the United States and considers which populations are allowed to thrive and which are repressed through institutional laws. In these projects as in her other social sculptures, Mun aims to provide a reflection and critique of political and social systems using a combination of artistic and scientific processes.

Prior to her current practice Mun worked with photographer Bruce Davidson in Central Park for several years, as well as communities in Mississippi, Lebanon, Spain, and Kyrgyzstan developing photographic workshops. Since 2004, she has developed web products for the United Nations, for which she won a Webby Award in 2006. She works in partnership with numerous community organizations including New York Beekeeping, New York Mycological Society, Newtown Creek Alliance, Genspace, and the Environmental Sciences Analytical Center at Brooklyn College.

Jody Wood

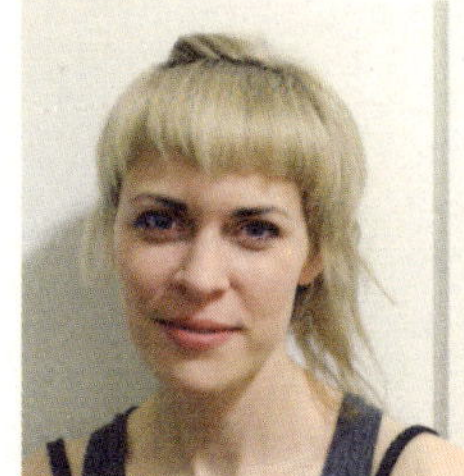

Jody Wood is an artist whose work is time-based and performative, utilizing video, installation, performance and community organization to engage with socially charged content. Primarily focusing on transitional experiences of death, trauma and social isolation, her work aims to unpack and meaningfully interpret these issues, often by working one-on-one with members of her community.

In *Preparing for Consumption* (2011), performed at Rivington Design House Gallery in New York City, Wood staged a formal dinner in slow motion, with a simultaneous audio installation of interviews exploring couples' reflections on death and dying. For *Spoken Stage* (2012), a community-based project in Seoul, South Korea, Wood worked with a community of senior citizens to develop and perform personal, poetry-based narratives centered on themes of loss, the body, the role of family, and society. And in *Dimensions of Air* (2013), Wood transformed narratives of paranormal experiences inspired by Internet chat rooms, dreams, visions, case files and interviews into video vignettes. Each of these works deals with the social preparations and rituals surrounding transitional moments, alongside the structure of interpersonal relationships—how they form, how they dissolve, and their delicate underpinnings.

Wood's work has been supported by organizations including Brooklyn Arts Council, Lower Manhattan Cultural Council, and Skowhegan School of Painting and Sculpture. A participant in the 2014 Open Engagement conference at the Queens Museum, she has presented collaborative community-based projects in New York City at El Museo Del Barrio, and in Seoul at Temporary Space Artist Residency, Seoul Art Space Geumcheon, One-Circle Community Theatre, and the Senior Welfare Center of Seoul.

Author Biographies

Jan Cohen-Cruz

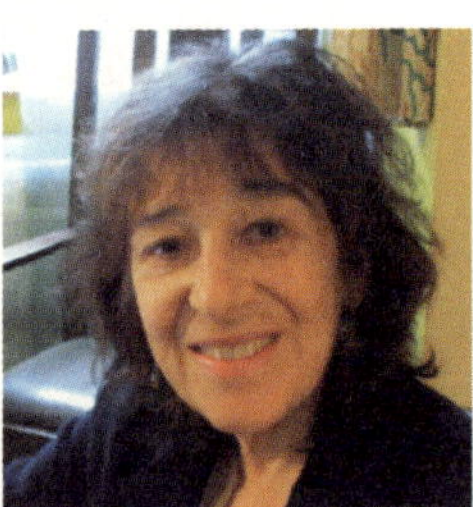

Jan Cohen-Cruz is senior editor and co-founder of *Public: A Journal of Imagining America* and a university professor at Syracuse University.
In addition to her new book, *Remapping Performance: Common Ground, Uncommon Partners*, Jan wrote *Local Acts: Community-Based Performance in the US* and *Engaging Performance: Theatre as Call and Response*; edited *Radical Street Performance*; and, with Mady Schutzman, co-edited *Playing Boal: Theatre, Therapy, Activism* and *A Boal Companion: Dialogues on Art and Cultural Politics*. As a longtime professor at NYU Tisch School of the Arts, Cohen-Cruz produced community-based arts projects with students and neighborhood partners. She directed the minor in applied theatre and Tisch's Office of Community Connections, and was among the founders of the Department of Art and Public Policy. She received the Association for Theatre in Higher Education's Award for Leadership in Community-Based Theatre and Civic Engagement (2012). She was the evaluator for the U.S. State Department/Bronx Museum cultural diplomacy initiative smARTpower, and is now Director of Field Research for A Blade of Grass.

Ben Davis

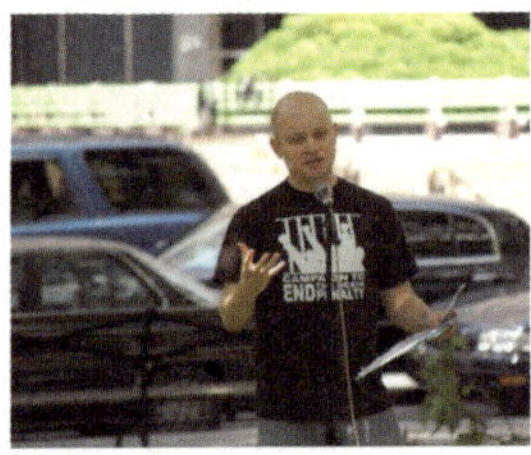

Ben Davis is an art critic living and working in New York City. He is currently National Art Critic for *artnet News*, and critic-in-residence at Montclair State University. He was formerly executive editor of Artinfo.com and was one of the editors of *The Elements of Architecture*, the catalogue for the 2014 Venice Architecture Biennale. His writings have appeared in *Adbusters*, *The Brooklyn Rail*, *Frieze*, *Slate.com*, *The Village Voice*, and many other venues. He is the author of *9.5 Theses on Art and Class* (Haymarket, 2013).

Charles Esche

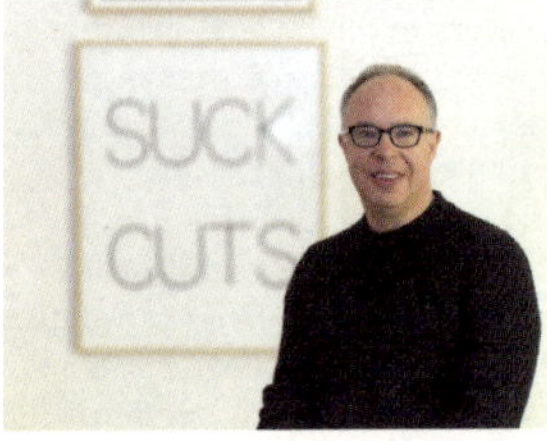

Charles Esche is a curator and writer. He is director of the Van Abbemuseum, Eindhoven, and co-editorial director and co-founder with Mark Lewis of *Afterall Journal and Books* based at Central Saint Martins, London. In 2014 he curated the São Paulo Biennale with a team of seven. In addition to his institutional curating, he has (co-) curated a number of major international exhibitions including U3 Triennale, Ljubljana (2011); Riwaq Biennale, Ramallah with Reem Fadda (2007 & 2009); Istanbul Biennale with Vasif Kortun (2005); Gwangju Biennale with Hou Hanru (2002). Currently, he is involved in the Jakarta Biennale 2015. He teaches at Central Saint Martins and the De Appel Curatorial Course, Amsterdam. He is a board member of CIMAM and chair of CASCO, Utrecht, NL. In 2012 he was awarded the Princess Margriet Award for Culture by the European Cultural Foundation; in 2013 the Minimum Prize by the Pistoletto Foundation and in 2014 the CCS Bard College Prize for Curatorial Excellence.

Tom Finkelpearl

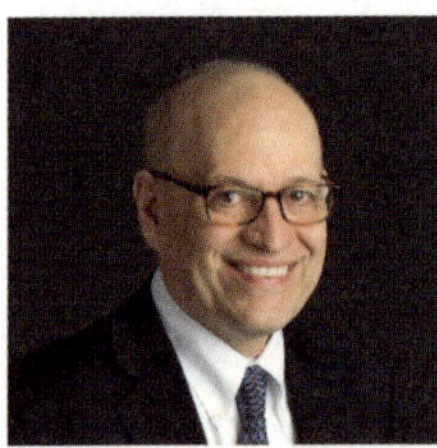

Tom Finkelpearl is the Commissioner of the New York City Department of Cultural Affairs. Prior to his appointment by Mayor Bill de Blasio, Commissioner Finkelpearl served as Executive Director of the Queens Museum for twelve years starting in 2002, overseeing an expansion that doubled the museum's size and positioning the organization as a vibrant center for social engagement in nearby communities. He also held positions at P.S.1

Contemporary Art Center, working on the organization's merger with the Museum of Modern Art, and served as Director of the Department of Cultural Affairs Percent for Art program. Based on his public art experience and additional research, he published a book, *Dialogues in Public Art* (MIT Press), in 2000. His second book, *What We Made: Conversations on Art and Social Cooperation* (Duke University Press, 2013) examines the activist, participatory, co-authored aesthetic experiences being created in contemporary art. He received a BA from Princeton University (1979) and an MFA from Hunter College (1983).

Deborah Fisher

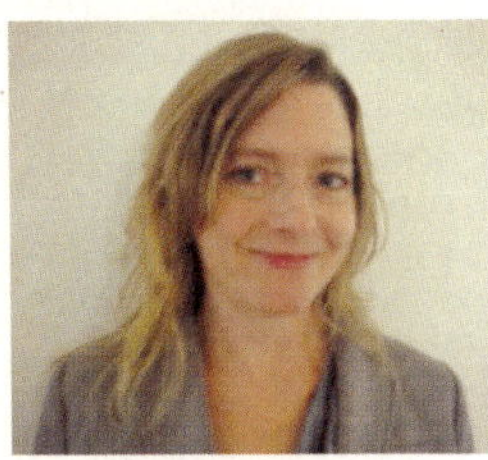

Deborah Fisher is the founding Executive Director of A Blade of Grass, and a strategic and philanthropic advisor to Shelley and Donald Rubin. She currently serves on the board of the Center for Artistic Activism. Fisher is a practicing artist and creative leader working to expand the roles art and artists play within communities. She has worked in many capacities at the intersection of art and civic life in New York City, including as studio manager at Socrates Sculpture Park, and as an educator and curriculum developer for the Brooklyn Center for the Urban Environment. She writes and lectures internationally about her own practice, arts funding, and socially engaged art; and participates in roundtables and planning sessions that seek to improve arts funding. Fisher's own art practice is largely organized around public sculpture and social projects, and is focused on how systems of value, waste, and meaning are created, both materially and socially.

Elizabeth M. Grady

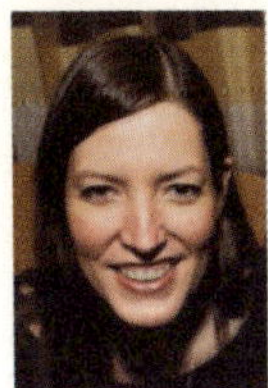

Elizabeth M. Grady is the Programs Director of A Blade of Grass, and a curator, critic, and scholar of socially engaged art. She was Program Manager of smART-power, a U.S. State Department program run by the Bronx Museum that sent artists to fifteen countries to do projects that engaged local communities (2010–2012). She served in the curatorial departments of the Museum of Modern Art, the Whitney Museum of American Art and San Francisco MoMA. As an independent curator, she did projects for the Moscow Biennial, the Biennial of the Canary Islands, and the Havana Biennial. For the latter, she curated *Proyecto Paladar*, a participatory food-based project at the Wifredo Lam Center (2012). She taught at FIT-SUNY in Art History and the Graduate School from 2002–2013. Among her many essays, articles and other publications, the most recent book was *Ten Dinners in Havana* (2013). She holds a Ph.D. in art history from Northwestern University.

Grant Kester

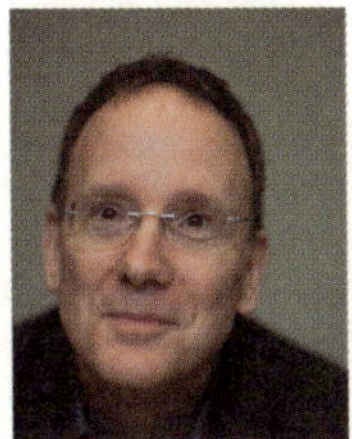

Grant Kester is professor of art history in the Visual Arts department at the University of California, San Diego and the founding editor of *FIELD: A Journal of Socially Engaged Art Criticism*. His publications include *Art, Activism and Oppositionality: Essays from Afterimage* (Duke University Press, 1998), *Conversation Pieces: Community and Communication in Modern Art* (University of California Press, 2004, second edition in 2013) and *The One and the Many: Contemporary Collaborative Art in a Global Context* (Duke University Press, 2011). He has recently completed work on *Collective Situations: Dialogues in Contemporary Latin American Art 1995–2010*, an anthology of writings by art collectives working in Latin America produced in collaboration with Bill Kelley Jr. which is under contract with Duke University Press.

Rick Lowe

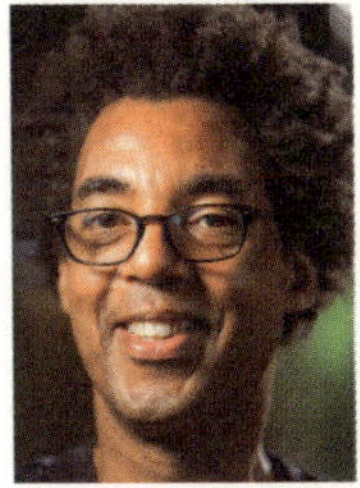

Rick Lowe is an artist whose community-based practice led him, along with six other artists, to found Project Row Houses (PRH), where he currently works as Founding Director, an organization that has transformed a neglected neighborhood in Houston into an expansive and visionary public art project. PRH, which started on a block and a half of derelict properties, is now an internationally recognized arts venue and community support center focused on transforming the community while preserving its culture. Among his honors are the Rudy Bruner Award in Urban Excellence, the AIA Keystone Award, the Heinz Award in the arts and humanities, Loeb Fellow at Harvard University, Mel King Fellow at MIT, Skowhegan School of Painting and Sculpture Governors Award, Skandalaris Award for Art/Architecture, and USA Artists Booth Fellow. For his vision and effort, President Barack Obama appointed Lowe to the National Council on the Arts in 2013, and Lowe was named a MacArthur Fellow in the class of 2014.

Laura Raicovich

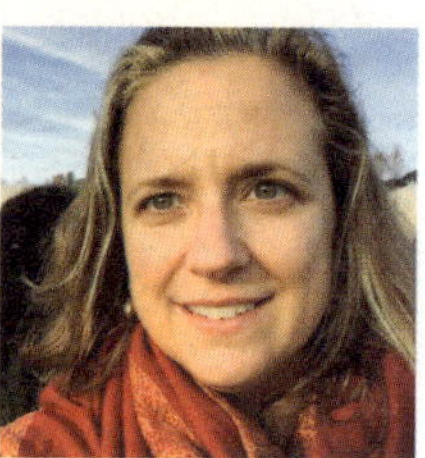

Laura Raicovich is President and Executive Director of the Queens Museum. Prior to this appointment she directed Creative Time's Global Initiatives, served as Deputy Director at Dia Art Foundation, and held positions at the Guggenheim and Public Art Fund. She is also a writer, lectures internationally, and has contributed regularly to The Brooklyn Rail. She is the author of "At the Lightning Field," a lyric essay and parallel text to Walter De Maria's renowned artwork, an excerpt of which was published in X-tra, Contemporary Art Quarterly; and "A Diary of Mysterious Difficulties," a book based on Viagra and Cialis spam recently put out by Publication Studio.

Gregory Sholette

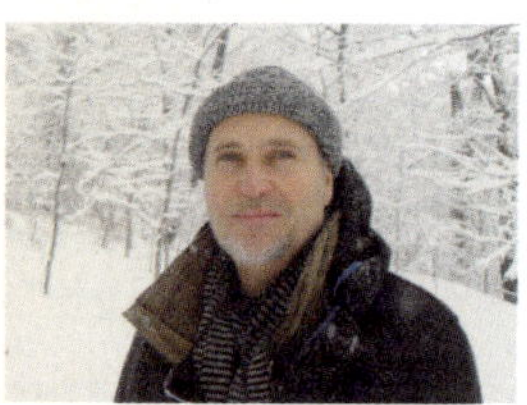

Gregory Sholette is an artist and writer whose publications include *It's the Political Economy, Stupid* co-edited with Oliver Ressler, *Dark Matter: Art and Politics in an Age of Enterprise Culture*, both Pluto Press UK, as well as *Collectivism After Modernism* with Blake Stimson, University of Minnesota Press, and *The Interventionists* with Nato Thompson, distributed by MIT. His recent art projects include *Collectibles, Action Figures and Objects,* at Station Independent Gallery, NY; *Imaginary Archive: Graz,* Rotor Art Center, Graz, Austria; *Exposed Pipe* at the American University Beirut Art Gallery; *Torrent* for Printed Matter Books in Chelsea, NY; *iDrone* for cyberartspace.net; and *Fifteen Islands for Robert Moses* at the Queens Museum. Sholette is an Associate of the Art, Design and the Public Domain program at the Graduate School of Design at Harvard University, a member of the Curriculum Committee of Home WorkSpace Beirut, and a faculty member of the Queens College Art Department, City University of New York where he helped establish the new MFA Concentration SPQ (Social Practice Queens).

Nato Thompson

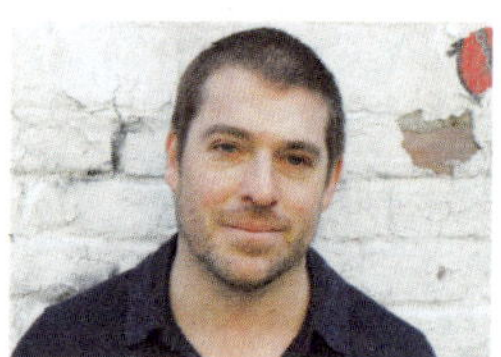

Nato Thompson joined Creative Time in January 2007. Since then, Thompson has organized such major Creative Time projects as The Creative Time Summit (2009–2015), Kara Walker's *A Subtlety* (2014), *Living as Form* (2011), Trevor Paglen's *The Last Pictures* (2012), Paul Ramirez Jonas' *Key to the City* (2010), Jeremy Deller's *It is What it is* (2009, with New Museum curators Laura Hoptman and Amy Mackie), *Democracy in America: The National Campaign* (2008), and Paul Chan's *Waiting for Godot in New Orleans* (2007), among others. Previously, he worked as Curator at MASS MoCA, where he completed numerous large-scale exhibitions, including "The Interventionists: Art in the Social Sphere" (2004), with a catalogue distributed by MIT Press. His writings have appeared in numerous publications, *Bookforum*, *Frieze*, *Artforum*, *Third Text*, and *Huffington Post* among them. In 2005, he received the Art Journal Award for distinguished writing. For Independent Curators International, Thompson curated the exhibition "Experimental Geography," with a book available from Melville House Publishing. His book *Seeing Power: Art and Activism in the 21st Century* was published in 2015.

Christian Viveros-Fauné

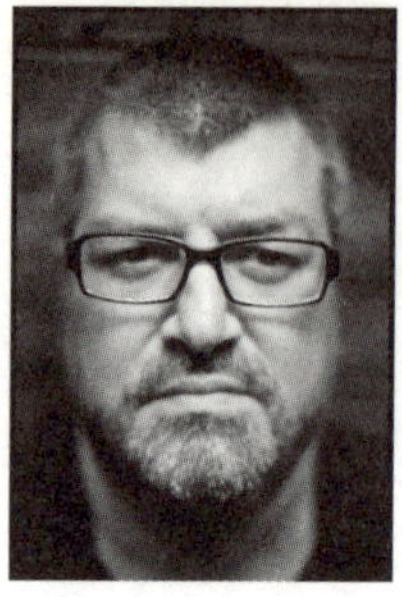

Christian Viveros-Fauné is a New York-based writer and curator. As a writer, he has written hundreds of catalogue essays for artists as varied as Joseph Beuys, Neo Rauch, Richard Mosse, Lisa Yuskavage and Philip Guston. The recipient of a 2010 Creative Capital/Warhol Foundation Arts Writers Grant, he was named inaugural Critic-in-Residence at the Bronx Museum for 2010/2011. He is currently the art critic for *The Village Voice* and *artnet NEWS*. A collection of his criticism, *Greatest Hits: Arte en Nueva York 2001–2011*, was issued in Spanish by Metales Pesados, S.A, in 2012. As a curator, Viveros-Fauné has organized many gallery and museum exhibitions around the world. These include shows at, among other venues, the Museo de Bellas Artes, Santiago; the Museo de Arte Contemporaneo de Monterrey, Mexico; the Museo de Arte Moderno, Mexico City; the Museo Amparo, Puebla, Mexico; the Centro Atlantico de Arte Contemporaneo, Spain; The Royal Hibernian Society, Dublin, Ireland; and the National Gallery of Art, Dublin, Ireland. Viveros-Fauné has additionally taught at various universities, among them Pratt Institute, the Gerrit Rietveld Academie, and Yale University.

Gabriela Ceja is an artist, researcher and educator. She explores working environments in Mexico and New York City in order to amplify the voices of people whose life paths have been affected by classism, racism, exploitation and alienation. Believing that art and education are tools for social change, she also designs programs that blur the boundaries between disciplines, institutions and publics.

Caitlin Hanson, MA, is the Director of School Based Health and Adolescent Medicine at the Institute for Family Health. Hanson currently manages three school-based health centers in Manhattan serving ten public schools, including the Washington Irving Campus. Before working with the Institute, Hanson spent four years working for Planned Parenthood League of Massachusetts.

Cheryl Maney is the Visual Arts and Dance Curriculum Specialist for Charlotte Mecklenburg Schools in Charlotte, North Carolina. She works with 250 visual arts teachers in 164 schools, serving 144,000 students. She also is the Supervision and Administration Division Director for the National Arts Education Association. Prior to working in the central office, she was the Integration Facilitator for University Park Creative Arts Magnet Elementary School. She resides in Concord, NC.

Nahomie Marcena is a hairstylist assistant at Just Because... Hair Therapy Salon in Fort Greene, Brooklyn. Her passion is to uplift and bring out the inner beauty of her clients. She is currently working toward a degree in massage therapy.

Tyler Norris is Vice President of Total Health Partnerships at Kaiser Permanente, the leading integrated health delivery system in the United States. For three decades, Tyler has served as a social entrepreneur and trusted advisor to philanthropies, health systems, governments, NGOs and collaborative partnerships working to improve the health of people and places. His work in the public, private, nonprofit and civic sectors has included initiatives with over 400 communities and organizations in the United States and internationally.

Claudia Nuñez de Ibieta works at an independent bookstore; from her home office, she reads, writes and translates. She founded the Hispanic Literature book group "La tertulia de la literatura hispana" in Tempe, Arizona, where she resides.

Cory Silverberg is a sexuality educator, author, and public speaker, and was a founding member of the Come As You Are Co-operative. He served as the chair of sexuality educator certification for the American Association of Sex Educators, Counselors, and Therapists (AASECT), and teaches on topics including sex and disability, sex and technology, and pleasure, inclusion, and access across North America. His book, *What Makes a Baby?*, the first in a series of three books for children about sexuality, was published by Seven Stories Press in 2013.

Danielle Wagner is a research assistant with a background in biochemistry. Prior to working on *Greenpoint Bioremediation Project*, she received her degrees in Chemistry and Sociology from the University of Florida. She lives in Brooklyn, NY.

Bryana Williams is a Community HealthCorps member currently serving as an Adolescent Health Educator at the Washington Irving Campus. Williams has been working directly with SexEd in the classroom, cafeteria and after-school outreach projects. She received her undergraduate education from Columbia University, where she volunteered with Peer Health Exchange for four years teaching alcohol awareness and sexual decision-making in New York City public schools.

Future Imperfect Acknowledgments

The ABOG Fellowship for Socially Engaged Art is truly a group effort, and we are grateful to have a pretty huge family of support.

A special, warm, XXXL thank you to our founder and Board Chair, Shelley Frost Rubin, for her passion for the ideas behind the fellowship, desire to make a truly different organization, and her generous spirit, and consistently brave leadership as we let the artists take us on a journey into the future. *We cannot do this work without her!*

We are equally indebted to our Board of Directors, present and past, whose effective stewardship, ambition, curiosity, and taste for adventure has enabled us to go much further, much faster, than any four-and-a-half-year-old organization probably has a right to have done. Thank you to our current board: Kim Brizzolara, Roxanne Mankin Cason, Jessica Duffett, Eva Haller, Carin Kuoni, John E. Osborn, Michael Premo, Basha Frost Rubin, Lee H. Skolnick, and Katherine Wilson-Milne! And to former board members Tom Finkelpearl, Zuzka Kurtz, Eileen Caulfield Schwab, and Daniel Schwartz, who have moved on in practice, but not in spirit.

Thank you ABOG Advisory Committee, for continually and generously ensuring that our work is relevant and impactful to the world outside ourselves: Ross Bleckner, Shannon Jackson, Marina McDougall, Anne Pasternak, Mark Shepard and Manon Slome.

In addition to our fantastic Advisory Committee, we relied upon advice and generous feedback from colleagues like Michelle Coffey from Lambent Foundation; Katie Hollander from Creative Time; Kemi Ilesanmi from The Laundromat Project; Edwin Torres from the NYC Department of Cultural Affairs; Laura Raicovich from the Queens Museum; Paul Ramirez Jonas; and Jason Schupbach from the National Endowment for the Arts.

We could not have done our first Fellowship Workshops without the generosity of John Ahearn and Mierle Laderman Ukeles, who offered their own public and social practices as models for aspiring ABOG Fellows. We also want to thank The 8th Floor and No Longer Empty for providing venues for these workshops, and Anne K. Goodfriend for videography.

Two committees read the proposals that came in through our open call, giving generously of their time and providing real insight to select these amazing projects. Thank you Hannie Chia, Maureen Connor, Jen Delos Reyes, Simon Dove, Helen Ho, and Sally Szwed.

The ABOG Fellowship was conceived, developed, and is administered by a staff that is truly astounding in its drive, courage, and care. Thank you Elizabeth Grady, Programs Director; Munira Khapra, Interim Programs Manager; Ellen Staller, Director of External Affairs; Joelle Te Paske, Programs and Communications Manager; Tom Anesta, Office Manager; and Anna Harsanyi, Programming Coordinator. And the Fellowship projects cannot truly be seen and understood without the careful listening and creative interpretation of Jan Cohen-Cruz, who does our evaluation work, and Rafael Salazar and Ava Wiland of RAVA Films. During the Fellowship year, we were honored to have learned Theatre of the Oppressed from George Emilio Sánchez, and Alexander Technique from Kim Jessor.

Our work is made possible by the generosity of our many financial supporters! We are grateful for leadership level support from our Groundbreakers Agnes Gund, Eva Haller, Shelley Frost Rubin, Linda Schejola; and everyone in our First Field of support who contributed to the Fellowship as we were implementing it. We are also grateful for the in-kind support we receive from Blue Medium, the 8th Floor, and Rubinfrost.

Supporters

GROUNDBREAKERS
Agnes Gund
Eva Haller
Shelley Frost Rubin
Linda Schejola

Janet Alvarez, Esq.
Janine Antoni and Paul Ramirez Jonas
Loreen Arbus
Monica Arora and Raj Goyle
Caron Atlas
Maria Bachmann and Josh Aronson
Sigmund R. and Elinor B. Balka
Regine Basha
Sasha Bau
Lois and Robert Baylis
Roberto Bedoya
James Benjamin
Gavin Berger
Amy Berkower and Daniel Weiss
Ross Bleckner
Holly Block
Annette Blum
Kim Brizzolara
Janisa Brunstein
Cindy and Ed Campbell
Roxanne Mankin Cason
Solana Chehtman
Emebet Cheru
Ruth Giorges Cheru
Lili Chopra and Simon Dove
Alice Faye Eichelberger-Cleese
Christopher Cormier
Beatrice Coron
Abigail Disney
Joyce Dubensky
Jessica Duffett and Edward Decker

Andrew Edlin
Joyce and David Edward
Koshin Paley Ellison and Robert Chodo Campbell
Hannah Entwisle
Mahnaz Fancy
Allison Feuer
Ben Feuer
Jack Feuer
Miles Feuer
Fine Arts Club, Grant MacEwan University
Tom Finkelpearl
Michael Fisch
Brock Forsblom and Jeremy Heimans
Alexander Gardner
Olivia Georgia
Anne Germanacos
Ellen Gesner
Julia Gesner
Rachel Gesner
Eran Geva
Lisa Gold
Julie Ann Gordon
Elizabeth Green
Gale Grinsell
Ray Grinsell
Agnes Gund
Eva and Yoel Haller
Jane Hammond
Donna Harkavy
Julie Harkins
John Hatfield
Libby Heimark
Herman & Susan Merinoff Charitable Trust
Naomi Hersson-Ringskog
Jeremy Hochman
Joshua Hochman
Lauren Hochman
Ronnie Hochman
Katie Hollander
The Home Depot Foundation
Kemi Ilesanmi
Alfredo Jaar
Marisa M. Jahn
Kim Jessor
The Joshua Mailman Foundation
Kim Kanatani
Juliette Kleiman
Ken Kleiman
Ava Krasner
Bob Krasner
Jesse Krasner
Melanie Kress
Carin Kuoni
MacQuesten Development, LLC
Francesca Mallows
Micaela Martegani
Kristin Marting
Brookie Maxwell
James P. McCarthy
Brian McFarland
Dylan McFarland
Luke McFarland
Nicole McFarland
Sofia Melograno
Ivana Mestrovic
Dara Metz
Lisa Mueller and Gara LaMarche
Sarah Murkett
No Longer Empty
John E. Osborn
Ari Peskoe
David Polakoff
Christine Ponz
Michael Premo
Laura Raicovich
Sara Reisman
Hillary Richard, Peter McCabe, and Jojo McCabe
Alyana Rubin
Amanda Rubin
Basha Frost Rubin and Scott Grinsell
Danil Rubin
Donald Rubin
Laurel Rubin
Marat Rubin
Shelley Frost Rubin
Gloria Sanchez
Henry G. Sanchez
Nelson Santos
Linda Schejola
Lisa Schejola and Jeffrey Akin
Schindler Cohen & Hochman LLP
Steven Schindler and Susan Kath
Clair Schneider
Eileen Caulfield Schwab
Daniel Schwartz and Csongor Kis
Joyce Pomeroy Schwartz
Alexandra Shabtai
Renee Simms
Richard Simon
Lee H. Skolnick
Manon Slome
Marina Staiano
Ellen Staller
Marie-Monique Steckel
Karen Stults
Sarina Tang
Derrick A. Te Paske
Pauline and Chris Tilley
Liz Valentin
Rachel Weingeist
Leticia Williams
Risë Wilson
Katie Wilson-Milne
Felicia Young
Beverley D. Zabriskie

Our 2015 initiatives are made possible through major contributions from the David Rockefeller Fund and Groundbreakers Agnes Gund, Eva Haller, Shelley Frost Rubin and Linda Schejola.

We are additionally grateful that our public programs are supported, in part, by public funds from the New York City Department of Cultural Affairs in partnership with the City Council.

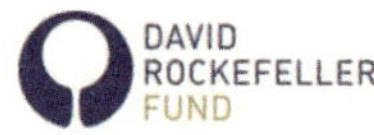

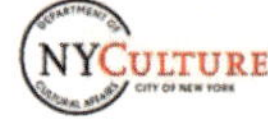

We would also like to thank City of New York, Mayor Bill de Blasio, Manhattan Borough President, Gale A. Brewer, Assembly Member, Richard N. Gottfried, City Council Speaker Melissa Mark-Viverito, City Council Members Jimmy Van Bramer, Corey Johnson, and Rosie Mendez, and the NYC Department of Cultural Affairs, Commissioner Tom Finkelpearl and Deputy Commissioner Edwin Torres.

Artist Acknowledgements

Pablo Helguera would like to thank:
Paco Cao
Chicago Cultural Center
Luis Croquer
Gabriela Galván
Alessandra Gomez
Henry Art Gallery
Lizzie Hurst
Kent Fine Art
Mexican Cultural Institute of New York
Nathan Murphy
Katrina Neumann
Jasmine Stein
Dannielle Tegeder
Caterina Toscano
Douglas Walla

Jan Mun would like to thank:
Newtown Creek Alliance
Jason Sinopoli, Co-Founder of the *Greenpoint Bioremediation Project*
Willis Elkins
Damion Lawyer
Gil Lopez
Mitch Waxman
Kate Zidar

Brooklyn College Environmental Sciences Analytical Center (ESAC)/NYC Urban Soils Institute faculty, students, and staff, including:
Natalie Buchins
Joshua Cheng
Alonso Cordoba
Sara Perl Egendorf
Jinyan Huang
Hermine Huot
Kate Lenahan
Lucy Lin
Maya Miller
Tatiana Morin
Theodore Muth
Diana Polonska
Colleen Simon
Liz Skolnick
Danielle Wagner
Wen Li Wang

61 Franklin Street Community Garden
596 Acres
Brooklyn Grange
Brooklyn Public Library
BuildItGreen!NYC
The Fortune Society
Java Street Community Garden
NYC Councilman Stephen Levi
Gary Lincoff
North Brooklyn Boat Club

SexEd would like to thank:
Sheryl Estafanous
Bec Susan Gill & Jayde Lovell
Caitlin Hanson and the staff of the 422 Health Center at Washington Irving High School Campus
Crystal Henry
Robert Hickerson
Nora Langknecht
Aaron Lazanksy aka DJ SpazeCraft One
Kerstin Pahl
Natalia Mehlman Petrzela
Cory Silverberg
Bryana Williams
The amazing students from the International High School at Union Square
Our incredible after school program participants

Jody Wood would like to thank:
Anna Adler
Jerry Anderson
Joseph Artale
Arté Salon
Erika Bansen
Nicola Benizzi
Body & Soul Hair Studio
Alex Branch
BRC Women's Shelter
Taneshia Brewster-Joseph
Broadway House Women's Shelter
Paolo Cirio
JoAnn Copeland
Neil Creedon
Dop Dop Salon
David Feeney-Mosier
Gabrielle Fishman
The Fortune Society
Tracey Goodman
Christian Hawkey
The Heights
Nate Hill
Just Because...Hair Therapy Salon
Sue Jeong Ka
Jackie Katz
Abbie Klensman
Matt Leibowitz
Magnolia House Women's Shelter
Nahomie Marcena
Jose Montanez
The New York Rescue Mission
Suhyun Park
Park Slope Women's Shelter
Rheaa Rao
Georgiana Rojas
John Rose
Randon Rosenbohm
Lulu Santiago
Nathan Schorr
Sherene the Queen
Caroline Sillstrop
Elisabeth Smolarz
Antonio Soddu
Efthemia Stefanou
Rachel Stevens
Studio 522
Sulon Hair Studio
Sylvia's Place
Carol Thomas
Urban Family Center
Valley Lodge
Vidal Sassoon
Ari Yaun

Index

Image Credits

P.10, photo: Cedoc-Funarte. Courtesy Instituto Boal. P.13, all photos: Deborah Fisher. P.27, courtesy Joe Alterio. P.28, photo: Frank Aymami. Courtesy Creative Time. P.29, bottom, courtesy Fallen Fruit. P.30, courtesy Conflict Kitchen. P.33, photo: Sam Horine. Courtesy Creative Time. P.34, collection of The Andy Warhol Museum, Pittsburgh © 2015 The Andy Warhol Foundation for the Visual Arts, Inc. / Artists Rights Society (ARS), New York. P.35, photo: Sara Pooley. Courtesy the artist. P.36, photo: David Robinson. Courtesy Project Row Houses. P.40, Dariusz. M. Wiszniewski, Zeskanowana praca ręcznie wykonanej kopii ogólnie dostępnej grafiki, April 23, 2011. P.42, film still of performance footage. Courtesy the artist. P.43, courtesy Akademie der Künste, Berlin—Walter Benjamin Archive. P.44, courtesy Gregory Sholette. P.46, courtesy Trades Union Congress Library Collections, London Metropolitan University. Pp.50–51, film still courtesy One Hundred Seconds. P.52, courtesy Operation Paydirt. P.53, courtesy Operation Paydirt. Pp.54–55, all images film stills courtesy One Hundred Seconds. Pp.56–57, photo courtesy McColl Center for Art + Innovation. P.59, top, diagram courtesy Operation Paydirt. P.59, bottom, image courtesy Operation Paydirt. Pp.60–61, film still courtesy RAVA Films. P.62, top, photo: Pablo Helguera. P.62, bottom, photo: Elizabeth Grady. P.65, top, photo: Pablo Helguera. P.65, bottom, film still courtesy RAVA Films. Pp.66–67, film still courtesy RAVA Films. P.69, courtesy Pablo Helguera. Pp.70–71, film still courtesy RAVA Films. P.73, top left, photo: Gabriela Ceja. Courtesy Fran Ilich. P.73, top right, photo: Gabriela Ceja. Courtesy Fran Ilich. P.73, center, photo: Gabriela Ceja. Courtesy Fran Ilich. P.73, lower left, photo: Juan Eduardo Navarrete Pajarito. Courtesy Fran Ilich. P.73, lower right, photo: Gabriela Ceja. Courtesy Fran Ilich. P.74, upper right, photo: Gabriela Ceja. Courtesy Fran Ilich. P.74, upper left, photo: Fran Ilich. P.77, upper left, photo: Fran Ilich. P.77, upper right, photo: Fran Ilich. P.77, center, photo: Fran Ilich. P.77, lower right, photo: Ellen Staller. P.78, top, courtesy Fran Ilich. P.78, bottom, film still courtesy RAVA Films. P.85, courtesy Kerlin Gallery, Dublin. P.89, photo: Pierre Huyghe. P.92, top, photo: Werner Maschmann. Courtesy the artist and Galerie Barbara Weiss, Berlin. P.92, bottom, photo: Peter Cox, Eindhoven, The Netherlands. Courtesy the artist and Galerie Barbara Weiss, Berlin. P.93, top, photo: Werner Maschmann. Courtesy the artist and Galerie Barbara Weiss, Berlin. P.93, bottom, photo: Peter Cox, Eindhoven, The Netherlands. Courtesy the artist and Galerie Barbara Weiss, Berlin. P.94 © Artists Rights Society (ARS), New York / VG Bild-Kunst, Bonn Photo: Imaging Department © President and Fellows of Harvard College. P.95, top, photo: Peter Cox, Eindhoven, The Netherlands. P.95, bottom, photo: Peter Cox, Eindhoven, The Netherlands. P.97, photo: Mon Iker. Courtesy The Natural History Museum. P.98, courtesy Observer Media. Pp.102–03, photo: Bethanie Hines. P.105, film still courtesy RAVA Films. P.106, top, film still courtesy RAVA Films. P.106, bottom, film still courtesy RAVA Films. P.108, photo: Bethanie Hines. P.109, photo: Bethanie Hines. P.110, photo: Bethanie Hines. Pp.112–13, photo: Nicola Benizzi. P.114, bottom left, photo: Jody Wood. P.114, bottom center, photo: Jody Wood. P.115, top, film still courtesy RAVA Films. P.115, center, photo: Nicola Benizzi. Pp.116–17, photo: Nicola Benizzi. P.118, bottom left, photo: Nicola Benizzi. P.118, bottom right, photo: Nicola Benizzi. P.119, top, photo: Nicola Benizzi. P.119, bottom, photo: Nicola Benizzi. P.120, photo: Nicola Benizzi. P.126, top, photo: Romain Lopez. Courtesy Dia Art Foundation. P.126, bottom, photo: Romain Lopez. Courtesy Dia Art Foundation. P.127, courtesy Women on Waves. P.129, top, courtesy Immigrant Movement International. P.129, bottom, photo: Neshi Galindo. Courtesy Immigrant Movement International. P.137, photo: Ramiro Chavez. Courtesy of the Queens Museum. P.139, courtesy of the United Nations Photo Library, Department of Public Information and the Queens Museum. P.140, courtesy of the New York City Department of Parks Photo Archive and the Queens Museum. P.141, courtesy of the New York City Department of Parks Photo Archive and the Queens Museum. P.144, photo by Norene Leddy. P.145, both photos by Bethanie Hines. P.147, photo by Mitch Waxman. P.148, both photos courtesy Operation Paydirt. P.149, film still courtesy RAVA Films. P.150, film still courtesy RAVA Films. P.151, photo, Pablo Helguera. Pp.155–56, film still courtesy RAVA Films. P.156, left, photo: Wen Li Wang. P.156, right, photo: Mitch Waxman. P.159, top, photo: Mitch Waxman. P.159, bottom, film still courtesy RAVA Films. P.160, top left, film still courtesy RAVA Films. P.160, top right, photo: Jan Mun. P.160, photos: Jan Mun. P.161, film still courtesy RAVA Films. P.162, top, courtesy Jan Mun. P.162, bottom, photo: Jan Mun. Pp.164–65, photo: Crystal Henry. P.166, film still courtesy RAVA Films. P.167, upper right, photo: Norene Leddy. P.167, center left, photo: Norene Leddy and Crystal Henry. P.167, center right, courtesy Norene Leddy and Liz Slagus. P.168, photo: Norene Leddy. P.170–71, photo: Norene Leddy. P.171, top, photo: Crystal Henry. P.171, bottom, film still courtesy RAVA Films. P.177, film still courtesy RAVA Films. P.180, open source image via Wiki Media Commons. P.185 Jan Mun portrait by Mara Catalan.

Published by
A Blade of Grass Books
137 Fifth Avenue, 10th Floor
New York, NY 10010
646-757-4599
www.abladeofgrass.org

Designed by
Project Projects

Managing Editor
Elizabeth M. Grady

Copy Editing by
Stephen Maine

Indexing by
Millis Indexing Services

ISBN: 978-0-9842307-3-0

Printed by
Szaransky, Poland

Cover photo by
Bethanie Hines